350
Trees, Shrubs
and Conifers

In Full Colour

350
Trees, Shrubs and Conifers

In Full Colour

Rob Herwig

DAVID & CHARLES
Newton Abbot   London

British Library Cataloguing in Publication Data

Herwig, Rob
    350 trees, shrubs and conifers in full colour.
    1. Shrubs – Dictionaries   2. Trees –
    Dictionaries
    I. Title   II. 350 bomen, heesters en coniferen
    en hun toepassing. *English*
    635.9′76′0321   SB435

ISBN 0-7153-8823-1

Translation by Marian Powell

© 1985 Zomer & Keuning Boeken B.V., Ede, The Netherlands
    Translation © David & Charles 1986

Typeset by Typesetters (Birmingham) Ltd,
Smethwick, West Midlands
and printed in The Netherlands
for David & Charles Publishers plc
Brunel House   Newton Abbot   Devon

FOREWORD

Shrubs are woody plants which produce new growth every year. In principle they therefore grow continually larger. Many of them are beautiful only when they are mature; others, such as roses, must be regularly pruned in order to remain attractive.

It is said that shrubs form the skeleton of every beautiful garden. This means that, after a good design has been worked out, a number of fixed points and lines are established by means of shrubs, after which the remaining space is filled in with other plants such as perennials. It is obvious that a century ago this was a logical theory, but does it also apply to the handkerchief-sized gardens unfortunately seen more and more often today?

To some extent it does. Needless to say it is impossible to frame a fairly small garden by a forest of oaks and beeches, with an inner ring of large conifers and a number of fine free-standing trees in the corners of a sloping lawn. Nevertheless gigantic trees are still seen in tiny front gardens. Blue atlas cedars seem to be particularly popular. Once I noticed a chestnut in a garden less than 3m deep. . . .

However, provided care is taken in the planning, shrubs can contribute a great deal to the small garden. In the first place there are of course shrubs which can be pruned to form a small hedge. Hornbeam may be as much as 2m high at a width of 50cm. I also believe that every garden, however small, should have a tree. Of course a small garden needs a small tree, for example a sumach, a *Koelreuteria* or a golden elm, to mention but a few. Some trees are available in 'Fastigiata' or 'Columnaris' shape which means that all the branches grow upwards, creating a tall narrow column which takes up little space. Also consider the many miniature shrubs, including numerous ground-covering plants and heathers. Next, climbing plants – just think how much they can contribute to a small garden! They grow vertically against a wall or pergola and thus take up practically no ground space – climbing roses, *Clematis*, honey-suckle, etc. Truly, even a small garden needs its shrubs.

The availability of shrubs is often a problem. This is logical: not every garden centre can accommodate large stocks. For that reason it will often be necessary to buy from specialist tree growers, many of whom supply private customers. They can be ordered by post and will be delivered in the planting season.

I wish you success in the purchase and especially the cultivation of shrubs in your garden.

Rob Herwig
Lunteren

Rob Herwig's Model Gardens in Lunteren, The Netherlands. In addition to original design, a great deal of attention has of course been given to the planting of these gardens. Apart from numerous shrubs there is a large selection of perennials.

CONTENTS

Genista aetnensis

INTRODUCTION

What are shrubs?

Shrubs are woody plants which, unlike herbaceous perennials, do not die down above ground every winter. The parts of the shrub above ground remain alive. Trees are shrubs, bushes are shrubs and conifers, too, are shrubs. A bush is often confusingly referred to as a 'shrub'. Having established that this book deals with woody plants, we further distinguish between needle-leaved and foliage trees. Needle-leaved trees, usually called conifers, produce needles instead of leaves – a striking difference. In a few cases the distinction is less clear-cut. *Gingko* is a conifer, but the foliage is leaf shaped.

A distinction may also be made between evergreen and deciduous shrubs. Evergreen shrubs retain their foliage in winter while deciduous shrubs drop their leaves in autumn. This applies to foliage trees and conifers alike. *Larix* and *Metasequoia* are well known deciduous conifers.

Next a word about the shape of a shrub. Where a trunk emerges from the soil we speak of a tree. When the plant comes up in multiple branches we are concerned with a bush.

Sometimes it is difficult to distinguish between the two; it depends on how the shrub is pruned.

How do shrubs grow?

Shrubs develop woody, perennial branches protected by bark. The bark covers the bast which protects the downward flow of the sap. Next comes the cambium, a one-cell layer. Though thin, it is extremely important, for it forms the bast on the outside and the wood on the inside. This is why trees may become constantly broader.

The young wood within the cambium layer is called sapwood. The upward flow of the sap passes through vascular bundles in this layer. Further inwards the wood becomes increasingly hard, until we reach the heartwood. Here no sap flows; the heartwood serves mainly to strengthen the tree or bush.

Winter-hardiness

As the parts above ground do not die in winter, they are exposed to frost and drying winds. Whether or not a certain shrub can withstand such circumstances depends on its natural qualities. Most of the shrubs discussed in this book are tolerant of low temperatures, but there are a

Winter protection for a standard rose

. . . and for Helianthemum

few less winter-hardy – but very beautiful – shrubs which may suffer in a severe frost. This means that the part above ground dies down entirely or partially, but that the shrub will usually sprout again from the roots. In the case of low-growing bushes this is generally no great disadvantage, but a tree which dies down again and again will never have a chance to grow into a proper tree. In other words, winter-hardiness is more important to trees than to bushes.

As a rule shrubs do not exactly freeze up, but they dry out because the roots are unable to absorb moisture from the solidly frozen soil. Evaporation continues through

Shape of a standard tree, depends on how the shrub is pruned.

Example of a bush shape

the branches and, in the case of evergreen shrubs, through the foliage, with the result that the shrub becomes parched and dies. Consider a row of *Thuja* conifers facing east in a severe winter, or a plantation of cherry laurels.

Frost damage may be prevented by planting sensitive shrubs in more sheltered positions, and also by covering the soil with vegetation – leaves, straw etc – so that it cannot freeze up. 'Tidy' gardeners who remove all fallen leaves before the arrival of winter will always have more frost damage than others. Protection against drying, usually east, winds can be provided by windbreaks consisting of reed matting, netting or special windbreak material. Low shrubs can be covered with large heaps of straw, rushes or conifer needles.

The use of shrubs

In large, classical gardens, shrubs were planted along the edges in order to break the wind, thus creating a more favourable microclimate for the other plants. The larger the garden, the bigger the shrubs along the boundary. Towards the centre they became increasingly small, beautiful and delicate. Large conifers such as *Chamaecyparis lawsoniana* are particularly suitable for the boundaries of larger gardens, since they break the wind in winter as well.

Naturally this method is unsuitable for the 5m × 8m garden of a terraced house. Here the protection has to be provided by the buildings and by the unwise neighbour who, in spite of warnings to the contrary, insists on planting a chestnut or a blue cedar in his small garden. Let him: provided the tree does not shade your garden, you can only benefit from the windbreaking effect of a large tree. In a small garden a small

tree is usually more than enough. *Aralias* and sumachs are popular, but when leafing through this book you will find a much wider choice. There will also be room for some lower growing bushes including, of course, heathers.

Be warned against making a hedge round a garden of less than 5m × 8m. In the course of a few years a healthy hedge will easily grow 50cm wide and you would lose half your available ground space (provided that you don't poach upon your neighbour's garden!). A better solution is to build a solid partition (wall, fence, railings) which can then be covered with climbers such as roses. Nearly all climbers are shrubs. They do not grow so wide, their flowers and foliage colours are more satisfying to look at, and the wall or fence will provide a windbreak.

The size of many gardens lies between this small 5m × 8m back garden and the country property of 2ha or more. In a bungalow garden of 0.1ha there will be plenty of scope for shrubs. Here hedges are ideal windbreaks. There can be a number of free-standing, medium-sized trees; creeping shrubs may serve as ground-cover; and the edges may be planted with ornamental

A pergola is ideal for climbing shrubs

The Rhododendron *is tolerant of shade*

shrubs, including evergreen shrubs tolerant of shade, for example rhododendrons. There can be a separate rose garden, a heather garden, a garden for rock shrubs, or whatever takes your fancy.

Combinations of shrubs, herbaceous perennials, bulbous plants, annuals and especially biennials, can be very successful. In fact, it is advisable to avoid a garden consisting solely of shrubs or conifers, otherwise your private property will look suspiciously like a municipal park or a cemetery.

Their ornamental value

Annuals and perennials are judged chiefly on the merits of their flowers, but shrubs give us a great deal more. To start with there are shrubs which flower very early, a reminder, in the middle of winter, of the coming spring. Well known examples are the winter jasmine (*Jasminum nudiflorum*) and the witch hazel (*Hamamelis*), but there are other early flowering species such as *Viburnum × bodnantense*.

The next stage is when the first foliage shoots appear. In some shrubs this provides a real treat – just consider the maples. But many conifers are also extremely beautiful when they start into growth. In

Small shrubs in a rock garden

Nyssa Sylvatica, *autumn colouring*

summer those shrubs which flower on their new growth display their colours, often for months on end, as, for instance, in long-flowering roses. Meanwhile many shrubs have developed fruits which ripen towards autumn. These can produce a magnificent effect, for example in the case of many of the *Cotoneasters* and crab apples.

Finally many shrubs delight us with their magnificent autumn colouring, usually at its best at the end of October. In this country the dazzling *Nyssa sylvatica* is unfortunately not winter-hardy, but there are many other shrubs with fine autumn display.

These are just a few of the obvious characteristics of shrubs, sufficient to demonstrate how much enjoyment they can provide.

Where to buy shrubs

In every garden centre, you will say. True, but not every firm can provide a wide enough choice, for it would not pay the average business to keep a few thousand species in stock. Only those shrubs which guarantee a reasonable turnover are therefore kept, while you might like to plant something that your neighbour has not got in his garden. Fortunately

there is another method of buying plants – in this case shrubs – namely directly from the specialised grower, who usually runs a mail-order business. There are, for example, specialists in heathers, in rare trees and shrubs, conifers, roses, fruit trees and so on.

All the shrubs mentioned in this volume are available somewhere or other, so do not be too easily discouraged.

Pruning

After a few years many shrub owners are worried by the question of how to prune them. Advice on this point is frequently conflicting and the courage to wield the knife is often lacking. The fact that as a result of increasing urbanisation we become more and more distanced from nature, is clearly seen when it comes to pruning.

In many cases, though not always, shrubs have to be pruned for a variety of reasons. Provided you possess good quality tools (pruning shears, possibly a pruning saw) it is not a difficult job. The long and short of it can be taught within five minutes.

Pruning for shape Young trees, but also bushes, have to be shaped

in good time. Trees do not always grow in the correct shape of their own accord: they may grow crooked, develop too much growth at the top, or the branches may cross and rub against each other. Look at the average woodland, it is very beautiful, but much of it is decayed. Nature does not economise on her children.

A correctly cultivated standard tree will have been shaped by the grower. As a rule a straight, vertical trunk is desirable, while the side branches should be regularly distributed and spaced round the trunk. They must all point outwards, in normal trees at an angle of between 30 and 60 degrees.

Shaping a Fothergilla

Climbing roses after pruning

Shaping a Malus tschonowskii

The result: an open crown

Metasequoia *before pruning*

Open top after pruning

ground in spring) to moderate (removing branches which have finished flowering). Naturally the correct or desirable shape can be taken into account at the same time. Before you get to work we must distinguish between shrubs which flower on new wood and woody plants which produce their flowers on mature (usually two-year-old) wood. In the former case the flowers appear on branches which have grown in the same season. Roses, for instance, start into growth early in spring. They develop shoots on which the flower-buds appear, and these open around 21 June, the longest day. This is how you can determine whether or not a shrub flowers on new wood – the flowers rarely appear before 21 June.

Flowering on two-year-old or more mature wood means that the flower-buds were formed before the onset of winter. All they have to do is to open their petals. Only then will the branches start into growth and, in the course of summer, the buds for the following spring will develop on these shoots. All shrubs flowering on two-year-old wood will bloom before 21 June. A good example is the *Forsythia*, but all May-flowering shrubs such as ornamental cherries, golden chain, apples, pears, rhodo-

After a few years in your garden something is bound to have gone wrong. The tree suddenly develops two tops, there are too many side branches interfering with each other, the branches grow at too small an angle, which in time will cause water to collect. All such faults must be corrected annually. Once it has reached a certain size the tree will need less treatment.

As an illustration, I had in my garden two magnificent chestnut trees, planted fifty years ago by the previous owner of the farmhouse. He had never heard of pruning for shape. There was no main trunk; each of the trees had three trunks

growing close together. I noticed that water had collected in the centre, causing considerable rotting. Treatment appeared to be useless. In a severe summer storm both trees fell through my thatched roof; the centre proved to be rotted through and through. The cause – insufficient shaping in the early days.

Pruning for rejuvenation Bushes, especially low-growing specimens such as *Spiraea*, roses etc, are repeatedly cut back to encourage growth and restrict their size. This might be called pruning in order to rejuvenate, and it varies from drastic (cutting down to just above the

Spiraea × bumalda: *spring pruning*

dendrons, also produce their flowers on two-year-old wood.

Knowing these facts, you will be able to understand the principles of pruning. Everything that flowers on that year's shoots, ie after 21 June, may be cut back early in spring, for new shoots with buds will develop. You will not sacrifice any flowers; on the contrary, cutting back will stimulate bud formation.

On the other hand, if shrubs flowering on two-year-old wood are pruned in the autumn, winter or spring, a large number of flower-buds will be removed. This does not matter if you do it on purpose, for instance when cutting a few

A standard rose before spring pruning

. . . and after

branches in January to be forced into flowering indoors; but it is a pity if you remove too much, for in that case the shrub will not flower that year. The time to prune such shrubs is immediately after flowering. In general the pruning of such species is restricted to shaping.

The technique of pruning The principles of pruning have been described above. We shall now deal with the technique. Pruning means cutting or, in the case of thick branches, sawing. Where this is done the shrub will try to start into growth again as close as possible to the cut surface. Shoots can only emerge from eyes, ie buds, which are sometimes very obvious, but in other cases almost invisible.

Once we know this, it is easy to forecast what the shrub will do after being pruned. The position of the eye determines the direction in which the new shoot will grow. Since as a rule we want the branches to grow from the centre of the tree or bush outwards, pruning is generally confined to just above an 'outside eye', ie a bud pointing outwards. There will now be no problem when you read about roses: 'prune in March to 3–5 eyes and retain 3–5 branches'. By this time the roses have frequently produced some new growth; in other cases the small eyes can be found on the circular marks of the shoots. Count from the bottom and cut just above the third, fourth or fifth eye, depending on which eye points outwards. Leave at most three, four or five shoots pointing in different directions if possible. That is all.

A shrub will not necessarily suffer if you make a mistake. Experiments have been made in public gardens, where in March rose bushes have been cut down with a grass-cutter to a height of 10cm. Naturally this saves labour and, lo and behold, in

Always prune just above an eye

summer the roses flowered as profusely as before!

Many late-flowering garden shrubs are cut back drastically in early spring, and early-flowering specimens are increasingly cut back severely immediately after flowering. In this way they remain compact and are more useful in smaller gardens. Further instructions concerning the pruning of individual shrubs will be found in the plant descriptions.

Cutting hedges

Straight hedges – for which in any case only a few shrubs such as beech, hornbeam, holly, tree of life, privet, hawthorn, box and yew are suitable – have to be pruned at least once a year to be kept in shape.

It is advisable to start pruning immediately after planting. There is only one correct shape, tapered, ie slightly wider at the bottom than at the top. This prevents hedges dying at the base as a result of lack of light. Hedges are usually cut with pruning shears. Cut along a taut string and don't be too cautious; if you don't cut enough the hedge will grow thicker and thicker. Some hedges may be cut back to the old wood when they have become too

Pruning a privet hedge

Ornamental pruning

Cutting a yew hedge with shears

large, and they will start into growth again. This applies for instance to privet, box and yew.

Personally I cut my hedges in the first half of June and again in the autumn, the latter chiefly to prevent conifer hedges collapsing under a weight of snow.

Planting techniques

When planting shrubs you must first take their eventual size into account, in order to judge the distance at which they are to be placed. Atlas cedars in 5m × 4m gardens are a joke, but they exist and I wonder what will happen to the house in fifty years' time. If the illustrations in this book are an insufficient guide you are advised to visit a botanical garden where the shrub of your choice has reached an age of ten or twenty years. Its future size will then no longer be a secret.

To turn to the plants themselves. In large gardens the type of soil may influence our choice of shrubs. Heathers, shrubs such as rhododendron and many conifers will not thrive in heavy clay. Real 'clay plants' are in any case rare.

In small gardens the type of soil is usually of less importance. As a rule the ground has been thoroughly

dug, and in places raised, when the house was built, so that little remains of the original soil. When the garden is being laid out the soil is easily turned into 'all-purpose garden soil', in other words, soil suitable for most garden plants. It contains sufficient humus, is porous, has a pH level of between 5 and 6, adequate soil life and a reasonable amount of nutrients. Its condition may be established by taking soil samples. The scope of this book does not allow a detailed discussion of soil improvement and digging; on these subjects you might consult an encyclopaedia of garden plants.

If it is impossible to improve the soil in the entire garden, a separate hole may be dug for each shrub, to be filled with a soil mixture suitable for the individual plant. That is, nice and acid for a rhododendron; drier, calciferous and porous for a rock shrub. Some people laugh when I advise them to dig down to the water level if necessary when making these plant-holes, and definitely to remove all soil along the house walls (pure sand and rubble); but in practice all this extra digging will prove rewarding. The shrubs will thrive and flower more profusely in extra large and deep planting-holes. In general a planting-hole is filled

with one part of the original soil mixed with peat, chopped turves, leafmould, stable manure, or a combination of these. The shrub is placed in the centre, preferably to the same depth as it was planted in the nursery, as can be seen on the stem; then the soil mixture is returned to the hole and firmly trodden down, in order to leave no hollow spaces round the roots. Gentle planting is bad planting! Now the soil is watered until the shrub is standing in a mud-pool. Trees are usually staked to give them some support in the first few years. The stake should not be creosoted and must be placed on the

Planting a staked tree

Loosen the netting round the soil-ball

side of the prevailing wind. The stake is hammered some way into the firm subsoil, before the hole is partially filled with improved soil. Now the tree is planted, the hole is filled in and the plant is watered. Next it is tied to the stake, leaving a gap of 5–10cm. This is best done with a plastic tree-tie; a small block supplied with the tie ensures the correct distance. Since the tree will drop a little in the first few months, it is better not to tighten the tie too firmly. This can be done at a later stage, in such a way that the wind cannot make the tie rub against the bark.

When a shrub is supplied with a soil-ball it means that it will not strike so readily as, say, a container grown plant. In a natural root-ball the clump will be filled with roots, but sometimes the grower has merely added a little soil. You will find out when you remove the netting – after placing the shrub in the planting-hole. This must be done with great care; try not to damage the root-ball.

Planting seasons

Deciduous shrubs without a soil-ball may be transplanted from the moment they have lost their foliage,

usually by the end of October. Planting may continue up to late April, except in times of frosty weather.

Evergreen shrubs, including many conifers, should be supplied with a soil-ball. In principle they can be transplanted throughout the year, but to avoid risks it is better done in May or September. Cloudy, rainy weather is an advantage, for then there will be little evaporation.

Shrubs are now often sold in containers. Like shrubs with soil-balls, these container plants may in principle be planted throughout the year. Naturally the container must first be removed, except in the case of the 'soluble' types, or of the slotted container in which brooms are sometimes supplied.

Keep an eye on newly planted shrubs in the first year. They may easily dry out in frosty or dry weather or in a severe wind. You yourself may like sunny weather, but your young garden plants prefer a drizzle.

Diseases

The primary cause of diseases (pests, mildew etc) is that the shrub has been planted in an unsuitable place, or you have forgotten to water and feed it regularly. If you plant a rose in damp soil in a shady spot you may be certain that it will languish. If you forget to feed it you will see fewer and fewer flowers. Plant a rhododendron in full sun in chalky soil and, if it does not dry out, it will certainly be attacked by pests.

Nature is very logical; there is a reason for all diseases. Man is more and more kept alive by means of pills, vaccines and operations, but originally it was a case of 'the survival of the fittest' and in the garden this jungle law still prevails – weak plants are unable to maintain their natural powers of resist-

ance and are affected. True, you need only go to the shop and buy a number of poisons, but these will only combat the effect, not the cause.

This is a general rule, but naturally there are exceptions. The spindle-tree, for example, may be attacked by the ermine moth even when well cared for, and old-fashioned roses are subject to mildew. Many limes are permanently covered in aphis, and oaks without gallnuts are rare. Sometimes it is necessary to combat such pests and diseases, but often they can be left alone.

If you decide that it is necessary to interfere, you should first try a harmless substance such as a mixture of soap and methylated spirits, or use products which only kill the parasite without affecting other aspects of nature (eg a bacterium preparation against caterpillars).

Feeding

No plant can live without food. Most of its nutrients are absorbed from the soil, but some types of soil are more nutritious than others. Good clay soil releases so many nutrients that feeding may be unnecessary. In sandy soil, on the other hand, nutrients are washed away

Stable manure for a climbing rose

The rewards of good care

fairly quickly and annual fertilising is by no means a luxury.

Soil analysis is generally accompanied by advice on manuring. Good advice, in fact, consists of two recommendations: one based on artificial fertiliser, the other on organic fertiliser. Many people dislike the former and prefer to use natural products such as dried blood, bone meal, cow manure etc, even though they are more expensive.

Many shrubs are extremely vigorous and consequently need a great deal of food. This certainly applies to hedging plants, which are frequently neglected. In such cases the roots will reach into other parts of the garden where the plants, in their turn, will be deprived of food. You will thus fall from the frying pan into the fire.

Fast-acting fertilisers, such as chemical products, must be administered when the plant starts into growth, that is, in May. More slowly acting fertilisers – some synthetic products, but mainly organic manure – are better given a few months earlier, for the nutrients will be released only after changes

have taken place in the soil.

For more demanding plants, including roses, a second manuring in summer is desirable to encourage continuous flowering. It is advisable not to feed after the beginning of August, for in that case the shrubs would continue to grow for too long. Growth must cease at the end of August, allowing the wood to ripen and harden before the onset of winter.

As regards the quantity of artificial fertiliser to be used, it is best to follow the instructions usually given on the packing.

Propagation

The more expensive a shrub, the more difficult it is to increase. The price itself will tell you whether or not you can do it yourself. Some people are more successful than others, and sometimes amateurs achieve good results even with notoriously difficult shrubs. Once you have been infected by the propagation bug there will be no holding you, and your garden will rapidly fill with presents for your friends and neighbours. The following methods of propagation may be considered:

from seed
division
layering
taking cuttings
grafting

From seed This is by no means the easiest way to propagate shrubs, but sometimes it is the only possible one. The method is effective only in the case of original species and varieties; as a rule strains will not grow true to type. However, there is always the chance of a spontaneous variety.

Shrub seed often lies dormant for a long time before it germinates. Growers usually keep such seed

frost-free in damp sand; this is called stratification. The seeds are lifted in spring and are germinated at a fairly low temperature. However, some seeds may germinate only after having lain dormant for a whole year – a slow business.

Division This is by far the easiest method and one with immediate results. Unfortunately it is possible only in the case of shrubs which emerge from the soil in several shoots. Such shrubs are lifted in the autumn or in spring and the clump is divided into several sections, either by hand or with a sharp

Dividing a Pachysandra

Layering a Clematis *in autumn*

Winter cuttings of Ribes

spade. The sections may be quite small, provided each of them has a root and a bud or shoot. They are placed in a nursery-bed, possibly protected in winter, and then grown on.

Layering A fairly easy method of increasing shrubs, but only bushes or climbing shrubs with pliable twigs can be layered. A cut is made in one or more twigs, where there is an eye. This section is bent down and buried in potting-soil in a hole in the ground. Autumn is a good time for this job. Usually it takes as much as a year for roots to develop from the wound; at that point the new plant can be cut from the parent plant and grown separately.

Cuttings These may be divided into summer cuttings and winter cuttings. We shall start with the latter, since they are easier.
Winter cuttings are taken from shrubs with thick, firm shoots, usually in October or November, but in many cases it can be done earlier. Straight branches, developed that year, are cut into 10–20cm sections. Often only the top parts are used, but where there is a shortage of material the lower sections may also be rooted. During the winter

the cuttings are kept frost-free in damp soil. They may be covered with glass or plastic to prevent drying out. In spring there will be few, if any, roots; but if they are potted up and some bottom heat is provided, they will soon start into growth. It is advisable to water in the autumn with a product which combats mildew; you will then lose fewer plants.

Summer cuttings are often more difficult to grow. Many deciduous and evergreen shrubs with thin twigs, and especially conifers, are increased by this method which takes place in the months of June, July or August. Cuttings of about 5–15cm, nearly always the tips of shoots developed in that year, are cut just below an eye, preferably with a small piece of bast. This is called a cutting with a 'heel'. The lower leaves are removed and the cutting is placed in a mixture of sand and potting-soil. The problem is that evaporation continues through the remaining leaves (needles in the case of conifers), while there are no roots to absorb moisture. Growers therefore keep the cuttings damp by means of a misting apparatus. It is essential to provide good light. You might try to protect the cuttings against evaporation by covering them with glass or clear plastic. It is advisable to use a product to combat mildew. Often the cuttings are first dipped in rooting powder, available in any garden centre. Additional bottom heat will encourage root formation. It is unlikely that you will immediately succeed in rooting a rhododendron, but you never know. Cuttings from conifers are often very successful, even though a great deal of material is lost.

Grafting This is the most difficult method of propagation. The principle is that the plant we want to

grow, the 'noble' plant or graft, is placed on stock which is often less 'noble', but which is more vigorous. In this way two different plants are linked. However, they must not be too different: you will not be able to graft a rose on a rhododendron, but a slight difference in species and even in genus is admissable.
There are various methods of grafting, for example whip grafting and rind grafting. Budding is another method of grafting, often used for roses. In this method of propagation a small bud is inserted in the bast of the stock.
With practice, grafting is not very difficult, but it can rarely be learnt from a book. For that reason it is not described in detail here.

General care

Like most other garden plants, young newly planted shrubs, as well as small shrubs, are easily overgrown by weeds. It is therefore desirable to control unwanted growth near shrubs during the first year. It has been proved that shrubs grow better in soil kept clean during the first few years.
On the other hand no weed control is necessary in the case of coarse

Hoeing between shrubs

shrubs or thicket bushes. These will look after themselves and will in fact suppress weed growth. However, their weaker brothers, such as rock shrubs, heathers and most roses, must constantly be freed of weeds, otherwise they will die.

In private gardens, weeds are usually removed by hand or with a hoe. There are chemical weedkillers which are harmless to shrubs, but not everyone likes to use such poisons. In a small garden there is in any case no need for them.

Mulching is an excellent method of suppressing weeds growing under the larger, non-creeping shrubs. All this means is that the ground is covered with a layer of some organic material such as grass cuttings, tree-bark, hay, wood shavings etc, after the soil has first been carefully weeded. The layer must not be too thin, otherwise the weeds will grow through it. A new layer must be added at least once a year, because weeds often germinate on top of the mulch. In my experience this is an effective way of using grass cuttings. The soil does not dry out so quickly, it is excellent for encouraging soil life and hoeing will be a thing of the past.

Another important element of general care is watering. I frequently hear people say that the plants will have to look after themselves. I fail to understand how a caring gardener, seeing his plants wilting in a dry summer, can be so cruel. Of course one should not water unnecessarily, but when, as happens quite often, dry weather persists for

A rose tied too tightly

weeks on end, it is essential to water thoroughly, especially where the soil is sandy.

Tying-in climbing shrubs also requires attention. By no means all climbers are self-clinging like the ivy. As a rule they are creepers, winding themselves automatically round branches or other objects. This winding movement is useless against a level wall, and if the plants are not tied they will never grow upwards.

I am no champion of climbing frames, since they are rarely attractive and often require maintenance. I prefer to use small brass hooks, screwed into the wall with the aid of rawlplugs. Several hooks can be screwed into the wall before the shrub starts to climb. The brass will soon turn black and become invisible and the screws will not rust. The climbers are tied to the hooks with twine, plastic-coated wire or plastic ties.

Tying a climbing shrub to a hook

Nomenclature

In this book all the shrubs are arranged under their botanical names. This has advantages and disadvantages. To find them under their English name you will have to consult the Index. Several plants have more than one English name – an important reason for using only the correct botanical name, of which there is only one.

However, even botanical names are sometimes changed by international committees with the result that, for example, the Russian vine, a well known plant at one time generally known as *Polyganum*, was changed some time ago into *Bilderdykia*, but it has now been discovered that the correct name is *Fallopia*. Many growers' catalogues still refer to *Polyganum*, even though this name is incorrect. I always use the latest name, while mentioning the old one. It is realised that the botanical names may cause some difficulty.

SHRUBS FROM A TO Z

Abelia

These rather unusual shrubs belong to the same family as the honeysuckle and are closely related to the *Kolkwitzia*. Most of them have arching twigs and a prolonged flowering season.
Situation   In northern regions they must be protected against cold north and east winds. A sheltered site against a sunny south- or west-facing wall is excellent.
Soil   Will thrive in ordinary garden soil.
Propagation   Cuttings are taken in summer and are rooted in a heated tray.

Abelia × *grandiflora* (syn *A. rupestris* var *grandiflora*): A hybrid of *A. chinensis* and *A. uniflora*, valuable because of its long flowering season from July until well into September. This *Abelia* is moreover partially evergreen. The largest number of flower plumes will be produced if the shrub is planted in a sunny spot.
Abelia triflora: Together with the previous species, this is the most winter-hardy *Abelia*. The shrub has erect-growing branches and plumes of fragrant pale-pink flowers in summer. Maximum height 3–4m.

Abelia × *grandiflora*

Abies balsamea var *hudsonia*

Abies

Silver fir

Imposing, winter-hardy conifers. A few dwarf forms are also referred to as silver firs. *Abies* is easily recognisable by its erect-growing cones, usually cylindrical in shape, which when ripe disintegrate, leaving only the core.
Situation   Provide a sunny, slightly sheltered position. The dwarf forms are attractive additions to a conifer collection or a rrock garden. Large silver firs are only suitable for large gardens or parks, as a background for other plants or free-standing. One of the smallest firs, in size midway between the dwarfs and the giants, is *Abies koreana*, also popular for its numerous, striking cones. The foliage colour of silver firs varies from the majestic deep dark green of *A. nordmanniana* to the steel-blue grey of *A. pinsapo*. Make sure that the surrounding vegetation does justice to the colouring of these trees.
Soil   Most species prefer standard to fairly acid soil. *Abies grandis* and *A. pinsapo* tolerate some lime and *A. cephalonica* likes chalky soil.
Propagation   Botanical species from seed, garden forms from cuttings; occasionally by grafting.

Abies koreana

Abies lasiocarpa var *arizonica*

Abies × arnoldiana: The result of crossing *A. koreana* and *A. veitchii*. Frequently confused with the real Korean silver fir, but faster growing and less suitable for small gardens.

Abies balsamea, balsam fir: Height 15–25m, 4–6m across. A tree with a cone-shaped habit; the dark-green needles face upwards and have two white stripes on the reverse. When rubbed they release an aromatic scent. The grey twigs are covered in short hairs; the red buds contain resin. The cones may grow to a length of 7cm. 'Nana' is a dome-shaped dwarf form with densely growing needles in double rows, height 80cm. The variety *hudsonia* grows to a height of 1m and 1.25m across.

Abies cephalonica, Greek fir: Cone-shaped tree, 10–20m tall; bare, bright-brown twigs and reddish-brown buds containing resin. Sharp, dark-green radial needles, up to 2cm long and facing upwards. The cones, 12–15cm long, have spreading scales.

Abies concolor: Height 25–50m, 4–5m across, fairly cylindrical in shape; horizontally spreading branches. The yellow-green twigs are practically bare; the buds contain a large amount of resin. Grey-green needles, up to 7cm long, often curved upwards, sometimes pointing backwards. Green cones, up to 10cm long. 'Argentea' has striking whitish needles. 'Candicans' bears bluish-white needles, initially almost white. In 'Violacea' they have a purplish hue.

Abies grandis, giant silver fir: Height 30–90m, but only 4–6m across. Pyramid shaped, with olive-green branches and buds containing resin. The needles, strikingly arranged in one plane, are 3–5cm long and have two white stripes on the reverse. This tree tolerates wind and prefers fairly rich soil.

Abies homolepis: Broad, cylindrical tree, up to 25m in height, with bare brown branches and blunt buds containing resin. The needles are dark green and glossy on the upper surface and have two broad white stripes on the reverse. They are blunt, at most 3.5cm long, and face forwards and a little upwards.

Abies koreana: A 15m tall fir with yellowish-grey branches and brush-like, erect-growing needles up to 1.5cm long, narrowing towards the base. Before they ripen the magnificent cones have a purplish colour.

Abies lasiocarpa: A narrow tree, up to 20m in height, with short, hairy branches and grey buds containing resin. The inflorescence is particularly fine; the male flowers are violet blue, the female reddish purple. The needles are less than 2mm wide, the purple cones up to 6cm long. The well known variety *arizonica* has fine blue needles and is very suitable for a free-standing position. 'Compacta', a cone-shaped dwarf conifer, has silvery, bluish-white needles.

Abies nordmanniana, Caucasian fir: A 25–35m tall tree, 4–6m across, with glossy dark-green needles, 2–3cm long, on bare or slightly downy grey-brown twigs. The blunt needles have two white stripes on the reverse and face forward. The resin-less, fairly small buds are a striking feature. The cones are up to 15cm long. This fir may suffer in a severe winter if there is bright sunlight on the south side, and also in a drying north or east wind.

Abies pinsapo, Spanish silver fir: Height 10–20m, width 5–7m. A tree with bare twigs and blunt buds rich in resin. The radially arranged 1–2cm long needles are whitish on both surfaces; brown, 10–12cm long cones. In 'Aurea' the needles are initially yellowish, later yellow green. In 'Glauca' they are glaucous.

Abies procera, noble fir: A cone-shaped tree up to 20m tall, with thick, bare twigs and blunt, strongly curved and furrowed blue-green needles. In 'Glauca' the needles have a magnificent blue-grey colour.

Abies pinsapo 'Glauca'

Acer cappadocicum

Acer

Maple

The genus *Acer* comprises hundreds of species and strains, cultivated for their fine shape, foliage colouring or bark marking. The colour of the leaves may vary considerably from one season to another. In spring many of the species bear clusters of flowers, sometimes very profuse and especially effective. Later winged seeds appear; these may flutter through the garden like tiny helicopters. An important characteristic of *Acer* species is the opposite position of the leaves.

Situation Maples vary considerably in size and habit and can therefore be used in many ways. Large specimens are often planted as striking free-standing trees in parks and large gardens, whereas the smaller forms of Japanese maple may be used even in the tiniest town garden. In general they do well in both sun and partial shade, but a vigorous species like the common maple tolerates so much shade that it can be planted under other trees. This maple can be pruned and may therefore be used for hedges.

The Japanese maples are much less hardy and consequently more demanding. They prefer a sheltered

Acer cissifolium

Acer japonicum 'Aureum'

position, protected against strong winds, as do the silver maple and the ash-leaved maple.

Where we wish to plant a dome-shaped standard tree other than the dome-shaped acacia, a maple may be a good choice. Many *Acer* species are suitable for avenues.

Soil Most maples prefer humus-rich soil, moisture retaining but well-drained. *Acer campestre*, *A. palmatum* and *A. rubrum* tolerate a certain amount of lime. Unlike other maples, *A. palmatum* and its many cultivars require damp soil and enjoy a position on the bank of a pond, where the soil may be acid. Rapidly growing species like *A. saccharinum* must be planted in a free-draining position in poor soil, where the shoots will grow less rapidly and break less easily.

Propagation Species are increased by grafting or from seed, the shrub forms also by layering. The seeds remain viable only for about six months. Cultivars are increased by grafting, bud grafting or from cuttings.

Acer campestre, common maple, field maple: Height to 20m, 8m across; the shrub forms are considerably smaller. Very vigorous and fast growing, both in sun and shade. The brownish-red twigs, sometimes covered in cork, are initially hairy. The 5-lobed leaves have beautiful autumn colouring. 'Nanum' is a dwarf form with a spherical crown. 'Elsrijk' has a cone-shaped crown and 'Albovariegatum' produces white-flecked leaves.

Acer capillipes: Height to 6m, 3m across; a tree with a striped trunk and branches. Greenish-white flowers in May; the foliage turns carmine red in autumn. Moderately fast growing.

Acer cappadocicum (syn *A. laetum*): Height to 20m, 8m across, a tree with initially red leaves turning yellow in autumn. Clusters of yellow flowers May–June. In 'Aureum' the foliage is at first bronze coloured, later yellow. The tree grows to 8m and has a broad crown with spreading branches.

Acer cissifolium (syn *Negundo cissifolium*): Spreading tree or shrub, up to 6m. In autumn the 3-lobed leaves turn orange red. Flowers profusely in May.

Acer ginnala: Shrub or tree, 3–5m tall and almost as much across; free-growing habit. Erect-growing plumes of white flowers in May. The 3- to 5-lobed leaves are green and glossy on the upper surface, pale green on the reverse; in autumn they turn yellow and red. Very fructiferous.

Acer griseum: Magnificent specimen tree with peeling bark and cinnamon-coloured bast. Height up to 12m and 5m across. Leaves grey green, green and felty on the reverse; in autumn they turn purple red. Yellow flower clusters in May.

Acer japonicum, Japanese maple: Graceful shrub or small tree, up to 5m in height and 3m across, fairly slow growing. The pale-green leaves are 9- to 13-lobed, usually deeply incised and doubly serrated; dark-red autumn colouring. Drooping clusters of purple-red flowers in May. 'Aconitifolium' may grow a little broader and is characterised by the large, pale-green very deeply incised leaves, initially bronze coloured and turning yellow-orange and red in autumn. 'Aureum' grows very slowly and has golden-yellow, slightly incised foliage and dense branches.

Acer lobelii: Initially a squat tree, a native of Italy. Later it grows into a narrow vase shape. The young shoots are glaucous. The leaves are 5 to 7-lobed, very similar to *A. platanoides*; their upper surface is dark green, the reverse grey green.

Acer negundo (syn *Negundo aceroides, N. fraxinifolium*), ash-leaved maple: Tree or shrub; height up to 15m, 8–10m across, with glossy green or glaucous twigs. Dioecius, therefore the male and female flowers are on different plants. The male flowers appear in clusters, the female in racemes; April flowering. The foliage is feathery. The fruits stay on the tree long after the leaves have dropped.

'Crispum' has crisped, frequently distorted leaves. The very well known forms, 'Aureovariegatum' and 'Variegatum', the golden and silver ash-leaved maple, are usually shrubs with multiple trunks and with yellow or white variegated leaves. 'Auratum' has yellow foliage.

Acer palmatum (syn *A. polymorphum*), Japanese maple: Tree or shrub, 5–7m in height and 2–3m across; very graceful in shape, with thin twigs. It should be planted in a sheltered position, where it may still be frost damaged, but in spring it will start into growth again. The pale-green, deeply incised leaves are 5- to 9-lobed and have fine autumn colouring. Brownish-red flower racemes in June. Forms with very finely divided foliage require a partially shaded position. Well known strains are 'Atropurpureum', which grows to 6–8m and has deeply incised, brownish-red leaves; 'Bloodgood', which is slower growing, to 4–6m, and has dark reddish-brown foliage. 'Corallinum' grows to a height of 3m and 2m across. The pale-green foliage is deeply incised and has beautiful autumn colouring; the bast is coral red; the red flowers appear in June. 'Dissectum' has a squat habit; the branches are often twisted. It grows to a height and width of 3m. The leaves are so deeply incised they look like ferns; in autumn the fresh green foliage turns deep orange. 'Dissectum Garnet' has equally finely incised foliage, but is brownish red in summer, changing in autumn to deep red. 'Dissectum' strains are sometimes planted in rock gardens.

Acer pensylvanicum (syn *A. striatum*), snake-bark maple: Tree up to 8m in height and 6m across, with white-striped bark and foliage which turns yellow in autumn. Hanging clusters of yellow flowers in May.

Acer platanoides, Norway maple: Broad-crowned tree, up to 20m tall and 10m across. Fast growing and tolerating shade. The 5-lobed leaves are fresh green, turning yellow in autumn. In April to May yellow-green flowers appear in erect-growing clusters. 'Crimson King', height

Acer palmatum 'Atropurpureum'

Acer palmatum 'Dissectum'

Acer platanoides 'Globosum'

Acer tegmentosum

8–10m, has reddish-brown foliage with a silvery tinge and a dense, asymmetrical, cone-shaped crown. 'Drummondii', height to 15m, 10m across, has pale-green leaves with a white margin. Branches which revert to type must be removed. 'Globosum' has a spherical crown and initially reddish-brown leaves. Height up to 5m and 10m across. Later the crown flattens and becomes umbrella shaped. 'Lobergii', to 15m in height, has fine, deeply incised leaves and a round crown. In 'Olmsted' the crown is pillar shaped; height up to 9m.

Acer pseudoplatanus, sycamore. A 20–25m tall tree with large leaves, rough to the touch, and a regularly shaped crown. An excellent tree for avenues. 'Brilliantissimum' grows to 7m in height and 5m across with yellowish, white-speckled leaves and yellow-green flowers in May. 'Costorphinense' grows up to 15m, it has a wide pyramid-shaped crown and foliage discolouring from bright yellow to dull green.

Acer rubrum, red maple: Height to 15m and 10m across, this tree produces red flowers March–April. Deep green, 3- to 5-lobed leaves, bluish on the reverse. Magnificent red autumn colouring.

Acer rufinerve: Height to 10m; its initially red 3- to 5-lobed leaves are pale green in summer, yellow to red in autumn. Young shoots and buds are glaucous.

Acer saccharinum (syn *A. dasycarpum*), silver maple: Height to 30m and 15m across, a tree for lime-free soil. Spreading, open crown and delicate-looking foliage. The 5-lobed leaves are pale green with silvery reverse, turning yellow in autumn. In 'Lacinatum' the deeply incised foliage is retained for a fairly long time.

Acer saccharum (syn *A saccharophorum*), bird's eye maple, sugar maple: Height to 25m, a tree with an oval to spherical crown. The 3- to 5-lobed leaves turn orange yellow to red in autumn. Wind resistant.

Acer tegmentosum: Height to 9m and 4m across; a tree with pale-green twigs, paler striped when mature. Yellow flowers in May.

Acer × *zoeschense*: The result of crossing *A. campestre* and *A. lobelii*. Resembles the field maple. The most frequently grown form is the cultivar 'Annae', a slow-growing tree with a dense round crown. Does not grow beyond 8m. The 5-lobed leaves are initially brownish red, but later assume an olive-green colour. Clusters of yellow-green flowers appear in May. This form tolerates a certain amount of shade; it is an attractive tree for small gardens, but may also be found lining streets.

Actinidia

Chinese Gooseberry

Deciduous climbers with simple leaves. They are dioecious plants so that, in order to grow your own Kiwi fruits, you need a male and a female plant.

Situation For covering walls and pergolas in sunny and partially shady positions. To avoid bleeding they should never be pruned in spring.

Soil Humus-retaining soil.

Propagation From seed and cuttings.

Actinidia chinensis, Chinese gooseberry, Kiwi: Climber, up to 8m in height and 2m across. In a sheltered position it may produce a large number of fruits. When young it should be protected in winter. It is a vigorous grower, with brownish-red, hairy twigs and round to oval, fresh green foliage. The yellow-white flowers appear in clusters May–June and are followed by hairy brown, vitamin C-rich fruits.

Actinidia kolomikta: Fragrant white flowers in May. In the male plants the leaves are red tipped.

Actinidia kolomikta

Aesculus hippocastanum

Aesculus

Horse Chestnut

Large, deciduous trees, with the exception of *A. parviflora*, which is a ground-covering shrub. Large, hand-shaped, composite leaves and somewhat prickly fruits.

Situation Beautiful free-standing trees for large gardens and parks, also suitable for lining avenues. A number of smaller growing trees are suitable for medium-sized gardens. Provide a sunny to partially shady position. Pruning is unnecessary, but is tolerated.

Soil Rich in humus.

Propagation From seed or by grafting.

Aesculus × carnea: Tree up to 15m in height and 12m across, with pale-red flowers in May. Bears little fruit and the husks are not very prickly.

Aesculus hippocastanum: Height up to 30m, 15m across, bearing white flowers in May, followed by very prickly fruits. The 7-lobed leaves develop in spring from large, sticky brown buds.

Ailanthus

Tree of Heaven

Large, deciduous tree, with enormous, composite leaves. It is fast growing and may develop an extensive root system. Very decorative.

Situation Beautiful in a free-standing position in full sun or partial shade. Occasionally used as a pioneer plant. Pruning is rarely necessary, but is tolerated. Light-wood (it tolerates little shade), resistant to smoke and pollution.

Soil Fairly indifferent to soil condition. The roots grow on the surface, providing little opportunity for undergrowth.

Propagation From seed or from root suckers.

Ailanthus altissima (syn *A. glandulosa*): Height up to 20m, 15m across, the twigs are covered in delicate down; when cut the branches reveal thick orange to pale-brown pith. The feathery leaves are up to 60cm long and consist of 13–25 leaflets, each 7–12cm long. The orange flower clusters which appear in June have a disagreeable scent; they are followed by yellow-green winged fruits.

Ailanthus altissima

Akebia quinata

Akebia

Beautiful climbers with graceful, hand-shaped leaves and purple-red flowers. As a rule they grow quite slowly in the first few years, after which they may cover an entire fence within one season. In mild winters the foliage is retained for a long time. Young plants must be given frost protection in winter, but older specimens are entirely winter-hardy.

Situation Decorative climber for sunny or partially shaded positions. May grow to a height of 10m and 5m across.

Soil Will grow in humus-retaining garden soil.

Propagation By layering and from cuttings.

Akebia quinata: The better known of the two species, with 5-fold, hand-shaped foliage. The leaflets themselves have short stems and are somewhat leathery. The plant flowers in April and May, when it is covered in fragrant purple clusters, sometimes followed by violet-coloured, gherkin-like fruits.

Akebia trifoliata: As the name indicates, this climber has 3-fold leaves. It does not grow as large as *A. quinata*. The chestnut-coloured flowers appear in May.

Alnus

Alder

Deciduous trees with a fairly regular crown. They are lightwood trees, which means that they tolerate little shade. In general alders are not very sensitive to wind. They are characterised by their early flowering catkins, their seeds and their stalked buds.

Situation Large gardens, boulevards, parks and – especially where *A. cordata* is concerned – streets. May be pollarded.

Soil *A. glutinosa* requires nutritious, damp soil. *A. incana* imposes few demands.

Propagation From seed, cuttings and by layering.

Alnus cordata: Height 15–20m; a tree with an oval crown. Dark-green, leathery, heart-shaped leaves, long retained in autumn and rarely attacked by the alder beetle. Tolerates sea wind, but its growth will be slowed down.

Alnus incana: A tree up to 20m in height, with delicately haired buds and twigs, silver-grey trunk and leaves which are blue grey on the reverse. 'Aurea', the golden alder, grows up to 6m in height and 4m across.

Alnus incana 'Aurea'

Amelanchier canadensis

Amelanchier

June Berry

Early flowering shrubs or small trees, with a profusion of flowers in spring and magnificent autumn colouring. All *Amelanchier* have a bushy habit and develop a large number of runners.

Situation Free-standing or in large groups of shrubs.

Soil Imposes few demands as to soil and moisture retention. Prefers lime-free, moderately damp soil.

Propagation From seed, rooted suckers or by grafting on *Crataegus monogyna* or *C. laevigata* stock.

Amelanchier canadensis (syn *A. oblongifolia*): When it starts into growth the foliage is green. A North American species with erect-growing flower racemes.

Amelanchier laevis: Broad shrub, 4–6m tall. Initially the twigs are somewhat hairy. White flowers, followed by brownish-purple edible fruits.

Amelanchier lamarckii (syn *A. canadensis*): When the tree starts into growth the foliage is reddish brown. Pink-white flowers and blue-black edible berries.

25

Amorpha

Bastard Indigo

Little known shrubs with, in summer, butterfly-like flowers attractive to insects. After a severe winter they must be cut back drastically in spring.

Situation In a sunny place in the shrub border, in damp, somewhat acid soil.

Soil Will grow in any standard or acid garden soil.

Propagation From cuttings or seed. Sow in spring, pod and all; the seeds will germinate after eight weeks.

Amorpha canescens: This shrub does not grow beyond 1m; the stems become woody at the base. Long spikes of violet-coloured flowers July–August.

Amorpha fruticosa: Large bush; it may grow to a height of 5m and 4m across. Spikes of purple flowers appear from June to August. Striking yellow stamens.

Amorpha nana: Similar in height and habit to *A. canescens*, but the violet-coloured flowers have orange stamens.

Amorpha fruticosa

Aralia elata

Aralia

Shrubs belonging to this genus have little ramification; the twigs are prickly. The large, long-stemmed multiple leaves have pale marking, and the white flowers are produced in plumes or clusters.

Situation Very suitable as a free-standing shrub in small gardens. Sometimes produce a large number of runners; if they are not removed you may end up with a forest of *Aralia* plants. Will thrive in full sun as well as in partial shade.

Soil Will grow in any garden soil rich in humus.

Propagation Runners are removed from the parent plant in the autumn, to be grown separately.

Aralia elata (syn *Dimorphus elatus*), Hercules' club: Decorative, tree-like shrub which may grow to 5m in height, 3m across. The leaves, which may be as much as 80cm long, are often prickly along the main vein, the reverse is grey green. The white flower plumes which appear in August and September are followed by black berries. There are two variegated forms: 'Variegata', in which the leaves have a white margin, and 'Aureovariegata' with yellow-edged foliage.

Araucaria

Norfolk Island Pine, Monkey Puzzle

Evergreen conifers with practically horizontal branches and needle-shaped scales.

Situation The Norfolk Island pine has a very distinctive appearance and makes an excellent specimen tree. Although it grows fairly slowly, it may eventually reach a height of 20m and a width of 10m, so that it is unsuitable for small gardens. Young specimens, in particular, are sensitive to frost. Protect them against frost and wind with netting. The best chance of reaching maturity is in coastal regions.

Soil Well-drained, acid soil, rich in humus.

Propagation From seed or cuttings.

Araucaria araucana (syn *A. imbricata*): Striking dark-green conifer with snake-like branches, densely covered in thick, sharply pointed triangular leaves which give the tree its name of 'Monkey Puzzle'. Cones are produced only when the tree is about thirty years old. Until that time it can only be increased from cuttings.

Araucaria araucana

Aristolochia macrophylla

Aristolochia

Birthwort

Climbing or trailing plants with large, beautifully shaped leaves and pipe-shaped flowers, which are visible only if we take the trouble to push aside the leaves behind which they are usually hidden.

Situation An excellent climber for covering walls, fences, sheds etc. Sometimes grown singly on a trellis. They are not self-clinging and must therefore be tied. In the first few years they grow fairly slowly.

Soil Will grow in any standard garden soil.

Propagation By layering shoots or from seed sown in a heated greenhouse.

Aristolochia macrophylla (syn *A. durior*, *A. sipho*), Dutchman's pipe: A trailer; the brown-green pipe-shaped flowers on long stems appear from June onwards. The plant may grow to a height of 10m and is winter-hardy. Will thrive both in full sun and in partial shade. The more shade, the deeper the green of the magnificent heart-shaped foliage.

Aronia

Choke Berry

Little known shrubs belonging to the rose family. It is a pity they are so rarely planted, for choke berries have great decorative value and impose few demands as to situation. Masses of white flowers in spring are followed by red or black berries. In autumn the foliage turns deep red.

Situation   In combination with other shrubs; also suitable as a windbreak. The smaller species are attractive free-standing shrubs for small gardens.

Soil   *Aronia melanocarpa* requires drier soil than the other forms, which prefer the soil to be slightly on the damp side.

Propagation   From seed or cuttings.

Aronia melanocarpa (syn *Mespilus arbutifolia* var *melanocarpa*, *Sorbus melanocarpa*, *Pyrus melanocarpa*), black choke berry. Flowers May–June, grows to 1m and develops root runners. The black berries drop in September.

Aronia prunifolia (syn *A. floribunda*, *Mespilus prunifolia*, *Pyrus floribunda*): Flowers May–June; red berries. Height 4m.

Aronia melanocarpa

Arundinaria pumila

Arundinaria

Bamboo

Though by no means all species are winter-hardy, these exotic looking plants can thrive in our regions. Bamboos originate in eastern Asia, where some species may reach a height of 10m. Here they will rarely grow beyond 3m; the bamboo in the photograph will not reach more than 60cm.

Situation   Excellent for use in grass gardens, stone-filled gardens and water gardens. *Arundinaria pumila* also makes good ground-cover. Provide damp soil.

Soil   Nutritious soil, rich in humus.

Propagation   The plants may be divided, or rooted runners may be removed and planted separately.

Arundinaria pumila (syn *Bambusa pumila*, *Pleiobastus pumilus*, *Sasa pumila*), dwarf bamboo: Evergreen, spreading plants with underground runners. In winter the foliage may turn yellow.

Arundinaria simonii (syn *Pleiobastus simonii*): Tall bamboo with yellow-green stalks. Must be covered in winter.

Aucuba

Spotted Laurel

Evergreen ornamental shrub requiring little light. It has beautiful foliage and produces cheerful berries. Unfortunately *Aucuba* is not entirely winter-hardy, which must be taken into account when choosing its position. Make sure that in winter the morning sun cannot reach it; this will solve the problem in not too severe winters. In general these shrubs develop best if they are not pruned.

Situation   Although not entirely winter-hardy, this is a very strong evergreen shrub which will thrive in situations unfavourable to other plants. May also be used to good effect in shrub borders.

Soil   Will do best in nutritious, moist soil, rich in humus.

Propagation   From cuttings.

Aucuba japonica: Evergreen shrub which may grow to a height of 2–3m within a decade. Insignificant flowers March–April, followed by red berries. The strain 'Variegata' has yellow-spotted foliage.

Aucuba japonica 'Variegata'

Berberis 'Bunch o' Grapes'

Berberis

Barberry

This large genus comprises evergreen and deciduous shrubs, all more or less thorny. The species which produce beautiful flowers and large number of fruits, and have fine autumn colouring, have exceptional decorative value. The barberry is a strong and easy-to-grow garden plant.

Situation   There is great variety in size, which means that barberries can be used in the smallest gardens as well as in public parks. Several species are suitable for forming loose hedges; they will create an impenetrable barrier, chiefly because of their thorns. A few species can also be used in formal hedges, since they are easily pruned. One example is *B. thunbergii* and its many strains. Always taper hedges at the top, otherwise they will grow bare at the base. Many species are planted in groups or are pruned into a square block, but they are equally valuable as free-standing plants. A number of barberries tolerate shade and may be planted under not too dense trees or on the north side of a building; for example *B. verruculosa*. Naturally they will produce fewer flowers and berries in such a situation. Low-

Berberis darwinii

Berberis × media 'Jewel of the Park'

growing forms such as *B. × media*, 'Jewel of the Park', can be used as ground-cover. Species with an abundance of berries are frequently incorporated in flower arrangements. In water they will last for a long time, eg *B.* 'Bunch o' Grapes'. Not all barberries will survive a severe winter without problems; they must be covered with pine branches. This applies, for example, to *B.* 'Bunch o' Grapes', *B. dictophylla* and *B. wilsoniae*.

Soil Most species make few if any demands on the soil condition. Deciduous species in particular prefer humus-rich soil with adequate nutrients.

Propagation Botanical species are sown immediately after the berries ripen: in November. Garden forms are increased from cuttings, by division or by layering.

Berberis 'Bunch o' Grapes': Compact, deciduous shrub growing to over 1m in height and 2m across. Yellow flowers in June, followed by berries in clusters resembling bunches of grapes. Initially erect, at a later stage the branches curve.

Berberis buxifolia (syn *B. dulcis*): Evergreen shrub, height up to 2m, with yellow, long-stalked pendent flowers in May, followed by large blue berries. In a sunny situation it may lose its foliage in winter. A well known form is the compact, 30–50cm tall 'Nana', a spherical shrub with orange-yellow flowers. May be pruned.

Berberis candidula: Evergreen barberry, growing to a height of 50cm, 1.5m across. In May it produces pale-yellow, single flowers, followed by dark-blue berries covered with bloom. The yellow twigs bear glossy dark-green leaves, strikingly white underneath. Mature leaves turn yellow in autumn. Also used in rock-, heather- and paved gardens. 'Amstelveen' is a very reliable cultivar, 1m tall, very winter-hardy, with a compact habit and fairly fast growing. 'Telstar' grows a little taller and has arching branches. The leaves are bluish white underneath.

Berberis darwinii: Evergreen shrub, height 1.5–3m, with dark-green foliage, pale green on the reverse, and a profusion of flowers April–May in dense, pendulous yellow clusters. In severe winters it may be damaged by frost.

Berberis gagnepainii var *lanceifolia*: Evergreen, erect-growing bush, 1.5–2m in height. In winter the dull-green foliage often turns reddish brown. Sulphur-yellow flowers May–June, followed by blue-black berries covered with bloom. Very winter-hardy, but a little sombre.

Berberis giraldii: Deciduous barberry growing to a height of 2m, 3m across. Bright-yellow flowers in June, followed by red berries. Egg-shaped dark-green foliage.

Berberis × hybridogagnepainii: The result of crossing *B. gagnepainii* var *lanceifolia* and *B. verruculosa*. Compact bush with green foliage. Beautiful strains are: 'Chenault', evergreen, to 1.5m tall and the same across. Compact habit, dull-green foliage, bluish white on the reverse. Purple-brown autumn colouring. 'Wallich's Purple' is also evergreen and grows to the same height, though somewhat less broad. Young foliage is brownish red, an attractive contrast to the glossy green mature leaves. The foliage is bluish green underneath. Very winter-hardy.

Berberis julianae: Evergreen shrub, height to 2m, the same across, with clusters of yellow flowers May–June. The leaves are dark green and glossy, partially turning red in autumn. Blue-bloomed berries. Very winter-hardy.

Berberis koreana: Erect-growing deciduous bush, to 1.5m in height, with dull-green leaves turning bright red in autumn. The yellow flowers which appear in May are followed by glossy, bright-red berries which are retained for a long time. Not affected by rust. 'Red Tears' thrives in dry soil.

Berberis linearifolia: Evergreen, erect-growing bush, to 1m in height, with glossy green leaves, curled at the edges. Clusters of large orange flowers in May. Very sensitive to frost.

Berberis × media: A semi winter-hardy hybrid, the result of crossing B. × *hybridogagnepainii* 'Chenault' and *B. thunbergii*. The best known strain is 'Jewel of the Park', to 1m in height and 2m across. The glossy dark-green foliage is partially retained in winter. A small number of yellow flowers appear May–June.

Berberis × mentorensis: Semi-hardy bush with slender habit. It grows to 1.5m in height and has dark-green foliage, partially turning orange yellow and red in autumn.

Berberis × ottawensis: Deciduous barberry, a cross between *B. thunbergii* and *B. vulgaris*, and frequently confused with the former. A bush growing to 2m in height, 3m across, with furrowed red-brown twigs. A profusion of yellow flower clusters in May, the calyxes red; red berries. 'Superba' is similar in size. It is a vigorous grower with red-brown foliage and pale-red autumn colouring. In the shade the foliage will remain green.

Berberis × rubrostilla: A variable, deciduous barberry, cultivated from seed and fairly sensitive to frost. 'Barbarossa' is a fine strain, growing to 1.5m in height and 2m across. A profusion of yellow flowers in June, followed by red berries.

Berberis sieboldii: Deciduous barberry, to 1m tall and 2m across. Yellow flowers in May, glossy red berries and fine red autumn colouring.

Berberis × stenophylla: Attractive green bush with gracefully arching branches; the result of crossing *B. darwinii* and *B. empetrifolia*. Height to 2m, 3m across. Yellow-orange flowers in May, followed by black berries covered in blue-white bloom. There are many useful, vigorous strains, such as 'Crawley Gem', 60cm in height, 1m across, and of loose habit. The yellow flowers are red outside. Often flowers for a second time in autumn.

Berberis sieboldii

Berberis × stenophylla

Berberis thunbergii 'Atropurpurea'

Betula costata

Berberis thunbergii: Deciduous bush; height and width to 1.5m. Yellow flowers May–June and conspicuous, glossy, bright-red berries in autumn. The foliage turns a beautiful shade of scarlet. 'Atropurpurea' is a very well known strain, with bronze-red foliage. Its dwarf form, 'Atropurpurea Nana', grows to about 40cm.

Berberis verruculosa: The branches of this evergreen bush, which grows to 1.5m, are covered in warts. Dark-green foliage, blue grey on the reverse; mature leaves turn red in autumn. Yellow flowers and dark-violet berries, covered with bloom.

Berberis vulgaris: Deciduous bush, native to most of Europe. Height and width to 2m. A profusion of pendent yellow flower clusters in May, followed by oblong red berries.

Berberis wilsoniae: Deciduous barberry, height to 1m, 2m across. Gracefully arching branches. Yellow flowers May–June and a profusion of salmon-red berries. The dense bush is closely covered in thorns. The dull, grey-green leaves turn red brown in autumn. It is a pity that this fine shrub is not more winter-hardy. 'Orangeade' grows less broad; it turns red in autumn and is a little less sensitive to frost.

Betula

Birch

Deciduous trees with sparse foliage, letting through a great deal of light. Because of their striking, peeling bark they are attractive at all times of the year. In general they are fast growing and will thrive even in poor soil. The leaves are well distributed over the branches, egg-shaped, with feathery veins. After a May shower the foliage may exude a delightful scent; it frequently turns golden yellow in autumn.

Situation Most birches are suitable only for planting in large gardens, parks and along streets in green verges. The only form suitable for small gardens is *Betula pendula* 'Youngii'. They are attractive planted singly, but a group of birches creates a very special effect. The birch is a lightwood tree and should therefore preferably be planted in full sun. Because of their rapid growth the trees are often used as windbreaks, sometimes only temporarily; once the other vegetation spreads the birches are cut down. *B. pendula* is a true pioneer. Birches should not be pruned in spring, for they might bleed to death.

Soil Poor, sandy or peaty soil is satisfactory. *Betula nigra* requires damp soil, while *B. jacquemontii* and *B.*

pubescens will thrive in both damp and dry soil.
Propagation From seed. Only *B. pendula* 'Youngii' is increased by grafting.

Betula albosinensis: Tree growing to 20m; very different in colour to the usual birch, being orange red to reddish brown. The bark peels very thinly. The variety *septentronalis* has a cherry-red trunk with a blue bloom.

Betula alleghaniensis, yellow birch: Height to 20m; initially the crown is narrow, but it later broadens. The elliptical leaves are 8–12cm long, dull yellow-green, with beautiful yellow autumn colouring. The peeling bark resembles that of the European bird cherry; it is greyish yellow in colour. A tree for parks, unsuitable for small gardens.

Betula costata: Grows to 15m in height and 10m across with a creamy yellow trunk which does not readily peel. The young shoots are initially brown. The tree branches fairly close to the ground, and is fast growing. Oval, erect-growing catkins follow the yellow-green flowers which appear April–May.

Betula ermanii: Height to 15m, with a compact oval crown and a vertical trunk. Fast growing, excellent for lining streets. The yellow-white bark remains smooth to a great age. The leaves appear early in the year.

Betula jacquemontii (syn *B. utilis* var *jacquemontii*): Tree growing to a height of 12m, 8m across, branching at a low level and with white, peeling bark. Leathery dark-green leaves with fine yellow autumn colouring. Fast growing.

Betula lenta, black birch: Height to 20m; narrow, erect-growing crown. The leaves are elongated oval, 6–12cm long, green and glossy, turning golden yellow in autumn. The bark is dark reddish brown, full of splits, but not peeling. This species is very similar to *B. alleghaniensis*, but is not quite so beautiful. A tree for parks.

Betula maximowicziana: Height to 15m; a tree with an airy crown and lime-like foliage which appears late in spring and turns golden yellow in autumn. The orange-grey bark peels in narrow strips.

Betula nana, dwarf birch: Grows to almost 1m in height and the same across with thin, downy twigs and almost circular grey-green leaves. Suitable for planting on slopes, in borders, and in heather- and rock gardens. Will grow in dry as well as in damp soil.

Betula nigra, river birch: To 10m wide and 20m tall, often with multiple trunks. Graceful habit. The red-brown bark peels in numerous curling strips. When mature it is characterised by the thick black patches of bark. The soft green foliage starts into growth late in spring.

Betula papyrifera, paper birch: Height to 12m and 12m across, often with multiple trunks. Snow-white bark, peeling in paper-thin strips; underneath the bark the trunk is red brown in colour. Faster growing than the common birch. Yellow-green flowers April–May,

Betula jacquemontii

Betula nigra

Betula pendula 'Youngii'

followed by pendulous catkins. If planted under other trees the bast will be brown.

Betula pendula (syn *B. alba*, *B. verrucosa*), common silver birch: Height to 20m, 10m across, with peeling white bark. In winter the tree is easily recognised by its twigs which are rough to the touch; it often has multiple trunks. Gracefully drooping branches. Branches more than one year old are initially brown, later turning white like the trunk. The covering bark is grey-green to black. 'Dalecarlica' has particularly fine leaves: fairly large, deeply incised and serrated. The tree grows to 8–10m and has an erect-growing trunk with gracefully arching branches. 'Fastigiata', over 10m tall, has erect-growing branches, somewhat erratically twisted. 'Purpurea', to 10m in height, has red-brown foliage, while the trunk is darker than in the other species. The autumn colouring is bronze green; fairly slow growing. 'Tristis', the weeping birch, grows to 8–12m in height, with a vertical trunk. The branches droop gracefully and retain their leaves for a long time. 'Youngii' is used for making arbours; this too is a weeping form, but without a vertical trunk. It grows to 4m in height, 6m across.

Betula pubescens (syn *B. alba*), common white birch: The new branches are downy to the touch. Height to 20m, with grey-green peeling bark. Will grow in marshy soil.

Broussonetia papyrifera

Broussonetia

Paper Mulberry

Deciduous, dioecious bush or small tree, with heart-shaped or deeply incised leaves. Originates in eastern Asia, but has become naturalised in southern Europe and in the eastern part of the United States. Tolerates a maximum of 15°C frost; in severe winters it must be protected.

Situation In a sunny or partially shaded position in the shrub border. To produce the brightly coloured fruits, a male and a female specimen must be planted together.

Soil Will grow in any soil.

Propagation By summer cuttings.

Broussonetia papyrifera, true paper mulberry: In its native country it may reach a height of 13m, but here it will not grow beyond 4m. The leaves are sometimes deeply incised, especially in young or severely pruned plants (see photograph). The large, serrated foliage is downy on the reverse and long stalked. The female flowers appear in May and are followed by orange-red berries.

Buddleia

Butterfly Bush

Graceful, summer-flowering bushes, flowering profusely every year. All species grow to between 2 and 4m.

Situation In warm, sunny places in the garden. *B. davidii* strains may be planted singly in small gardens. *B. alternifolia* may also be used in combination with other shrubs or hanging over a low wall.

Soil Dry to moderately moist, friable and nutritious garden soil, which may contain a certain amount of lime. Should be fed every year.

Propagation The species from seed, cultivars from cuttings. *B. alternifolia* is increased by grafting.

Buddleia alternifolia: A shrub from north-western China, it reaches a height of 3m and grows very wide. It is the only *Buddleia* species with alternating leaves. All other species have opposite-growing leaves. The long, thin arching twigs give the shrub a graceful appearance. Fragrant, violet-coloured flowers appear in June on the previous year's wood and for that reason these plants must not be pruned in spring. Pruning may be restricted to the removal of old wood. *B. alternifolia* is completely winter-hardy.

Buddleia davidii (syn *B. variabilis*), butterfly bush: A native of China, 2–3m tall. In the course of several years a large number of fine strains have been cultivated. Flowers on the new wood, from August until well into the autumn. It should be pruned to 30cm above ground level every year, preferably just before it starts into growth. The arching branches bear 15–25cm long leaves, downy white on the reverse. The fragrant terminal flower plumes, 10–25cm long, attract a large number of butterflies. Some of the most important cultivars are 'Black Knight', with large, dark-purple racemes; 'Border Beauty', a strongly branching bush, not very large, with a profusion of lilac-coloured flower plumes; 'Empire Blue' where neither the bush nor the deep-blue flowers grow very large; 'Fascination', with purple-pink, 'Royal Blue' with purple-red and 'White Profusion' with white flowers.

Buddleia Nanhoensis hybrids is the new name for a group of cultivars resulting from crossing *B. davidii* var *nanhoensis* (syn *B. farreri* var *crispa*) and strains of the ordinary *B. davidii*. They are low, spreading bushes with thin twigs, rarely growing beyond 1m. The original colour is pale purple-violet, but in 'Nanho Purple' the colour is deeper. The flowers have small, orange-yellow centres. In the coming years other cultivars will no doubt be developed.

Buddleia alternifolia

Buddleia davidii 'Fascination'

Buxus

Box

Evergreen shrubs which are easily pruned into a variety of shapes. The foliage has a distinctive scent, especially in the sun and in the course of pruning. The insignificant flowers are attractive to bees. The plant is poisonous.
Situation Sunny or partially shaded positions, not too dry. Can be used singly or in hedges, the taller-growing species also in the shrub border.
Soil Standard garden soil.
Propagation From cuttings and by layering.

Buxus sempervirens: Slow-growing bush or small tree, to 8m tall, with angular green twigs and leathery foliage. Greenish flowers April–May. 'Argenteovariegata', to 2m in height and 1m across, has egg-shaped to elliptical white-flecked foliage. 'Aureovariegata' reaches the same dimensions and has yellow-blotched foliage. 'Suffruticosa' is a dwarf variety, to 1m in height, 50cm across.

Buxus sempervirens 'Suffruticosa'

Callicarpa bodinieri var *giraldii*

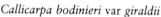

Callicarpa

Deciduous shrubs, chiefly grown for their colourful berries. In autumn the foliage is often beautifully discoloured, and after the leaves have fallen the berries often remain for nearly a month. In a mild climate *Callicarpa* may grow to 2–3m, but in severe winters they often freeze down to the ground and in the following season grow to only 1m and flower a little later.
Situation In a sunny or partially shaded position in front of a shrub border.
Soil Standard, nutritious garden soil.
Propagation From seed, by layering or from cuttings taken in late spring, early summer or during the dormant season.

Callicarpa bodinieri var *giraldii* (syn *C. giraldii*). Erect-growing bush, producing insignificant violet-coloured flowers in summer. Cross-pollination encourages fruits to set; for that reason *Callicarpa* bushes are generally planted in groups. 'Profusion', in particular, bears numerous purple berries.

Calluna

Heather, Ling

This genus consists of only one species, but there are very many garden forms. The common heather is native to Europe: it is found in all heathlands. The species flowers August–September, but the flowering season of the cultivars varies considerably: some flower as early as June, others not until November or December. Heathers can be conspicuous for their unusually coloured foliage as well as for their flowers. To avoid the plants becoming bare, they should be regularly pruned in spring; remember that our finest heathlands are pruned by sheep.

Situation Notably the heather garden, which has become so popular in recent years. However, heather can also be attractive in borders and as ground-cover. The species is suitable for use in wild gardens, where it will flower more profusely in sunny and partially shaded positions than in full shade. The multicoloured foliage will also show to good advantage in the light.

Soil In Europe, and especially in regions where the climate is affected by the Atlantic, there are large heathlands only occasionally interrupted by birches, grass species and the odd juniper bush. The soil is poor, humus rich, porous and lime free. Unless our garden soil resembles this condition it must be improved with conifer-needle compost, peat, leafmould and, to loosen the soil, sand. If your garden consists of calcareous clay soil, heather would not thrive and you would do better to forget about a heather garden.

Propagation By layering and from cuttings. Propagation from cuttings is very simple. Non-flowering tip shoots, about 7cm long, are cut in August or September; the lower leaves are removed. The shoots are placed at 1cm intervals in a tray or pot containing a mixture of potting soil and sharp sand. Water them with an anti-mildew product such as Captan. Keep them frost free under plastic during winter and provide bottom heat in spring. When they have rooted, the cuttings are pricked out.

Calluna vulgaris: Height 40–70cm; the dark-green, evergreen leaves are up to 3cm long, often scale shaped with two small ears at the base. The flowering season and the colour of the flowers vary; usually the flowers are purple pink, sometimes white. The erect-growing inflorescence is cluster- to plume-shaped. As a rule, heather branches strongly. The already large number of garden cultivars is still increasing. The following are some of the recommended strains:

'Alba Erecta' grows to 50cm, the foliage is bright green and the white flowers appear in August and September. 'Alba Plena', 40cm, spreading habit, with dark-green

Calluna vulgaris 'Alba Erecta'

Calluna vulgaris 'Golden Rivelet'

Calluna vulgaris 'H.E. Beale'

Calluna vulgaris 'Multicolor'

foliage and double white flowers from August to October.

'Alba Praecox', 40cm; spreading, erect-growing habit, dark-green foliage and white flowers from June to August.

'Alportii', 70cm; purple-red flowers August–September.

'Barnett Anley' has a spreading, bushy habit, to 50cm tall; purple flowers August-September.

'Blazeaway', 30cm, spreading habit. Yellow foliage; purple-red flowers July–August.

'Boskoop', 40cm; broad, spreading habit and bronze-green foliage turning orange red in winter. Pink flowers August–September.

'County Wicklow' has a compact habit, to 25cm. Green foliage and pale-pink flowers August–September.

'Cuprea' is erect growing, to 45cm; bronze-yellow foliage turning dark bronze in winter. Purple flowers August–September.

'C.W. Nix', to 70cm; dark-green foliage and reddish-purple flowers August–September.

'Elegantissima', 50cm; grey-green foliage and white flowers August–September.

'Elsie Purnell', 60cm; graceful habit with pale-pink to silvery flowers September–October.

'Flore Pleno', 60cm; double, pale lilac-pink flowers August–September.

'Foxi Nana', compact, spherical shape and not more than 15cm high. Purple flowers July–November.

'Golden Rivelet', 20cm; broadly spreading habit, yellow foliage turning bronze yellow in winter. Pale-purple flowers August–September.

'Gold Haze', 50cm; yellow foliage, white flowers August–September.

'H.E. Beale', 60cm; grey-green foliage. Silvery-pink double flowers September–October.

'J.H. Hamilton', 25cm; green foliage turning bronze in winter. Double, salmon-pink flowers August–September.

'Long White', 70cm; white flowers September–October; they may be cut for use indoors.

'Mrs Ronald Gray', creeping habit, to 8cm in height. Purple flowers August–October; bright-green foliage.

'Multicolor', 20cm; broad habit. The bronze-yellow foliage discolours. Purple flowers August–September.

'Peter Sparkes', 60cm; double deep-pink flowers September–October. Useful in dried flower arrangements.

'Robert Chapman', 40cm; orange-hued foliage which turns bronze red in winter. Purple-pink flowers August–September.

'Sunset', 30cm; broadly spreading habit, bronze-yellow foliage. Pink flowers August–September.

Calycanthus

Allspice, Jamaican Pepper

Aromatic, deciduous shrub with fairly large leaves and fragrant velvety red-brown flowers.

Situation   For sunny and partially shaded spots in the shrub border, or free standing. Pruning is rarely necessary, but is tolerated.

Soil   Prefers humus-rich, somewhat damp soil.

Propagation   From soft, half-ripe or hardwood cuttings, by layering and from seed.

Calycanthus floridus: Height to 3m and 2m across. A bush with dark, initially felty twigs, delightfully scented when cut. The oval to round leaves are up to 10cm long, grey green and hairy on the reverse. Fragrant red-brown flowers, 4–5cm in diameter, from May to July.

Calycanthus occidentalis: Height to 3m and 2m across; a bush with pointed oval leaves. The red-brown flowers which appear from June to August soon fade. Flowers much less profusely than the previous species.

Calycanthus occidentalis

Camellia japonica

Camellia

Beautiful, ornamental evergreen shrubs, unfortunately not very winter-hardy. Fine, mature specimens may be found in coastal areas, where they have survived many a winter thanks to a sheltered position and extra care. Elsewhere the camellia is better grown as a tub-plant.

Situation   Plant singly in a partially shaded position with a carpet of evergreen ground-cover to catch the faded flowers. It is essential to provide protection against east and north winds. The flowers will keep for a long time in water.

Soil   Acid, nutritious and preferably damp soil.

Propagation   By layering, from cuttings and from seed.

Camellia japonica: In China and Japan these shrubs may grow to as much as 10m in height, but in this country we are satisfied if they reach 1–2m. The flowers appear between January and April. They are white, pink, red or a combination of these shades; single, semi-double or double. Camellia plants have a shallow root system and the surrounding soil must be treated with care.

Campsis radicans

Campsis

Trumpet Flower

A climber with graceful, feathery foliage and conspicuously coloured trumpet-shaped flowers. Not entirely winter-hardy.
Situation A climber for a sunny, sheltered position, for example against a south-facing wall. Although it possesses clinging roots, it nevertheless requires some vertical support. Flowers rarely appear in the first year. During that period the plants should be cut back drastically, so that they can spread and do not grow bare at the base. Once they have grown sufficiently wide at the base, prune every spring to just above last year's growth. Do not be afraid to remove flower buds; the trumpet flower blooms on new wood.
Soil Nutritious soil.
Propagation From seed, cuttings or by layering.

Campsis radicans (syn *Bignonia radicans*): A 10m tall and 5m broad climber with twigs covered in fine down; at a later stage they develop roots. Orange flowers July–September. 'Praecox' flowers a little earlier; 'Yellow Trumpet' has yellow flowers.

Carpinus betulus

Carpinus

Hornbeam

Fast-growing tree, which can be pruned and is frequently used as a hedging plant.
Situation In parks or for lining avenues and, since it is satisfied with little light, also as undergrowth. It is particularly suitable for creating a fine, fast-growing hedge. Provided it is adequately fed and correctly pruned, the hedge may grow to 2m in height within five years, while it need not be more than 50cm wide. Should be pruned at least twice a year.
Soil Prefers calcareous soil, rich in humus.
Propagation From seed; cultivars from cuttings.

Carpinus betulus, common hornbeam: A tree growing to 20m, with yellow-green flowers in June. The deciduous foliage is bright green, oval, with downy veins on the reverse. 'Fastigiata' develops a dense, pyramid-shaped crown and grows to about 15m. 'Incisa' has deeply and irregularly incised leaves. In 'Purpurea' the foliage is initially brownish in colour, later green. 'Quercifolia' has a fairly broad habit. The foliage resembles that of the oak. 'Variegata' has yellow-blotched leaves.

Caryopteris

Shrubs with aromatic foliage and fine, violet-blue flowers late in the season.

Situation *Caryopteris* is not entirely winter-hardy and must therefore always be planted in a sheltered position. It is advisable to cover the plant in winter to protect it from drying cold winds. In spring it may be drastically cut back since the flowers appear on the new wood. Full sun and a well-drained position are essential if the plant is to flower profusely.

Soil Nutritious, humus-rich soil. Some lime is tolerated.

Propagation The species from seed, strains from summer cuttings.

Caryopteris × *clandonensis*: To 1.25m in height and the same across. Blue flower plumes September–October. The small oblong leaves are grey green and smooth edged. The fine cultivar 'Heavenly Blue' has deep-blue flowers and remains a little smaller.

Caryopteris incana (syn *C. mastacanthus*, *C. sinenses*, *C. tangutica*): Height at least 50cm; fragrant violet-blue flowers August–September.

Caryopteris × *clandonensis* 'Heavenly Blue'

Castanea sativa 'Glabra'

Castanea

Chestnut

Deciduous trees with serrated leaves. The male inflorescence is long and erect, the female is shorter. The fruit is enclosed in a prickly husk.

Situation Beautiful trees for a sunny or partially shaded position. The variegated forms are particularly suitable for planting singly. If the trees are grown for their fruits there should be level ground-cover on which the chestnuts can be easily found.

Soil Avoid heavy clay or very dry soil.

Propagation From seed.

Castanea sativa (syn *C. vesca*, *C. vulgaris*), sweet chestnut: Height to 20m, up to 10m across. The buds are covered in fine down; the narrow, leathery and glossy dark-green leaves, up to 18cm long, are rounded or broad wedge-shaped at the base, Initially the underside is hairy. Conspicuous greenish-yellow flower racemes appear in June, followed by very prickly fruits. There are a number of cultivars, varying in the colour and shape of the foliage, eg 'Glabra', which has dark-green and glossy leaves.

Catalpa

Indian Bean

Large-leaved deciduous trees which start into growth very late in spring. The magnificent flowers have an unusual scent. Conspicuous, long, very thin pendent fruits in winter.

Situation Fine specimen trees for warm and sunny positions. In a severe winter they may be damaged by frost, especially the unripened wood. If the Indian bean is surrounded by a lawn, manuring in late summer must be avoided, otherwise the *Catalpa* will continue to grow for too long.

Soil Standard, preferably nutritious garden soil, not too damp.

Propagation From cuttings.

Catalpa bignonioides: Tree growing to 10–15m, half as much across, with an umbrella-shaped crown. Oval leaves, to 20cm long; when rubbed they exude a disagreeable scent. Clusters of white flowers June–July.

Catalpa × erubescens (syn *C. bignonioides × C. ovata*): Richer flowering, and the flower clusters have a more compact shape. Oval leaves, initially brown in colour.

Catalpa bignonioides

Ceanothus hybrid 'Gloire de Versailles'

Ceanothus

Californian Lilac

Deciduous shrubs, usually producing lilac-like flowers in late summer. Not entirely winter-hardy; the root system must be covered in winter.

Situation Plant only in warm, sheltered positions, preferably in full sun. If they have suffered from frost they must be cut back to a level of 20cm; but their flowers will delight us the same year, for they appear on the new growth. May be used as a climber against a south-facing wall, but in that case the plant must be wrapped throughout the winter, so that we do not have to start every year with a small plant.

Soil Nutritious soil, which may contain lime.

Propagation By layering or from cuttings; the species also from seed.

Ceanothus americanus: White flower plumes July–August. Maximum height 1m.

Ceanothus hybrids: The result of crossing *C. delilianus* and *C. pallidus*. 'Gloire de Versailles' is reasonably winter-hardy and bears large clusters of pale-blue flowers. 'Marie Simon' and 'Perle Rose' have pink flowers.

Cedrus

Cedar

Magnificent evergreen conifers which may eventually grow to enormous size. In general they are quite winter-hardy.

Situation Because of their size they are definitely unsuitable for small gardens and should be planted only in large gardens and in parks. Cedars are at their finest when they can develop freely. Pruning is unnecessary and undesirable. The trees should be planted at least 5m away from paths. Provide a sunny position and low undergrowth.

Soil Well-drained standard garden soil. A certain amount of lime is tolerated.

Propagation Botanical species from seed, cultivars by grafting or from cuttings.

Cedrus atlantica (syn *C. libani* ssp *atlantica*, *C. libanotica* ssp *atlantica*), Mount Atlas cedar: A conifer up to 30m in height and 10m across, pyramid shaped and fairly loosely branched. Grown in a free-standing position it will retain even its lowest branches. Fairly fast growing. The needles are up to 2.5cm long, usually blue green to silver grey, rarely pale or dark green. The barrel-shaped cones are 5–7cm long, 3–5cm in diameter. The tree is reasonably winter-hardy, but in very severe winters even Mount Atlas cedars will freeze, certainly in an unsheltered position. The minimum acceptable temperature is approximately −20°C. Up to a great age the branches grow upwards, but eventually they attain a horizontal position. 'Aurea' is a golden-yellow form which grows to only 3–5m and may therefore be planted in a small garden; not entirely winter-hardy. A winter-hardy form is the well known blue cedar, *Cedrus atlantica* 'Glauca', which attains the same height as the species and has blue-green to blue-grey needles. Usually selected from seedlings and consequently somewhat variable. The weeping form of this cultivar is called 'Glauca Pendula'.

Cedrus deodora, Himalayan cedar: Tree growing to 20m and 8m across; somewhat sensitive to frost. Pyramidal shape, the main branches spread horizontally, the side-shoots droop. Dark blue-green needles, to 5cm long. Trees less than forty years old rarely produce cones. 'Aurea' has the same pyramid shape, but grows more slowly than the species; golden-yellow needles in spring and summer, more greenish yellow in autumn and winter.

Cedrus libani ssp *libani* (syn *C. libanotica*), cedar of Lebanon: Tree growing to a height of 40m and 12m across; slow growing. When young it has a broad pyramid shape; later the crown levels off and the branches attain their typical horizontal position. Dark-green needles, to 3cm long, in bundles of 30–40. The aromatically scented wood is red brown.

Cedrus atlantica 'Glauca'

Cedrus deodara

43

Celastrus

Staff Tree

Deciduous, winter-hardy climbers with brightly coloured fruits and occasionally fine autumn shades. The winding twigs may strangle a trunk or a branch to death by halting the sap stream.

Situation Fast-growing climbers for covering walls, pergolas and insignificant trees. They will grow both in full sun and in partial shade; they dislike strong winds.

Soil Any standard garden soil.

Propagation By layering, from seed or from half-ripe cuttings.

Celastrus orbiculatus (syn *C. articulatus*): Fairly inconspicuous yellow-green flowers in June. May grow to as much as 10m. The leaves vary in shape. The fruits are yellow, with orange-red seeds.

Celastrus scandens: Dioecious climber with oval leaves. Grows to 5–7m and has yellow-orange fruits.

Celastrus orbiculatus

Cephalotaxus harringtonia

Cephalotaxus

In the wild it is pyramid shaped, but in cultivation it is nearly always round, in our regions reaching a height of 3–6m. Like the *Taxus* it is an evergreen as well as poisonous conifer. *Cephalotaxus* tolerates pruning, but as a rule it is only necessary to trim the tips of the branches.

Situation May be used as a hedging plant or to create a low screen, but also in groups of conifers. The cultivar *C. harringtonia* 'Fastigiata' is beautiful planted singly. Provide a sunny or partially shaded position in moderately damp soil. These conifers dislike warm, dry winds.

Soil Standard to slightly acid garden soil.

Propagation From seed or cuttings.

Cephalotaxus harringtonia (syn *C. drupacea* var *pedunculata*): The 3–5cm long needles are arranged in two rows; they have silvery stripes on the reverse. 'Fastigiata' has a broad, pillar-shaped habit. The needles are arranged in spirals round the branches. Purplish, 3cm large fruits, which ripen only after two years. Initially slow growing.

Ceratostigma

Deciduous semi-shrubs, unfortunately not 100 per cent winter-hardy. Nevertheless the striking gentian-blue flowers give a special distinction to the garden in late summer, when other plants are fading. For that reason they deserve to be used more often. Very suitable for small gardens.

Situation The shrubs are related to the *Plumbago*, which is used as a house plant. However, *Ceratostigma* is a true garden plant, able to survive many a winter provided a number of factors are taken into account. In the first place they become winter-hardy only when they are well established, and the best planting season is therefore between May and July. In the second place they should be given a sheltered position in well-drained soil. Damp soil is unsuitable, as is a position open to severe winds in frosty weather. The plants may also be protected against frost by covering them. Spring pruning consists of removing twigs which have frozen. The shrub will grow both in full sun and in partial shade. *C. willmottianum* is attractive in the shrub border or planted singly. *C. plumbaginoides* is a fine edging plant, deriving its charm from the discolouring autumn foliage as well as from the flowers. Both plants are indispensible in blue borders, where they may be combined with the blue of bugloss and delphinium, of lungwort, speedwell and gentians.

Soil Dry, preferably somewhat calcareous soil.

Propagation From cuttings and by division.

Ceratostigma plumbaginoides: Height 30–40cm. A semi-shrub with a creeping trunk and angular, reddish twigs covered in short hairs. The plant is densely branched. The leaves are oval, almost sessile, 4cm long, green, turning red brown in autumn. Since this species has the character of a herbaceous perennial rather than of a shrub, it stands up better against cold weather. After a severe winter it usually starts into growth again from the roots. The small heads of gentian-blue flowers do not appear until September or October.

Ceratostigma willmottianum: A shrub to 1m in height, with bristly, angular twigs, reddish in colour. The diamond-shaped leaves are scattered along the branches; they are sessile, grey green in colour. The flower heads appear successively from July to October. The colour is not pure blue, rather purple violet. This species was introduced into England from China in 1908 and was distributed from there. Because it is not very winter-hardy its use in this country is restricted. Most specimens are found in coastal areas and even there they usually have to be replaced after a severe winter.

Ceratostigma plumbaginoides

Ceratostigma willmottianum

Cercidiphyllum

Cercidiphyllum japonicum

These shrubs are planted chiefly for their fine ramification and variable foliage colouring. The leaves resemble those of the *Cercis*, but in spring, when both plants are in flower, the difference is clearly noticeable; *Cercis* has a rich inflorescence, that of *Cercidiphyllum* is inconspicuous.

Situation Planted singly or in groups, in a partially shaded position.

Soil Nutritious, adequately damp soil.

Propagation From seed.

Cercidiphyllum japonicum: A native of China and Japan, where the tree may grow to 30m. In our regions it is a shrub or small tree, attaining a maximum height of 10m. In winter the red-brown twigs bear carmine-coloured buds. When it starts into growth the foliage is red; in summer the upper side of the leaves is green, the reverse blue green, in autumn discolouring to luminous yellow. The red flowers appearing April–May are insignificant. The straight fruits contain brown seeds.

Cercis siliquastrum

Cercis

Judas Tree

In southern countries *Cercis* is frequently used to line streets, but in this country it is insufficiently winter-hardy for this purpose. The flowers which appear on the bare wood before the leaves develop, are easily damaged by late night frosts.

Situation In a sheltered position in full sun it makes a fine specimen tree. The Judas tree can also be trained as an espalier.

Soil Nutritious, if necessary somewhat calcareous, garden soil, adequately moist.

Propagation From seed sown out of doors after mid-May. Seedlings must be kept frost-free in the first winter.

Cercis siliquastrum: A small tree or shrub, with multiple trunks. It can grow to a height of 7m, 5m across, but is usually smaller. A profusion of small purple flowers April–May, followed by kidney-shaped leaves, blue green underneath. The fruits of this butterfly-like bush are pod-shaped. 'Alba' is a strain with white, or very pale pink, flowers.

Cestrum

Evergreen bushes belonging to the potato family. They are not winter-hardy, but are suitable for a warm or unheated greenhouse. Since in this country they can only be grown as tub-plants they are not well known.
Situation The species described below requires a temperature of between 5 and 10°C in winter and will therefore just survive in an unheated greenhouse. When there is no more danger of night frost, the plants may be placed outside in a sheltered position in the sun or in partial shade. In October or, in a warm autumn, in November, they must be brought indoors.
Soil Nutritious, calcareous soil, which must be replaced every year if the plant is grown in a tub.
Propagation From cuttings.

Cestrum elegans (syn *C. purpureum*): A graceful climber, to 3m in height, with reddish-purple flowers April–September.
Cestrum newellii (syn *Habrothamnus newellii*): Height up to 3m, almost as much across; a shrub with red flowers May–September. Its parentage is unknown.

Cestrum elegans

Chamaecyparis lawsoniana 'Albovariegata'

Chamaecyparis

False Cypress

Evergreen conifers, distinguished from most other cypresses by their flat branchlets. In addition the cones are smaller. These plants occur in endless variation, from low to tall, and in various shapes and colours. You will notice the variety when you sow its seeds: the difference among the seedlings may surprise you. The species *lawsoniana*, in particular, has numerous ornamental forms. One of the deviations which occurs is the permanent retention of young foliage, which in the species disappears after a time. In addition to normal ramification, double twigs or leaves are encountered.
Situation False cypress trees grow best in a sunny or partially shaded position. The golden varieties require a little more light than the green forms. Garden cultivars with an unusual habit, such as the cone-shaped *C. lawsoniana* 'Ellwoodii', the compact *C. obtusa* 'Nana Gracilis' and *C. nootkatensis* 'Pendula' with its drooping twigs, are beautiful specimen trees. *C. lawsoniana* 'Alumnii' or 'Triomphe de Boskoop' may be used as hedging plants. For the rock garden there are miniature forms such as *C. pisifera* 'Plumosa Minima'. Most

Chamaecyparis lawsoniana 'Alumii'

Chamaecyparis lawsoniana 'Ellwoodii'

dwarf cypresses tolerate pruning; in some cases regular pruning is actually essential in order to achieve a fine, compact shape. *C. obtusa* may be pruned at various levels to create the shape so suitable for Japanese gardens. The last-mentioned type is sensitive to strong winds, as are *C. lawsoniana* and *C. nootkatensis*. They will thrive in a cool, damp environment. All false cypresses have poisonous elements.

Soil False cypresses prefer nutritious, well-drained soil, rich in humus, but adequately moist. They will do better in sandy or peaty soil than in clay.

Propagation Botanical species from seed, garden cultivars by layering and from cuttings. The easiest method is to take cuttings in summer and root them under mist, but when the number of successful rootings is of no importance, you might try to plant some cuttings out of doors. In this way you will quickly assemble an attractive collection. Make sure that the plantlets are not placed too close together. They will develop only if they have adequate space and are lit from all sides.

Chamaecyparis lawsoniana (syn *Cupressus lawsoniana*): Height to 35m, 10m across. Narrow, cone-shaped habit. The flat brown twigs bear pointed, blue-green scales, turned in at the tips, and with bluish margins on the reverse. In March to April it may flower profusely; at that time the tree appears to be covered in a red haze, from which the wind blows clouds of pollen. There are a large number of cultivars, only a few of which can be mentioned here:

'Albovariegata', a shrub growing to 7m in height, 4m across, with a compact round shape. The variegated foliage is retained if it has a sheltered position in winter, possibly with additional protection against drying, freezing winds.

'Alumnii' is a popular form, which grows rapidly to a maximum of 20m, 8m across. The dark-green foliage is smooth to the touch and is initially covered in blue bloom. Like the species it is used for hedge making.

'Columnaris' is cultivated on a large scale. It is a dense, narrow, cone-shaped tree with erect-growing dark-green twigs, bluish underneath.

'Dow's Gem', 3m in height and across, is an attractive, low and spreading cypress with twigs drooping at the tips. The foliage resembles that of the *Thuja*.

'Ellwoodii' is a well known type which may grow to 6m in height, 2m across; but it is a slow grower, with a squat, cone-shaped appearance. The foliage is blue green. May also be used as a tub-plant.

'Ellwood's Gold', like the previous example, but with pale-yellow foliage.

'Erecta Aurea', slow growing, height to 4m, 2m across. Golden yellow; the needles broaden into scales. Numerous spherical cones when the tree is a few years old.

'Filiformis', a loose, broad pyramid shape, to 4m in height. Thin, drooping branches and thread-like twigs.

'Filiformis Compacta' grows more slowly, to 2m, and also has fine, thread-like foliage.

'Fletcheri' a tree growing to 12m, 4m across, columnar and often with multiple trunks; blue-green foliage.

'Forsteckensis', a low, spherical bush with frizzy foliage, rather like moss; green.

'Gimbornii', to 80cm tall and broad. Slow growing, with purple tips to the leaves. Should be left to grow naturally; do not prune.

'Green Hedger', as the name implies, is particularly suitable for hedges. The foliage is fresh green.

'Howarth's Gold' has a squat, cone-shaped habit. The foliage is golden yellow.

'Intertexta', a weeping form, to 20m in height and 10m across with fairly thick branches with few side branches. Because of its open, upward-growing habit and gracefully drooping twigs it creates an elegant effect, but it is not suitable for small gardens.

'Lane', one of the finest golden-yellow strains, with a slender, upward-growing habit and spreading branches. To 6m in height, 3m across.

'Lutea' is also golden yellow, but the branches are more drooping than in the preceding cultivar. Narrow, columnar, to 10m.

'Minima Aurea' is very slow growing and reaches a maximum height of 1.5m. The colour is at its best in winter.

'Minima Glauca' grows to the same size as the preceding form, but has blue-green foliage and a more spherical habit.

'Nidiformis' resembles a large, blue-green bird's nest. To 1.5m tall, 2m across; excellent for a small garden.

'Pembury Blue' develops into a circular column. The young foliage is a beautiful bluish shade; in the second year it turns green.

'Pendula', height to 20m, 10m across, is a fine weeping form with branches reaching to the ground. Dark-green foliage and numerous male, purple-red flowers.

'Pygmaea Argentea', slow growing, height to 1m, the same across. To avoid scorched leaf-tips they must be protected against too bright sunlight and frost.

'Silver Queen' is a well known, pyramid-shaped form with striking creamy-white colouring.

'Spek', also called 'Glauca Spek', is a slender, erect-growing tree with fine pale-blue foliage.

'Stardust' has sulphur-yellow foliage and a broad cone shape; feathery ramification.

'Triomphe de Boskoop', a very popular form, also suitable for hedges. It must be pruned to remain compact. May grow to over 15m, 4m across. The twigs are rough to the touch; the foliage is covered in blue bloom. Fairly wind resistant.

'Winston Churchill' is another of the best golden-yellow strains, retaining its fine colouring throughout the year. Grows relatively slowly, maximum height 8m.

Chamaecyparis nootkatensis (syn *C. nutkaensis, Cupressus nootkatensis*): Tree growing to 40m in

Chamaecyparis lawsoniana 'Intertexta'

Chamaecyparis lawsoniana 'Minima Aurea'

Chamaecyparis nootkatensis 'Pendula'

Chamaecyparis pisifera 'Filifera Aurea'

height, with a slender pyramid shape. Yellow-brown, usually square, twigs and dark-green foliage. There are variations with yellow or blue-bloomed foliage, but the finest strain is undoubtedly 'Pendula', a weeping form, to 10m in height. The more or less horizontal branches are widely distributed and bear limp, pendent twigs with green scales, coarse to the touch.

Chamaecyparis obtusa (syn *Cupressus obtusa*, *Retinispora obtusa*): A tree growing to 30m; in cultivation usually a shrub, to 8m in height and 6m across, with brown, compressed twigs bearing blunt, bright-green scales with a blue margin, especially on the reverse, creating Y-shaped marking. The cones are up to 1cm long.

'Cripsii' grows to 3–5m in height; open habit and yellow foliage. Must be protected against severe frost.

'Filicoides', to 1.5m in height; very graceful, with fern-like branching. Dark-green foliage.

'Nana Gracilis' is the best known strain. A slow grower, to 2.5m, cone shaped, with characteristic fan-shaped branching. Moss-green foliage.

'Pygmea' has a broad spherical shape, to 75cm tall, with red-brown spreading twigs. Suitable for the rock garden.

'Tetragona Aurea'. Must be pruned to create a good shape and dense growth.

Chamaecyparis pisifera (syn *Cupressus pisifera*, *Retinispora pisifera*): A tree growing to 30m, with widely spreading, flattened brown twigs and pointed scales, dark green with a blue-white margin on the reverse, creating an X-shaped marking. The garden forms are lower growing.

'Boulevard', to 4m in height, 3m across, has a dense, broad cone-shaped, squat habit. The needle-shaped (young) foliage has a striking grey-blue colour.

'Compacta', to 50cm tall, a little more across, with a flattened spherical shape. The bluish-green foliage turns brown green in winter.

'Filifera', to 6m in height, has fine, thread-like foliage. Broad, cone-shaped habit.

'Filifera Aurea', with similarly shaped, golden-yellow foliage, grows to approximately the same size.

'Filifera Nana' is a very dense, spherical shrub with grey-green drooping foliage. To 50cm in height, 1m across.

'Nana' is very compact, to 60cm, dome shaped with green foliage. Excellent for the rock garden.

'Plumosa Aurea Nana' also remains compact, but grows to 1.5m in height and almost the same across. A very slow grower, it retains its fine golden colouring in winter. Like all Plumosa types it has needle-shaped scales, to 4mm long.

'Plumosa Minima', to 1m in height, 1.5m across; a bush with an irregular spherical shape and feathery foliage which appears to be soft, but is somewhat prickly.

'Pygmea', a slow-growing, compact, cone-shaped shrub, to 2m tall and approximately the same across. Densely

covered in young growth. Foliage bluish and frizzy.
'Squarrosa' has a dense, broad habit, to 10m. Squarrosa types have 1cm long, needle-like scales.

Chamaecyparis thyoides (syn *C. sphaeroidaea, Cupressus thyoides*): Not so well known; a 20m tall tree of slender pillar shape with branches at varying levels. Small, dark-green scales with a blue-white margin on the reverse, creating X-shaped marking. The tree produces numerous small cones.

'Ericoides' is an upward-growing, bronze-green conifer, retaining its youthful foliage, which discolours to reddish purple in autumn. To 2m in height and half as much across.

Chamaecyparis thyoides 'Ericoides'

Chamaedaphne calyculata var *nana*

Chamaedaphne

Evergreen bush, belonging to the heather family. The name does not indicate that this little shrub resembles an *Andromeda* rather than a *Daphne*. It is a native of polar regions and is therefore very winter-hardy.

Situation In damp, sunny or partially shaded positions in the heather garden, preferably planted in groups. Also attractive as an evergreen patch in the rock garden.

Soil Acid, humus-rich soil.

Propagation From seed or from cuttings taken from ripe wood.

Chamaedaphne calyculata (syn *Andromeda calyculata, Cassandra calyculata, Lyonia calyculata*): Height to 50cm; an evergreen bush with dark-brown, scaly, arching twigs and spreading habit. The oblong leaves, often facing upwards, are scaly on both surfaces. The urn-shaped white flowers appear April–May at the tips of the previous year's shoots. The dwarf variety, *nana*, 30cm in height and 50cm across, is smaller and more compact, with horizontal branches. More beautiful than the species!

Choenomeles hybrid

Choenomeles japonica

Choenomeles

Dwarf Quince

Deciduous shrubs (previously called *Chaenomeles*) with thorny twigs, flowering on wood developed in the previous year. Their ornamental value is chiefly derived from their single or double white, orange-red or red flowers and the greenish-yellow fruits in autumn; the latter are used in jam making.

Situation Shrubs for sun or partial shade. In a sheltered position they will flower early in the year. The low-growing species are used as ground-cover, in window-boxes or in the shrub border; in small gardens or in rock gardens they are sometimes planted singly. The taller growing forms may serve as an impenetrable, airy hedge, or they may be planted in a group in the shrub border or trained against a wall. Because they flower on the previous year's wood they should be very lightly pruned. The dwarf quince may be grafted on stock of the standard quince to form a weeping cultivar. In general the species require damp soil, the hybrids will grow in drier soil. Branches look attractive in a vase.

Soil Garden soil rich in humus.

Propagation The species from seed, strains from cuttings or by layering.

Choenomeles hybrids: The result of crossing C. *japonica* and C. *speciosa*. Well known forms are: 'Boulde de Feu', to 2m, with orange-red flowers before most of the foliage has developed; 'Fascination', to 1m tall, 1.5m across, with scarlet flowers; 'Nicoline', to 80cm in height, 1.5m across, flowers profusely with large, open, deep-red flowers.

Choenomeles japonica (syn *Cydonia japonica, C. maulei, Pyrus japonica*): Height to 2.5m, a little larger across. A very winter-hardy shrub with red flowers March–April, followed by fragrant yellow-green fruits. The twigs bear a number of warts. Dark-green, oval leaves, 3–5cm long. 'Sargentii', to 75cm, is a beautiful strain with spreading habit and a profusion of salmon-coloured flowers.

Choenomeles speciosa (syn *C. lagenaria, Cydonia japonica*), Japanese quince: To 2m in height and 1.5m across, with much stronger thorns than the previous species. Glossy, spear-shaped, dark-green leaves, to 8cm long. Red flowers April–May; yellow-green fruits. 'Brilliant' to 1.25m in height, flowers profusely; the flowers are deep red. 'Nivalis', to 2m, has white flowers. 'Simonii' is a dwarf shrub with spreading branches, to 50cm tall, 1.25m across. Single or semi-double red flowers March–April.

Choisya

This genus comprises only one species, an evergreen bush originating in Mexico and therefore not entirely winter-hardy.

Situation It is definitely worth trying in a very sheltered position, for example in a patio garden. Otherwise the *Choisya* can be used as a tub-plant: in summer in a sunny spot out of doors, in winter in good light in an unheated greenhouse. In mild climates the plant is also grown against walls.

Soil Nutritious garden soil.

Propagation Half-ripe cuttings are taken in late spring or in summer.

Choisya ternata: An evergreen bush, growing to 1m in height and the same across. Leathery, 3-lobed leaves appear on the grey-green twigs which are covered in short hairs; the foliage is glossy and aromatic. The delightfully scented flowers appear in large plumes May–June. If the temperature in its winter quarters is raised a little in January, it may flower as early as February.

Choisya ternata

Cladrastis kentukea

Cladastris

Yellow-wood

A deciduous tree with multiple trunks, which in this country grows to a maximum of 10m. In its native country, the south-eastern part of the United States, it may grow twice as tall. The wood is very fragile.

Situation Beautiful tree for a free-standing position; the foliage discolours in autumn. A sunny position is essential. Not to be used in areas where hares and deer are numerous, for they will damage the wood.

Soil Nutritious, loamy soil.

Propagation From seed sown after mid-May, or from root cuttings taken in December.

Cladastris kentukea (syn *C. tinctoria, Virgilis lutea*): When bare, the tree is characterised by its smooth bark and the buds which almost disappear in the marking. The faintly scented flower clusters, which may be as much as 30cm long, appear May–June. The florets are white, with a conspicuous, speckled red stain at the base of the upper petal. The composite leaves are irregularly pinnate, with short-pointed, smooth-edged oval leaflets. The compressed pods contain 4–6 seeds.

Clematis

Clematis alpina 'Willy'

Clematis hybrid 'Hagley Hybrid' (jackmanii-type)

This genus embraces numerous hardy climbers with brilliantly coloured flowers, and also a number of perennials which will not be dealt with in this context. The fairly small-flowered botanical species make few demands on their situation. Some of them actually grow so rampant that we are more inclined to curb than to encourage them. The large-flowered hybrids are less easily satisfied, but exuberantly repay extra attention.

The clematis has opposite growing leaves, single, ternary or pinnate. It drops in winter. The leaf-stalks frequently turn into tendrils. The flowers are flat and open, or bell-shaped, and are sometimes followed by very decorative down.

Situation The large-flowered climbers, in particular, are usually grown against walls, but they are also very suitable for covering pergolas, fences and other partitions. The wild Virgin's bower, *Clematis vitalba*, is particularly vigorous. Together with *C. montana* and a number of other small-flowered species, it tolerates a dry position. The early-flowering species *C. alpina* and *C. macropetala* are not very well known. The particularly charming bell-shaped little flowers appear as early as May. The plants are winter-hardy and relatively disease free. Clematis plants prefer fresh, adequately moisture-retaining soil. The base of the plant is particularly important; be sure to keep it out of the sun. A roof tile is often used to protect it, but a small evergreen bush is a much more attractive solution. However, remember that the root systems may compete. The upper parts of the plants enjoy full sun, especially in the case of large-flowered hybrids. Clematis should be planted against west- or east-facing walls rather than those facing south. Sun and frost may have such a drying effect that the plant freezes, especially in a draught. A well-chosen position and, in the case of young or early-flowering plants, protection by means of pine branches, may prevent a number of problems. A clematis grows best where it is able to develop freely. Coarse netting may provide good support. Young plants should be trained a little at first; later the tendrils will look after themselves.

Where pruning is concerned a distinction is made between spring- and summer-flowering plants. The former are cut back after they have flowered; the latter may be pruned in spring. Clematis flowers will keep well in water.

Soil Large-flowered hybrids require very nutritious soil, rich in humus. Always make a large planting hole and fill it with rotted cow manure, leaf mould, compost, peat etc. Clematis likes calcareous soil. In the autumn they should be given a second feed consisting of dried blood or well-rotted cow manure. Small-flowered species are less demanding.

Diseases The large-flowered clematis, in particular, may suddenly die back in winter as a result of soil mildew. The plants may already be infected when they are bought. The infection can be arrested with a fungicide such as Benomyl.

Propagation From seed or cuttings, or by layering. The seed should be sown soon after it is gathered, since it takes a long time to germinate and is only viable for two years. Grafting on roots of *C. flammula*, *C. vitalba* and *C. viticella* is also possible.

Clematis alpina: A climber growing to a height of 3m, with red-brown twigs and usually double leaves arranged in groups of three. Single, bell-shaped flowers, violet blue, with large honey sacs. 'Willy' flowers from May to July; purple-red flowers followed by attractive fruits. Should be pruned early in August. Will thrive in fairly dry soil.

Clematis × durandii: The result of crossing *C. integrifolia* and *C. × jackmanii*. A shrub growing to 1.5m, not a real climber, although it can be tied to a trellis. Large, dark-violet flowers June–September.

Clematis flammula: A fine climber for a sheltered position; to 4m tall, covered in delightfully scented small white flowers late in the season.

Clematis hybrids: This group embraces the large-flowered climbers which usually grow to 5m in height and flower between May and September. They are divided into five groups:

Lanuginosa 'Lilacina Floribunda', deep purple-blue; Lincoln Star, pink with a purple-brown centre; 'Madame Le Coultre', white, large flowers; 'Nelly Moser', very well known, lilac-pink flowers with darker veining; 'The President', dark violet-blue.

Patens 'Lasurstern', very dark blue flowers; 'Miss Bateman', white with brown stamens; 'Vyvyan Pennell', double, purple-red flowers.

Florida 'Duchess of Edinburgh', double white flowers.

Jackmanii 'Comtesse de Bouchaud', soft satin-pink; 'Gipsy Queen', dark red with paler veining; 'Hagley Hybrid', profusely flowering, red purple; 'Jackmanii-Alba', white; 'Jackmanii Superba', vigorous, growing to 10m; a profusion of violet-blue flowers.

Viticella 'Ernest Markham', one of the best known, has a profusion of red flowers; 'Lady Betty Balfour', velvety purple; 'Ville de Lyon', a reliable, richly flowering plant with carmine-red flowers.

Clematis integrifolia: A graceful, not entirely winter-hardy shrub bearing violet-blue, bell-shaped flowers June–August; height, 0.8–1.5m. A lower garden form, growing to 25–50cm, is called 'Hendersonii'. The violet-coloured flowers appear in groups of four. The great advantage of these shrubs is that they do not need tying.

Clematis × jackmanii: The result of crossing *C. lanuginosa* and *C. viticella* and itself the parent plant of other cultivars. A climber, to 4m, with large, violet-blue

Clematis hybrid 'Nelly Moser' (lanuginosa-type)

Clematis integrifolia

Clematis montana 'Rubens'

Clematis vitalba

flowers, 10cm in diameter, July–October. It is a strong plant, a vigorous grower. The leaves are usually grouped in threes.

Clematis macropetala: A very graceful climber with double groups of three leaves and a profusion of bell-shaped violet-blue flowers May–June. Bushy habit; height to 3m; very winter-hardy. 'Maidwell Hall' grows to the same height, but has single flowers. In 'Blue Bird' the flowers are larger and of a magnificent deep-blue colour. 'Markhamii' has pale-red flowers.

Clematis montana: A strong climber, fast growing, possibly to a height of 12m. Will do well in fairly dry soil or against a north-facing wall. Flowers profusely May–June with white or pink four-petalled flowers. 'Alba' has white, 'Rubens' pale-red and 'Tetrarose' purple-red flowers. The latter form is larger in all its parts, with flowers up to 8cm in diameter.

Clematis tangutica: Unlike most *Clematis* this species has pale-yellow, bell-shaped flowers. It is also remarkable for its late flowering season of August to October. Like other late-flowering *Clematis* plants it may be combined with climbing roses; when the roses are no longer in flower, *Clematis* takes over. *C. tangutica* may grow to 6m and is a fairly vigorous grower. The foliage is feathery, grey green. The flowers are followed by striking silvery down.

Clematis vitalba, old man's beard, traveller's joy: A very strong climber which may reach a height of 15m; a rapid grower tolerating much more shade than other *Clematis* plants. In woods it climbs tall trees; sometimes the scent of the flower plumes reaches us before we notice the little creamy-white flowers. The flowering season extends from July to September. In autumn the plant is covered in silvery down. The red-brown twigs bear feathery leaves.

Clematis viticella: A climber growing to 3m, with violet-red flowers August–September. Hairy, red-brown twigs with leaves in groups of three or pinnate. 'Albiflora' has white flowers; 'Kermesina', wine red, is the best known form; 'Minuet' has purple-red and 'Purpurea' reddish-purple flowers; 'Multiplex' is a double-flowered purple cultivar; the crimson 'Ville de Lyon' flowers profusely.

Clerodendrum

Small, deciduous tree with large, fragrant flower clusters in late summer, sometimes followed by berries.
Situation A beautiful specimen tree for small gardens, for example in a lawn or in a bed of low-growing ground-cover. Will do best in a sheltered position in full sun.
Soil Standard, nutritious garden soil.
Propagation From seed, root suckers, root cuttings or cuttings taken from half-ripe shoots.

Clerodendrum trichotomum: A tree with a round crown; height to 6m. The oval, 10–25cm long leaves are downy on the reverse; they are largest in young plants. When rubbed, the leaves have a disagreeable scent. White flowers appear in broad clusters August–September. The calyx is red, providing an attractive contrast to the white flowers and also to the blue berries. As a rule the branches will be damaged by frost in winter, but in spring they will start into growth again; at that time the dead wood is removed. The variety *fargesii* is more winter-hardy and has smaller flowers and leaves.

Clerodendrum trichotomum var *fargesii*

Clethra alnifolia 'Rosea'

Clethra

White Alder

Deciduous shrubs with delightfully scented flowers in late summer, and often with fine autumn colouring.
Situation In full sun or partial shade in fairly damp soil. Attractive grown singly in a water garden or in the shrub border. The flowers are very attractive to butterflies. Given suitable soil, *Clethra* will also thrive in salty and windy coastal areas. Further inland they look well when planted against the edge of a wood.
Soil *Clethra* species require acid soil, adequately moist and humus-retaining.
Propagation By layering, from seed or from cuttings taken from soft or half-ripe wood.

Clethra alnifolia: A shrub growing to about 2m, with obovate, pointed leaves. White flowers in erect-growing racemes July–August. Berries will be retained throughout the winter.
Clethra barbinervis: A little less winter-hardy; height 4m. White flowers and yellow and red autumn colouring.

Colutea arborescens

Colutea

Bladder Senna

Shrubs with butterfly-like flowers, often with a prolonged flowering season, rapid growth and large, inflated seed pods. These strong shrubs will do well even in the poorest soil. Plants which have grown bare will start into growth again at the base after drastic pruning.

Situation In large gardens, where their prolonged flowering season, graceful foliage and attractive fruits make them a welcome addition to shrub combinations. Because of its rapid growth the bladder senna is sometimes used as temporary infilling in wild plantations. After about four years it is removed.

Soil Will grow in any soil.

Propagation From seed and cuttings.

Colutea arborescens: Erect-growing shrub, to 3m in height and as much across. Graceful, pale-green feathery foliage and yellow flower clusters June–August. These are followed by seed capsules which do not burst open.

Colutea × media: Brown-red flowers throughout the summer. A little smaller than the preceding species. The foliage is blue green.

Cornus alba 'Argenteomarginata'

Cornus

Dogwood

A large genus consisting of deciduous shrubs, greatly varying in height, popular because of the beautiful colour of the wood, the inflorescence or the bright autumn colouring. *Cornus canadensis* and *C. suecica* are herbaceous plants and are attractive when used as ground-cover in partially shaded spots.

Situation Most dogwood species will thrive in full sun or in partial shade, but *C. amomum* prefers the former. The yellow dogwood will tolerate a fair amount of shade, but in that situation will flower less profusely. In general they like damp, somewhat acid soil. Dogwood species which do not need a damp position are: *C. kousa*, *C. mas*, *C. nuttallii* and *C. sanguinea*; *C. mas* and *C. sanguinea* will tolerate the least moisture. *C. mas* can be used for hedges, because it accepts pruning. Because of its early flowering season and red berries it is also attractive planted singly, but it is used in groups or in combination with other shrubs as well. The other dogwood species are planted singly in the case of *C. controversa*, *C. florida* and *C. kousa*, or in groups in the case of *C. alba*, *C. sanguinea* and *C. sericea*. All these shrubs are too large for small gardens.

Soil All dogwood species prefer humus-rich soil.
Propagation *C. alba*, *C. stolonifera* and all garden forms are increased by layering. *C. florida*, *C. kousa*, *C. mas* and *C. sanguinea* are propagated from seed. The last-mentioned species and *C. sericea* can also be grown from cuttings.

Cornus alba (syn *C. tatarica*), white dogwood: A shrub growing to 3m and almost as much across, with elliptical green foliage, blue green underneath. These erect-growing shrubs have a conspicuous red bark. White flowers May–June, followed by white to pale-blue berries. There are a number of beautiful garden forms. 'Argenteomarginata' has foliage with a white margin; in 'Gouchaultii' the leaves are blotched with yellow and pink. 'Kesselringii' grows stiffly upwards and has very dark, almost black twigs and foliage which is initially red to red-brown; brown-red autumn colouring. 'Siberica' is very well known for its striking red wood which looks so cheerful in winter; the green foliage discolours to red in autumn. In 'Spaethii' the foliage is initially bronze coloured, later with golden-yellow blotches and margins.

Cornus amomum: A fairly compact shrub, to 4m in height, with yellow-white flowers May–June and bright-blue to blue-black berries. The oval green leaves, pale green on the reverse, grow on dark-purple twigs. Fine autumn colouring.

Cornus controversa (syn *C. brachypoda*): A tree or shrub to 6m in height; the twigs are usually covered in bloom. Broad oval green leaves, to 15cm long, with a short point; whitish underneath. The branches are well spaced and grow level. White flowers June–July, followed by dark-blue berries. 'Variegata' has white-blotched foliage.

Cornus florida: A shrub growing to 6m in height and 4m across, with a fairly irregular habit and bloomed twigs with invisible buds. Green, rounded oval leaves, to 14cm long, whitish underneath and turning deep scarlet in autumn. Inconspicuous yellow-green flowers in May; these are surrounded by four large white bracts which contribute a great deal to the plant's ornamental value. When the shrub ceases to flower the bracts turn pale red; red berries. 'Rubra' is a fine strain with reddish-purple bracts. 'White Cloud' bears a profusion of white flowers.

Cornus kousa var *kousa*: A shrub to 6m in height, with plain brown twigs and dark-green foliage, blue green on the reverse, and magnificent red autumn colouring. A profusion of greenish-yellow flowers surrounded by white bracts in June, followed by attractive raspberry-like pale-red fruits. In the variety *chinensis* the bracts are even larger and whiter.

Cornus mas, yellow dogwood: A shrub or small tree, to 7m in height and 4m across, fairly slow growing. Oval green leaves, pale green underneath. Small yellow flower umbels appear in February, before the foliage. These are

Cornus alba, fruits

Cornus kousa var *kousa*

Cornus mas

followed by edible red fruits. This is the only *Cornus* species which tolerates lime. 'Aurea' has yellow leaves, later turning more yellowish green. 'Variegata' has a white margin along the leaves.

Cornus nuttallii: A shrub or small tree, up to 6m in height and 4m across, with rounded oval green foliage, whitish underneath. The twigs are not bloomed. It flowers in May when it catches the eye with its bright white, fairly flat to slightly curved, bracts. Magnificent autumn colouring.

Cornus sanguinea, common dogwood: A fast-growing shrub, to 5m in height, with somewhat arching branches. The blue-green twigs are often reddish on the side facing the sun; in winter they are dark red. The hairy green foliage turns scarlet in autumn. White flower panicles appear May–June, followed by black berries. A tenacious shrub.

Cornus sericea (syn *C. stolonifera*): A densely branched shrub, to 3m tall and as much across. The twigs are self-rooting at the base. Fresh green foliage and white flowers May–June, followed by white berries. A much cultivated strain is 'Flaviramea', conspicuous by its yellow-green bark in winter. In public gardens it is often combined with the red bark of the white dogwood.

Corylopsis pauciflora

Corylopsis

Winter Hazel

Early flowering shrubs with fragrant, bell-shaped yellow flowers and foliage which resembles that of the hazel. However, these plants belong to the *Hamamelis* family, whereas hazels are related to the birch. In autumn the foliage turns yellow.

Situation Their size makes them suitable for small gardens. They enjoy a sunny or partially shaded position, preferably somewhat sheltered, so that the early inflorescence cannot be damaged by night frosts.

Soil Lime-free porous soil, rich in humus.

Propagation From cuttings taken from soft or half-ripe wood and by layering.

Corylopsis pauciflora: A spreading shrub, to 1m in height, bearing pale-yellow flower clusters in March or April, depending on the temperature. The oval leaves are blue green on the reverse.

Corylopsis spicata: A 1–2m tall shrub which may flower as early as February. Pale-yellow flowers in pendent spikes. The foliage remains attractive in summer and turns yellow in autumn.

Corylus

Hazel, Filbert

Hazels are planted for the sake of their nuts, the beautiful colour of their foliage or their unusual habit. They are winter-flowering trees or shrubs with alternate leaves.

Situation The common hazel is a fast grower and is very suitable for creating a windbreak especially as it tolerates shade. The nut harvest is usually greatest in coastal areas, where there is less chance of night frosts. Hazels are occasionally planted along streets. The corkscrew hazel and the filbert are attractive specimen trees for small gardens.

Soil Standard or calcareous soil.

Propagation The species from seed, cultivars by layering, or by grafting on *Corylus colurna* stock.

Corylus avellana, common hazel: The following are beautiful ornamental forms: 'Contorta', height 2–3m, with twisted branches; 'Pendula', the weeping form; 'Aurea' with yellow to fresh green foliage and 'Fuscorubra' with purple-red foliage.
Corylus maxima, filbert: 'Purpurea' has magnificent dark reddish-brown foliage.

Corylus avellana 'Contorta'

Cotinus coggygria

Cotinus

Wig Tree, Smoke Tree

Deciduous ornamental shrubs with unusually coloured foliage and conspicuous inflorescence, to which they owe their common name. They are freely branching; the leaves are evenly distributed. The trunk of older specimens is grey-brown in colour, the branches are pale grey-brown, smooth, while young twigs are glossy, sometimes with numerous lenticels.

Situation The colouring of the foliage shows to best advantage in full sun. Their size makes these shrubs unsuitable for small gardens. The red-leaved strains are useful for creating a contrast; in the shrub border the dark-red leaves might be combined with grey-green or variegated foliage. Wig trees are also planted in groups and in shrubberies. In addition to their unusual inflorescence they have striking autumn colouring. Timely pruning will prevent the shrub growing bare at the base.

Soil Standard garden soil; lime is tolerated.

Propagation From cuttings and by layering.

Cotinus coggygria (syn *Rhus cotinus*): A shrub to 3m in height and 2m across. Broken twigs exude a disagreeable scent. Up to 8cm long, the obovate, blunt green

Cotinus coggygria 'Royal Purple'

leaves turn yellow orange to deep purple in autumn. The leaves are blue green on the reverse. The large plumes of green flowers appear June–July, and while the fruits are ripening the violet coloured, hairy and sterile stalks lengthen, giving the inflorescence the appearance of a tangled wig. The fruits are lop-sided. 'Purpureus' has green foliage, but purple-red flower-stalks and hairs; rarely grown. 'Royal Purple' is a vigorous grower with large, dark red-purple leaves with a metallic sheen. As the season progresses, the colour becomes deeper. In 'Rubrifolius' the foliage is also dark red-purple. In severe winters the branches may be damaged by frost, but the shrub will start into growth again in spring. 'Red Beauty' is a fine new cultivar with larger leaves than 'Royal Purple', but paler in colour.

Cotinus obovatus (syn *C. americanus*, *Rhus cotinoides*): Up to 6m in height, 3m across, a shrub or small tree with red twigs and green flower plumes June-July, again with the typically lengthening flower-stalks, purple-red twigs and green leaves, to 15cm long, turning orange red in autumn. The beauty of this species is chiefly due to its fine autumn colouring.

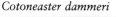

Cotoneaster dammeri

Cotoneaster

Rose Box

This extensive genus comprises deciduous as well as evergreen shrubs, whose ornamental value depends mainly on their graceful habit, the striking colours of their fruits and their autumn foliage; occasionally on the abundance of flowers which are attractive to bees. *Cotoneaster* species belong to the rose family. The buds are evenly distributed, sometimes arranged in double rows; the leaves are undivided and smooth edged. The flowers appear in groups of five; the red or black berries contain 2–5 seeds.

Situation The low-growing, evergreen species – *Cotoneaster dammeri* is a good example – are ideal as ground-cover. *C. horizontalis* is a typical wall-shrub, very attractive with its ferny branching. *Cotoneaster simonsii* may be pruned to form a close hedge, others are suitable for more open hedges. *Cotoneaster* species with graceful habit and abundant fruit formation, such as *C. salicifolius* and *C. watereri* hybrids, make excellent specimen plants. Species with arching branches are sometimes grafted on stock and sold as standard trees. Lower growing species may be planted in groups in the shrub border. They are often grown in troughs.

The foregoing shows the many ways in which *Cotoneaster* species can be used. It is therefore unfortunate that the genus's sensitivity to fireblight has, at the time of writing, led to a warning against the use of some species in public gardens, eg *C. bullatus*, *C. praecox*, *C. salicifolius*, *C. salicifolius* var *floccosus* and *C. watereri*. Frost is another enemy of the *Cotoneaster*. The taller growing species which cannot be covered with snow (eg *C. dammeri*) are particularly subject to frost damage. Since 1984 the number of rose box plants has diminished considerably as a result of bacterium infection and frost. Their importance as ornamental shrubs has been drastically reduced.

Soil Rose box makes few demands on soil type, but is out of place in damp, very calcareous soil.

Propagation The species from seed, cultivars by layering and grafting.

Cotoneaster adpressus: A deciduous creeping shrub, to 30cm tall, with dull-green foliage, downy on the reverse in the early stages. Pink flowers May–June, followed by bright-red berries.

Cotoneaster bullatus: Fast growing, with a spreading habit, up to 3m in height and bearing pink flowers May–June, followed by red berries. The oval leaves, to 8cm long, are blistered on the upper surface and are retained in winter.

Cotoneaster dammeri var *radicans*: Vigorous evergreen ground-cover. Height to 20cm, creeping habit and rooting branches. The branches will arch gracefully over a low wall. Oval, dull-green leaves, to 3cm long, which may turn brown or drop in winter. At that time the branches may also die back, but the plant will soon recover. White flowers in May; red berries. Tolerates a great deal of shade. 'Major' is a slightly larger and more winter-hardy plant. In late autumn it may have some orange-yellow leaves; few berries. 'Coral Beauty' is fast growing, to 50cm, with projecting, arching branches. A profusion of coral-red berries. 'Skogholm' is even larger, but bears far fewer berries. Both plants are very winter-hardy.

Cotoneaster dielsianus (syn *C. applanatus*): A shrub growing to a height of 2m, with arching branches. Dark-green oval leaves, grey and felty underneath, turning red in autumn and dropping in winter. White flowers in June, numerous red berries. Fast growing.

Cotoneaster divaricatus: A deciduous shrub, to 2m in height, with thin, arching twigs. Glossy green, broad oval to round oval leaves with beautiful autumn colouring. Pale-red flowers in June; red berries.

Cotoneaster franchetti: Height to 2m. Deciduous, upward growing shrub with arching branches. Glossy green foliage, yellow grey and felty underneath. Fine autumn colouring. Pale-red flowers in June, followed by oblong red berries which are retained for a long time.

Cotoneaster horizontalis: A dense shrub, to 1m in height, 2m across, with buds arranged in two rows.

Cotoneaster dielsianus

Cotoneaster horizontalis

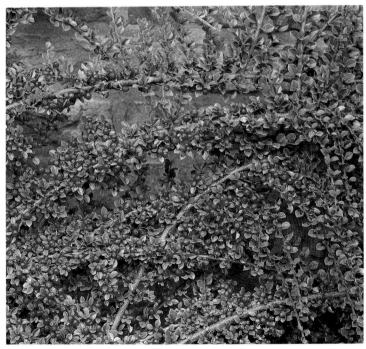

Cotoneaster salicifolius

Cotoneaster Watereri hybrid 'Cornubia'

Short, pointed oval leaves, to 1.5cm long, green and glossy, discolouring to purple red in autumn. Characterised by its flattened, horizontal habit. Flowers May–June; red berries. A wall plant, also suitable for slopes.

Cotoneaster praecox: Height to 60cm, small dull-green leaves with a wavy edge. Few orange-red berries, except in the cultivar 'Boer', which is therefore to be preferred to the species. Very winter-hardy.

Cotoneaster racemiflorus: A deciduous shrub, to 2.5m in height, with hairy grey twigs. Up to 4cm long, practically circular dull-green leaves, greyish on the reverse. White flowers May–June, followed by early ripening berries. There are two varieties.

Cotoneaster roseus: A large, strong shrub, up to 3m in height and 5m across. In June the arching branches bear white flowers, followed by numerous red berries. The dull-green foliage drops in winter.

Cotoneaster salicifolius: An evergreen shrub, to 3.5m in height, with felty, arching branches and spear-shaped glossy green, willow-like leaves. White flowers June–July and later an abundance of red berries. A particularly fine variety is *floccosus*, with very gracefully arching branches and a profusion of red berries. 'Parkteppich' is a small, spreading shrub, to 50cm tall; the leaves are covered in blue-white down on the reverse; few red berries. 'Repens' is even lower growing, to 30cm, and forms a dense carpet.

Cotoneaster simonsii: Height to 3m; an erect-growing shrub with hairy twigs and glossy foliage, retained in winter. White flowers June–July, followed by numerous red berries, which stay on the plant for a long time. Must be protected against severe frost.

Cotoneaster watereri hybrids: To 4.5m tall shrubs with deciduous, smooth foliage. White flowers in June, followed by numerous red berries. The following are fine cultivars: 'Brandkjaer', the most winter-hardy; 'Cornubia', erect growing, with pale-red berries; 'Pendula', a weeping form.

Cotoneaster zabelii: Deciduous shrub, to 2m in height. Thin, gracefully arching twigs. The broad-elliptical leaves, blunt, to 2.5cm long, are dull green, but grey green and felty underneath. White flowers, tinged with purple, May–June. The berries are bright red, spherical, and appear in pendent clusters.

Crataegus

May, Hawthorn

Deciduous trees or shrubs, usually thorny, the leaves distributed along the branches which in spring bear white or red flowers. In the autumn they may be conspicuous both for their autumn colouring and for their red, yellow or black, apple-like fruits.

Situation If the hawthorn is allowed to grow, its size makes it suitable only for use in parks and large gardens. In order to encourage flowering they are given a sunny situation, but they tolerate partial shade; some will thrive in a shady position. The hawthorn's attractive winter shape, its fresh green spring foliage and flowers, and its autumn colouring and fruits, make it popular as a free-standing tree. Hawthorns may also be used as loose or as clipped hedges. At present we are advised against the use of single or bifurcated hawthorns because of their sensitivity to fireblight.

Soil Standard garden soil. Calcareous soil is ideal.

Propagation The species from seed; cultivars are grafted.

Crataegus laevigata (syn *C. oxycantha*): A hawthorn with two or more trunks. A shrub or small tree, up to 5m in height, with white or rose-red flowers May–June. Broad oval leaves with 3–5 short serrated lobes. The fruits contain 2–3 pips, in contrast to those of species with a single trunk, which contain only one pip. There are many garden varieties, including 'Alboölena', with double white flowers and spreading habit; 'Gireoudii', with white-flecked green foliage, sometimes with pinkish, large fruits; 'Mutabilis', with double white flowers in June, the buds being pale red, 'Paul's Scarlet' with double red flowers, one of the best known varieties; and 'Punicea' which produces single, rose-red flowers.

Crataegus × lavallei: Moderately fast-growing, compact tree, to 5m in height, with red-brown twigs and long thorns. When it starts into growth the leaves are reddish in colour, later dark green, glossy and leathery. Large white flowers in dense, felty clusters in June, followed by large orange berries.

Crataegus monogyna: A tree or shrub to 8m in height. The leaves are much more deeply incised than those of the forms with multiple trunks. Long, straight thorns. White flowers May–June, followed by berries with a single pip; they are crowned by lanceolate sepals. 'Stricta' is columnar; 'Pendula' is a tree or shrub up to 8m in height, with drooping branches and twigs.

Crataegus × mordenensis: Only known in the shape of its cultivar 'Toba', a small tree or large shrub with 5–7cm long, deeply incised leaves. The double flowers appear May–June. Initially they are creamy white, later turning pale red. An excellent winter-hardy hawthorn, originating in Canada.

Crataegus laevigata 'Paul's Scarlet'

Crataegus × lavallei

Crataegus pedicellata: Shrub or tree, to 5m. The thorns are 3–5cm long; the leaves 5–9cm, broad oval, dark green. White flowers in May, followed by red berries. Able to withstand wind and very suitable as hedging, since pruning is tolerated.

Crataegus × prunifolia: The result of crossing *C. crusgalli* and *C. succulenta*. A shrub or tree, to 4m in height, with olive-coloured twigs and broad oval leaves. White flowers in felty clusters May–June; bright-red berries. Fine autumn colouring. 'Splendens' is the best known variety; it has a very broad crown and red berries which may be retained until the end of the year.

Crataegus punctata: A tree or shrub to 6m in height with, as a rule, very thorny twigs. White flowers in June are followed by yellow-red, downy berries.

Crataegus succulenta (syn *C. macracantha*): Tree or shrub to 5m in height, with red-brown twigs and numerous strong thorns. Umbel-shaped pale-red flower clusters in May.

Crataegus monogyna 'Pendula'

Cryptomeria japonica 'Elegans'

Cryptomeria

Japanese Cypress

A genus of evergreen conifers comprising a single species but with numerous strains. They are little known conifers demanding a sheltered position to be at their best.

Situation Japanese cypresses should be given a sunny or partially shaded position in well-drained soil which must nevertheless be adequately moisture retaining. The species grows into a fairly tall tree, excellent for planting singly, and producing a magnificent effect in a large lawn. The strains remain lower, but are worth growing for their beautiful shape and the colour of the foliage. They, too, make fine specimen plants, if not as impressive as the species. Dwarf forms, such as 'Globosa Nana' and 'Pygmea' are attractive in the rock garden, but are also suitable elsewhere in small gardens. They may also be grown in tubs on the terrace. The natural shape of *Cryptomeria* plants is so beautiful that pruning should be restricted to a minimum.

Soil Acid soil, rich in humus.

Propagation The species from seed, cultivars from cuttings taken in September.

Cryptomeria japonica: A pyramid-shaped to columnar tree, to 25m in height and 5m across. The reddish bark peels off in long strips. The needles are up to 1cm long, dark green and sickle-shaped, arranged round the twigs in five spirals. The pointed oval cones are 2–3cm long and are retained at the tips of the twigs for several years. 'Banda-Sugi' is an irregularly shaped dwarf form with fine green needles, turning bronze in autumn. It is not entirely winter-hardy.

'Compacta', to 15m tall, is densely branched and has blue-green needles.

In 'Cristata' the twigs are deformed at the tips and resemble a cock's comb. The foliage has a magnificent fresh green colour. Grows to 3m in height and 2m across.

'Elegans' is a broad shrub, not entirely winter-hardy, with green foliage, soft to the touch and turning bronze-coloured in autumn.

'Globosa Nana' is a shrub with a maximum height of 2m and 3m across, with a rounded crown and compact habit. The densely arranged needles are yellowish green in summer, more blue green in winter.

Cryptomeria japonica 'Globosa Nana'

× Cupressocyparis

A genus of conifers resulting from crossing *Cupressus* and *Chamaecyparis*. It comprises a single species, but several strains. All are winter-hardy conifers with pale-green, grey-green or gold-coloured scales. × *Cupressocyparis* grows extremely quickly and tolerates pruning.

Situation Provide a sunny or partially shaded position in well-drained soil. The combination of rapid growth and tolerance of pruning makes them ideal hedging plants.

Soil Standard garden soil.

Propagation From cuttings.

× *Cupressocyparis leylandii*: A conifer growing to 20m in height, 3m across, with twigs which appear square in section, and with pale-green or grey-green scales. The cones are up to 2cm long. As a hedge it needs space and must be tapered at the top. 'Castlewellan Gold' has golden-green, 'Haggerston Grey' grey-green, foliage. These two strains also grow very rapidly.

× *Cupressocyparis leylandii* 'Castlewellan Gold'

Cydonia

Quince

Large shrubs or small trees with beautiful flowers, attractive foliage and fruits which are tasty and aromatic when preserved.

Situation Ornamental shrubs, often planted in farmyards, along ditches and in windbreaks. Quinces are also cultivated as standard trees; there are several cultivars, grafted on hawthorn stock. They will grow in full sun and in partial shade. Pruning is rarely necessary, but is tolerated.

Soil Any adequately damp soil.

Propagation From cuttings or seed. The seedlings do not always grow true to type.

Cydonia oblonga (syn *C. vulgaris*): An erect-growing, deciduous shrub or tree, to 6m in height. Fairly large, white or pink flowers May–June; but attractive when the isolated flowers are still in bud. The oval leaves are covered on the reverse in dense hair, which makes them appear greyish white. The large, felty yellow fruits have an unusual fragrance.

Cydonia oblonga

Cytisus ardoini

Cytisus

Broom

In spring, broom produces a profusion of butterfly-like, predominantly yellow, flowers. The green wood and the graceful habit make it attractive in winter also. Not all species are entirely winter-hardy. Least sensitive to frost is *Cytisus × praecox*, which is why it is most frequently grown. It is interesting to note that species with square twigs suffer more from severe winters than those with round twigs. In a square stem the surface is larger, with the result that there is more evaporation and consequently drying. Broom should be supplied in a pot, for without a soil-ball the shrub will not easily strike. It is practically impossible to transplant mature, long-established broom species.

Broom flowers on the previous year's wood and should therefore be pruned only immediately after flowering. Low-growing species need only be shaped a little, since their natural growth is all that can be desired. Taller growing species sometimes grow somewhat bare at the base and it is therefore advisable to cut them back a little. In small gardens this is the only way to create a compact bush.

Situation Broom needs a sunny position; it is suitable for large and small gardens, depending on its size. *Cytisus scoparius* may also be used in wild gardens. Several of the smaller species are suitable for rock gardens, where the recumbent twigs can droop gracefully over a stone. Taller species are frequently planted in heather gardens. C. × *praecox* may be used to create a loose hedge.

Soil Light, acid soil. Feeding is rarely necessary. C. *purgans* will also grow in calcareous soil.

Propagation Species from seed, cultivars from summer cuttings.

Cytisus ardoini: Small bush with recumbent twigs; up to 20cm in height, 1m across. Yellow flowers April–May. Not entirely winter-hardy; requires dry soil.

Cytisus × dallimorei: Lower growing and less winter-hardy than *Cytisus scoparius*. It is a cross between the latter and C. *multiflorus*.

Cytisus decumbens (syn *Sarothamnus decumbens*): A creeping shrub, to 1m tall, 2m across, with numerous yellow flowers May–June. The twigs are slightly hairy. Not 100 per cent winter-hardy. Only suitable for dry soil.

Cytisus × kewensis: The result of crossing C. *ardoini* and C. *multiflorus*. Grows to 60cm in height, two and a half times as much across. Creamy yellow flowers in May. Winter-hardy.

Cytisus multiflorus: A shrub growing to 3m, frequently used for cross-breeding. Not entirely winter-hardy. In May to June the pale-green arching twigs bear small, creamy white flowers.

Cytisus × praecox: The result of crossing the preceding species with C. *purgans*. A bush growing to 2m tall and broad, with a profusion of very fragrant pale-yellow flowers April–May. 'Allgold' is more golden yellow, 'Zeelandia' red purple. The species and its cultivars are all very winter-hardy.

Cytisus purgans: A densely branching shrub, to 1m in height. Small, spear-shaped leaves which soon drop. The golden-yellow flowers appear in April.

Cytisus purpureus (syn *Chamaecytisus purpureus*): A shrub to 60cm in height and more than twice as much across, with pale-red flowers June–July. 'Albus' has white, 'Atropurpureus' dark purple-red, flowers.

Cytisus scoparius (syn *Sarothamnus scoparius*): A shrub growing to 2m, native to Western Europe. The erect-growing or arching branches bear butterfly-like flowers May–June, followed by elongated pods. There are many magnificent cultivars with colours varying from pale yellow to dark red. 'Andreanus Splendens', for example, produces yellow-red flowers in May and grows to 2.5m in height.

Cytisus × praecox

Cytisus scoparius

Daboecia

Irish Heather

A small evergreen shrub belonging to the heather family and thriving in similar conditions. However, the Irish heather is slightly more sensitive to frost and should therefore be given a sheltered position or be covered in winter. Prolonged flowering season; bell-shaped flowers.

Situation Sun or partial shade. As a rule it is used in the heather garden, but it is attractive in other spots as well.

Soil Light, humus-rich soil, on the acid side. *Daboecia* will do well even in fairly dry soil.

Propagation From cuttings; the species also from seed.

Daboecia cantabrica (syn *D. polifolia*): An evergreen little shrub, to 40cm tall, with erect-growing hairy twigs. The oval leaves are up to 1.5cm long, curled at the margins. The upper surface is dark green and glossy, the reverse felty white. Clusters of urn-shaped purple flowers June–September. In 'Alba' the flowers are white, in 'Bicolor' striped white and purple. 'Pracyerae' is low growing, but somewhat sensitive to frost.

Daboecia cantabrica 'Praegerae'

Daphne × *burkwoodii*

Daphne

Small deciduous or evergreen shrubs with leaves distributed along the branches and delightfully scented flowers in spring. The bark of *Daphne mezereum*, in particular, is very poisonous and causes irritation of the skin. The berries are poisonous as well.

Situation Because of their size these shrubs are very suitable for small gardens and also for the rock garden. In general they do well in partial shade, but *Daphne cneorum* requires sun and *Daphne laureola* tolerates a great deal of shade. The flowers are pastel coloured and are easy to combine with other species. Pruning is rarely necessary.

Soil Somewhat acid, humus-rich soil. *Daphne cneorum* will grow in calcareous soil, while *Daphne mezereum* loves lime. *Daphne cneorum* dislikes salt.

Propagation The species from seed, cultivars from cuttings. The plants can also be layered. The berries should be sown just before they are fully ripe.

Daphne acutiloba: Spindly, evergreen shrub, to 1m. Leathery, spear-shaped leaves with a sharp point. The greenish white flowers do not appear before July; they are followed by fine red berries.

Daphne altaica: An erect-growing, bare, deciduous bush, not beyond a metre in height. Dull-green, spear- to spatula-shaped leaves, at most 6cm long. Pure white flowers in sessile terminal clusters. They appear in May to June and have a delightful fragrance.

Daphne × burkwoodii: Partially evergreen shrub, to 50cm tall, the result of crossing *D. caucasia* and *D. cneorum*. The twigs are covered in short hairs and bear leathery, spatula-shaped leaves, to 4cm long. The white or pink flowers in groups of 15–20 have a delightful scent. In a severe winter this cultivar has proved to have suffered little and it may therefore be considered winter-hardy. 'Somerset' grows to over 1m in height and in May to June produces white and pale-red flowers. In 'Burkwood' the white flowers discolour to pink.

Daphne cneorum: A recumbent evergreen shrub, to 30cm in height, with somewhat hairy twigs and spatula-shaped, leathery leaves, green and glossy and up to 2cm long. Fragrant pale-red flowers in dense groups of 6 to 8 May–June. Prefers dry soil and should be protected against severe frost. There is a white form 'Alba', with a very spreading low habit. 'Eximia' is a little larger in all its parts than the species, and its flowers are red purple.

Daphne laureola: Evergreen shrub, approximately 50cm in height, with glossy green, spatula-shaped leaves, up to 8cm long, and yellow-green flowers March–April. These are followed by poisonous black berries. Not entirely winter-hardy. Likes damp soil. The variety *philippii* is more winter-hardy. It is a dwarf form with firm branches and its flowers have a pink tinge. Attractive in the rock garden.

Daphne mezereum: A deciduous shrub, to 1m in height, with purple-violet, particularly fragrant flowers April–May. The poisonous berries are scarlet in colour. The bare twigs bear grey-green, spear-shaped leaves, to 8cm long. The flowers appear before the foliage. Winter-hardy. 'Alba' is a fine cultivar with white flowers and yellow berries. 'Grandiflora', a shrub growing to 2m, flowers earlier, sometimes even in autumn, when the flowers are larger and darker in colour. 'Ruby Glow' has large, dark purple-red flowers.

Daphne pontica: This evergreen little shrub has obovate leaves, to 6cm long; their upper surface yellowish green and glossy. The stalked clusters of fragrant yellow-green flowers with linear sepals appear in May, sometimes as early as April. Not 100 per cent winter-hardy.

Daphne cneorum

Daphne mezereum

Datura suaveolens

Datura

Trumpet Flower

Large shrub with trailing white flowers. Beware of its seductive fragrance, for the plant is very poisonous.

Situation *Datura* shrubs should be treated as conservatory plants. In winter they must be kept in a frost-free greenhouse. After mid-May, when the danger of night frosts has passed, they are planted in a sunny and sheltered position out of doors, preferably in soil mixed with some additional rotted manure and loam. They will also flower well when grown in tubs. Bring them indoors again before the onset of night frosts. It is also possible to keep them permanently in an unheated greenhouse.

Soil Nutritious clay or loam.

Propagation Shoots are rooted in February; provide some bottom heat. In the first winter the temperature should be kept at between 10 and 15°C.

Datura suaveolens (syn *Brugmansia suaveolens*): A shrub growing to 5m, with a fairly thick, densely branched trunk. From August to October it bears fragrant pendent trumpet-shaped flowers. In the strain 'Flore Pleno', the flowers are double.

Davidia involucrata

Davidia

Handkerchief Tree

A deciduous shrub or small tree with thick, bare twigs and purple buds in winter. The flowers are insignificant, but the white bracts are all the more conspicuous, hence the common name. In China, where the tree was discovered by a French missionary, the tree can grow to 20m; but here it rarely exceeds 10m.

Situation Beautiful planted singly. When young it is somewhat sensitive to frost, but mature trees are entirely winter-hardy.

Soil Will grow in any standard garden soil which is adequately moisture retaining.

Propagation By layering, from shoots rooted in summer, or from seed.

Davidia involucrata: A tree with a disagreeable scent. The leaves, somewhat similar to those of the lime tree, are oval, pointed, coarsely serrated and hairy on the reverse. In the variety *vilmoriniana* the leaves are practically bare underneath. The flowers and the up to 15cm long cream-coloured bracts appear May–June. They are followed by nut-like fruits, green with a tinge of red or purple.

Decaisnea

A graceful deciduous shrub with very striking fruits and fine foliage. It comes from China.
Situation A valuable specimen plant for sunny or partially shaded sites; very winter-hardy.
Soil Porous soil, rich in humus.
Propagation From root cuttings and from seed.

Decaisnea fargesii: The sole representative of the genus. In a sheltered position the shrub will reach a height of 2.5 to 3m. In winter it is recognised by the fairly large, shield-shaped markings – the scars of fallen leaves – on the branches. Feathery leaves appear at the tips of the thick, glossy yellow-brown and slightly bloomed twigs. The leaflets are oval, pointed, smooth edged, and a striking bluish colour on the reverse. Clusters of bell-shaped yellow-green flowers May–June are followed by steel-blue, gherkin-like fruits, up to 10cm long. As a rule they are arranged in groups of two or more. They contain black seeds.

Decaisnea fargesii

Deutzia × hybrida 'Mont Rose'

Deutzia

Japanese Snow-flower

Hardy deciduous shrubs, usually producing an abundance of white or red flowers in June. Oval to spear-shaped opposite leaves; flower plumes borne in the axils or terminal. Outside the flowering season they are sometimes taken for jasmine plants, but the difference is that the twigs of *Deutzia* are hollow inside, those of *Philadelphus* contain white pith.
Situation The Japanese snow-flower prefers a position in full sun or partial shade and not too dry soil. In dry soil the leaves will soon droop and the flowers will drop, while in winter the plant will be more sensitive to frost. Most *Deutzia* species are of modest size and they are therefore suitable for small gardens. However, since outside the flowering season they are not so attractive, they should not be planted in a free-standing position. These plants are often used in shrub borders – low-growing species in front, taller forms at the back. The flowers are suitable for cutting. Pruning keeps the shrub compact and encourages flowering. *Deutzia* species flower on mature wood and must therefore be pruned immediately after the flowering season. Thick old branches should always be removed.

Deutzia × lemoinei 'Boule de Neige'

Deutzia scabra 'Macropetala'

Soil Nutritious soil is best, to encourage flowering.
Propagation From cuttings.

Deutzia crenata (syn *D. scabra*): A well known, erect-growing species, 2–3m in height. The oval to oblong leaves are 8cm long, slightly crenate, with a small tooth at each incision. White or pink-tinged flowers in erect-growing plumes June–July. 'Candidissima' has double white flowers; 'Macropetala' has large, single white. 'Plena' is double flowered, white; the outside of the petals is pink striped in the centre. 'Pride of Rochester' resembles the previous strain, but the pink stripe is less obvious.

Deutzia × elegantissima: The result of crossing *D. purpurascens* and *D. scabra*. Pink flowers in loose, large clusters May–June. An erect-growing shrub with pointed oval leaves.

Deutzia gracilis: A small shrub, to 1m in height, with white flowers May–June. On the upper surface the leaves are more hairy than on the reverse. Frequently forced by nurserymen; it will then flower February–March.

Deutzia × hybrida: The result of crossing *D. discolor* and *D. longifolia*. The upward growing twigs bear oval leaves and, in June, large, lilac-pink flowers, often paler along the margin. 'Mont Rose', to 2m, is a bushy shrub with an erect-growing habit. 'Contrast' has arching branches and a graceful appearance. The lilac-pink flowers are wine red on the outside.

Deutzia × kalmiiflora: The result of crossing *D. parviflora* and *D. purpurascens*. A 1–2m tall shrub with gracefully arching branches, bearing oval to spear-shaped leaves, finely serrated. They are up to 5cm long and pale green underneath. Clusters of flowers in May, white inside, pink outside.

'Fleur de Pommier' has lilac-pink flowers with fairly long sepals. In 'Boule Rose' the flowers are paler in colour and the sepals are shorter.

Deutzia × lemoinei: A bastard of *D. parviflora* and *D. gracilis*. Up to approximately 1m in height, it bears a profusion of white flowers in June. The flower clusters are almost spherical. 'Avalanche' has very large white flowers in profusion. 'Boule de Neige' is an erect-growing bushy shrub with large white flowers in very dense clusters.

Deutzia × magnifica: The result of crossing *D. scabra* and *D. vilmorinae*. An erect-growing shrub, 2.5m tall and across, with plumes of double white flowers in June. Peeling brown twigs with up to 8cm long, oval to oblong leaves. 'Erecta' has crenate leaves and erect-growing plumes of large white single flowers. 'Nancy' has large plumes of double white flowers.

Deutzia ningpoensis: A little known species from China, it is a tall shrub with 8–12cm long, elongated oval leaves with a sharp point. Single white flowers in large clusters June–July.

Deutzia × rosea: The result of crossing *D. gracilis* and

D. purpurascens. Densely branched shrub, about 1m in height. The arching branches have peeling brown bark. In June to July it is covered in bell-shaped flowers, white inside, purple on the outside. The flower plumes are short and broad. 'Campanulata' is the best known strain; it has fairly profuse clusters of white flowers with purple calyxes.

Deutzia scabra (syn *D. sieboldiana*): A shrub up to 1m in height and the same across, with peeling brown twigs. Oval to oblong, fairly coarsely serrated leaves, to 7cm long and fairly narrow at the tip. Loose, broad plumes of white flowers with hairy stalks in June.

Deutzia taiwanensis: To 1.5m in height, a little more across; a shrub with elliptical, finely serrated leaves and a profusion of white flowers in slender racemes in June.

Deutzia vilmorinae: Up to 1.5m tall and as much across. A fast-growing shrub with pale-brown, gracefully arching twigs, peeling at a later stage. White flowers in loose broad clusters in June.

Deutzia vilmorinae

Dipelta ventricosa

Dipelta

Little known deciduous shrubs, somewhat similar to *Weigela*, to which they are related. In early summer they bear fragrant flowers, a little smaller than those of *Weigela*.

Situation Sunny or partially shaded site in damp soil; in a shrub border, singly or in groups.

Soil Nutritious soil.

Propagation From winter and summer cuttings.

Dipelta floribunda: This is the best known species, to 4m tall, with arching brown twigs, peeling at a later stage. The oval to spear-shaped green leaves, up to 12cm long, are smooth-edged, sharply pointed and practically bald. The fragrant flowers appear in scant clusters May–June. The corolla is pink outside, yellow orange inside. The fruits are enfolded in two large, shield-shaped bracts.

Dipelta ventricosa: Up to 2m in height. Lightly serrated leaves and heart-shaped bracts round the fruit. The flowers appear June–July.

Elaeagnus angustifolia

Elaeagnus × ebbingei

Elaeagnus

Oleaster

This genus embraces evergreen and deciduous trees and shrubs. The evenly distributed leaves are characterised by small golden or silver scales on the reverse; these serve to limit evaporation. The flowers are inconspicuous, but very fragrant. The twigs are usually thorny. The deciduous species, in particular, are extremely hardy.

Situation The oleaster is very resistant to sea winds and is therefore often grown in coastal areas, sometimes to stabilise the sand in dunes. The species with silvery leaves are attractive in borders with a colour scheme of pink-blue-purple with grey foliage. Species such as *Elaeagnus × ebbingei* and *E. multiflora* can be pruned and may therefore be used for hedges. Deciduous oleasters will grow in very poor and silty soil. All species will do well in sun or in partial shade.

Soil Any garden soil; deciduous forms will thrive even in very poor sandy soil.

Propagation From seed and cuttings or by layering.

Elaeagnus angustifolia: A narrow-leaved tree or shrub, up to 7m in height and 5m across, usually thorny, with twigs covered in silvery scales. The narrow, spear-shaped leaves are 8cm long, grey green on the upper surface, silvery underneath; they drop in winter. Inconspicuous yellow flowers in June, followed by yellow berries with white scales.

Elaeagnus commutata (syn *E. argentea*): This thornless deciduous shrub grows much more slowly than the preceding species and does not exceed 2.5m. The twigs are covered in red-brown scales and bear oval, 8cm long leaves, silvery on both surfaces, making this the most beautiful of the silver-leaved shrubs. It develops runners. Both the flowers and the fruits are silver coloured. The flowers appear in June.

Elaeagnus × ebbingei: The result of crossing *E. macrophylla* and *E. pungens*. A valuable evergreen shrub which in a sheltered position may grow to a height of 3m. It is wind resistant, but in a windy situation it will not grow quite so tall. To obtain a beautifully compact shrub the plant should be cut back severely in the early stages. Often develops suckers which must be removed from the base as soon as possible. Initially brown, later grey-white, twigs with elliptical leaves, to 10cm long. The upper surface is dark green and glossy, the reverse silvery white. Inconspicuous white flowers with a delightful fragrance in autumn.

Elaeagnus multiflora (syn *E. edulis*): A spreading shrub, to 2m tall. Very dark brown twigs with oval leaves, to 8cm long, green on the upper surface, silver grey underneath. Pale yellow, barely scented flowers April–May, followed by orange-red fruits, edible but very sour.

Elaeagnus pungens: An evergreen shrub, to 5m tall, usually with thorny twigs covered in brown scales and bearing pointed, oval, to 9cm long leaves, dark green on the upper surface, silvery on the reverse. Fragrant white flowers October–November, followed by brown to red fruits. The green-leaved species is rarely encountered in gardens, but it is a strong shrub, particularly suitable for coastal areas since it is resistant to sea winds. Frost is tolerated less well. Variegated forms are more popular. The best known is 'Maculata', in which the leaves are yellow in the centre. 'Aurea' has a narrow yellow or creamy-white margin along the grey-green leaves. The new form 'Goldrim' has glossy green foliage with a bright-yellow margin. Branches with green shoots appearing on variegated forms should immediately be removed, otherwise the shrub will revert to green.

Elaeagnus umbellata (syn *E. crispa*): A deciduous shrub, to 4m in height, with yellow-brown twigs, usually thorny. Oblong, to 8cm long leaves, silvery on the reverse. Fragrant white flowers May–June, followed by white fruits.

Elaeagnus × *ebbingei* 'Limelight'

Empetrum nigrum

Empetrum

Heath-like evergreen shrubs, indigenous to most parts of Europe; members of the Empetraceae family.
Situation Will thrive in sunny or partially shaded positions in damp, but also in somewhat drier, soil. They look attractive in the heather garden, but may also be used in wild gardens, rock gardens or as ground-cover. Regular pruning is not essential.
Soil Must contain humus. Some lime is tolerated.
Propagation From seed and cuttings or by division.

Empetrum nigrum: Height to 25cm, 40cm across. The twigs are densely covered in linear leaves, to 6mm long and rolled along the edges. The creeping twigs grow erect at the tips. Red-purple flowers appear in May in groups of three; they grow in the axils and are inconspicuous. They are followed by glossy black, round berries, enjoyed by birds, including crows.

Enkianthus

Heathery, deciduous shrub with attractive flowers and magnificent autumn colouring.

Situation *Enkianthus* shows to best advantage in a partially shaded position, preferably sheltered, in a heather garden or a Japanese garden. It will also look well near a water garden, surrounded by ground-cover such as *Patrinia triloba*, *Waldsteinia* or *Galium odoratum* (woodruff). Protection against strong wind is essential if the plant is to develop its full potential.

Soil Acid, humus rich and adequately moisture retaining.

Propagation By layering, from seed or from cuttings of ripe wood.

Enkianthus campanulatus: An erect-growing, spreading shrub, to 3m in height, with pendent clusters of pale-red, urn-shaped flowers in May. There is a white-flowered cultivar called 'Albiflorus'. Flowers will keep for a long time in water. The smooth grey branches bear fresh-green, oval and finely serrated leaves. The fruits are brown. In autumn the foliage discolours to yellow and red.

Enkianthus campanulatus

Erica ciliaris 'Globosa'

Erica

Heather, Heath

This genus covers hundreds of evergreen species, of which few are native to our regions. Most of the species grow in the mountains of tropical Africa, a few in the Mediterranean area. The small needle-shaped leaves, arranged in circles round the twigs, are a common feature of all the species. The spikes of bell-shaped flowers are frequently very brightly and cheerfully coloured. Some of the species have large numbers of valuable cultivars. The flowering season is so varied that it is possible to have heather flowering in the garden throughout the year, even in winter, under snow. When planting, it must be borne in mind that not all species are equally winter-hardy. Some originate in southern Europe and in our climate need extra protection in winter.

Situation Heather should be planted in full sun or partial shade. For *Erica cinerea* full sun is essential. Heathers are of course used in heather gardens, but they can be used in many other ways. Species tolerating lime, in particular, are very suitable for the rock garden. Many others make excellent ground-cover, attractive in the border in combination with other low shrubs and perennials; they are also suitable for planting in front of shrub borders. The tree-shaped heather plant looks attractive planted singly in a small garden. A compact shape can be maintained by pruning. As a rule heather species are planted in groups in order to create striking patches of colour. Heather is also suitable for planting on graves.

The plants are pruned just before they start into growth in spring. While *Calluna*, ling, is cut back every year, the pruning of *Erica* plants is restricted to the removal of dead flowers and lanky stalks.

Soil In general *Erica* does best in acid soil, rich in humus. Garden soil is improved by the addition of peat and conifer-needle compost. To keep the soil friable and to restrict weed growth, the ground between the plants is covered in peat fibre. A number of species will thrive in calciferous soil: *E. herbacea*, *E. × darkeyensis* and *E. erigens*. All species require adequately damp soil.

Propagation By division, from cuttings or seed, and by layering. Cuttings, a few centimetres long, are inserted into sharp sand with a top layer of sifted heathland soil, in shallow bowls or pots. To avoid mildew they should not be placed too close together and must be pressed down well. Rooting may take several months. The glass covering the bowls must be dried every morning. When the cuttings have rooted they are hardened off and in the autumn are planted out under glass. In spring they are potted with some soil adhering to the roots, and are again hardened off. Next they are planted out in a nursery-bed. In September they are cut back severely to encourage bushy growth. The young plants cannot be used in the garden until the following year, when there is no longer any danger of night frost, that is, in May.

Erica ciliaris, Dorset heath: A small shrub, to 25–50cm tall, with erect-growing, downy twigs and oval leaves, usually rolled, covered in downy hair. Oblique urn-shaped flowers in elongated umbels, red purple, June–July. 'Globosa' with its greyish-green foliage is the most winter-hardy. It grows to 35cm and bears numerous red-purple flowers from July to October.

Erica cinerea: A completely winter-hardy species with recumbent or erect-growing twigs. Height 10–40cm. The twigs, covered in fine hair, bear leaves up to 7mm in length, usually arranged in circles of three. Flowers predominantly purple in colour, in simple or branched clusters. The anthers do not project from the corolla. There are a large number of cultivars, some of them slightly sensitive to frost. 'Alba', pure white, 25cm in height, has pale-green foliage, spreading habit and flowers August–September.

'Alba Minor' flowers from June to October; it has a bushy habit. Height 15–20cm.

'Atrosanguinea' is a spreading, erect-growing bush, 20cm in height, with rose-red flowers July–October.

'C.D. Eason' is one of the best known cultivars, 35cm tall, with red flowers June–September.

Erica cinerea 'C.D. Eason'

Erica × darleyensis 'Darley Dale'

Erica herbacea 'Heathwood'

Erica vagans 'St Keverne'

'Cevennes', height 25cm, erect-growing habit; purple flowers in elongated umbels August–October.

'Coccinea' has a creeping habit; height to 20cm. Red flowers June–August.

'Golden Drop' is a compact plant, 25cm in height, with golden-yellow and bronze-coloured foliage. Few flowers, red purple in colour, July–August.

'Pallas', reliable cultivar, winter-hardy, with erect-growing habit, to 35cm, has a profusion of purple flowers June–September.

'P.S. Patrick' has deep-purple flowers in August and September. Erect habit, 40cm.

Erica × *darleyensis*: The result of crossing *E. herbacea* and *E. erigena*. Larger flowers than in *E. herbicea* and twice as tall. 'Darley Dale', 40cm tall and 1m across, is a fine strain. Red-purple flowers December–May.

Erica erigena (syn *E. mediterranea*): Erect-growing, dense and bushy shrub, 1.5m in height and almost as much across. Fragile woody stalks. Pendulous red flowers in large, loose clusters March–May.

Erica herbacea (syn *E. carnea*): A very well known creeping heather, to 40cm in height. The bright-green needle-shaped leaves are arranged in circles of four round the erect-growing stalks. The flesh-coloured flowers are borne in the axils and have conspicuous, projecting brown stamens.

'Aurea' is a strain with golden-yellow foliage, height to 20cm. Purple-pink flowers February–April.

'Heathwood', to 25cm, has dark-brown twigs with dark-green foliage and red-purple flowers between December and April.

'Myretoun Ruby', height to 30cm, has a dense, creeping habit and dark-green foliage on brown twigs. Red-purple flowers from December to April.

'Praecox Rubra', spreading habit, height to 20cm, purple-red flowers, sometimes as early as November and continuing to March.

'Snow Queen' is a well known white-flowered strain, 15cm tall, flowering December to March.

'Springwood White', clump-forming, 25cm in height; white flowers February–April.

'Vivelli', height 20cm, has bronze-coloured foliage and purple-red flowers March–April.

'Winter Beauty' has a compact habit, 15cm; dark purple-red flowers from December to March.

Erica tetralix, common heather: Erect-growing hairy twigs, to 40cm in length. The elongated oval, grey to grey-green leaves are usually arranged round the stalks in circles of four. Urn-shaped, pendent pink flowers from June to September. Indigenous in western Europe.

'Alba' has silvery-grey foliage and white flowers from June to September. Erect habit, to 30cm.

'Ken Underwood' flowers in the same period; flowers red purple. The foliage is grey green. Height 30cm.

Erica vagans, Cornish heath: A 30–50cm tall shrub with fresh-green leaves arranged round the stalks in circles of 4–5. A profusion of purple-red flowers in elongated

clusters, from July to September. 'George Underwood' is more winter-hardy than the species; red-purple flowers August–September; height 25cm. 'Lyonesse', 30cm in height, bears creamy-white flowers in the same period. 'Mrs D.F. Maxwell', height 35cm, red flowers August–October. Dense, compact habit.
'St Keverne', red-purple flowers August–September. Compact growth, to 35cm.
Erica × watsonii: The result of crossing *E. ciliaris* and *E. tetralix*. In spring the twigs are bronze coloured. 'Truro' has red-purple flowers from July to October. Spreading habit, to 15cm in height.

Erica × watsonii 'Truro'

Escallonia hybrid

Escallonia

This genus includes deciduous and evergreen shrubs, not entirely winter-hardy, although they are resistant to sea wind and fairly resistant to drought.
Situation From the above it may be concluded that *Escallonia* is very suitable for cultivation in coastal areas. The plants are preferably planted in the shelter of a south-facing wall or as a loose hedge. The cultivar 'Donard Seedling', in particular, is frequently used for this purpose. Together with the evergreen 'Red Elf' this is one of the most winter-hardy strains. 'Edinburgh' is suitable for training against a sunny, south-facing wall. Many hybrids flower at a time when there are few other flowering woody plants – all the more reason to try out these versatile shrubs.
Soil Nutritious, humus-rich soil; the plant will also do well in calciferous soil.
Propagation From winter cuttings.

Escallonia hybrids: The results of crossing *E. virgata* and *E. rubra*. Approximately 2m tall shrubs with fresh-green, glossy foliage and pink or red flowers July–August.

Eucalyptus niphophila

Eucalyptus

Blue Gum

Rarely grown, evergreen or deciduous trees with beautiful grey foliage, very aromatic. As a rule young leaves differ from the mature ones. They are fast-growing trees; when mature the bark peels and flowers are produced. Most species are not winter-hardy in our regions, but some of the trees will tolerate a degree of frost, provided they are planted out of the wind. Only really suitable for coastal areas.

Situation Plant *Eucalyptus* in a sunny spot, where north and east winds cannot reach it. The condition of the soil is less important, provided it is well drained. Can also be grown in tubs.

Soil Standard garden soil.

Propagation From seed.

Eucalyptus niphophila: The most winter-hardy species, able to withstand 10°C of frost in a suitable situation. A deciduous tree, to 7m in height and 3m across, only bearing leaves of the mature shape. Green flowers June–July.

Euonymus alata

Euonymous

Spindle Tree

This genus embraces evergreen as well as deciduous shrubs. The deciduous species are grown for the sake of their berries, the shape of a cardinal's hat, and also for their fine autumn colouring. Evergreen species often have attractive variegated foliage. In nearly all species the leaves are single, opposite, and the flowers are inconspicuous. The corky ridges on the twigs are a characteristic feature.

Situation The deciduous species prefer full sun. Although they will also grow in shade, their inflorescence, berries and autumn colouring will be far less attractive and abundant. The evergreen forms tolerate more shade, but to encourage fine marking in the variegated strains, partial is better than full shade. *E. fortunei* can be used in hedge making. Its twigs may develop roots; it is sometimes grown against walls. Some cultivars of this species make excellent, fast-growing ground-cover. The deciduous species are grown singly or in groups, also in window-boxes. The common spindle tree is frequently planted in windbreaks; its berries are a treat to birds.

Soil Standard garden soil, adequately moist.

Propagation The creeping species are increased from runners. Deciduous species are increased from basal shoots, runners and from seed, which rapidly loses its power to germinate. Evergreen species are grown from cuttings.

Euonymus alata: Height 2m, the same across. The initially bare green twigs bear elliptical green leaves with beautiful autumn colouring; afterwards the foliage drops. Two-year-old and older branches have striking corky ridges. Brown-red berries with orange seeds.

Euonymus europaea, common spindle tree: A deciduous shrub, 4m in height, with blunt square green twigs. Oval leaves, to 7cm long. Pink fruits with orange seeds. 'Atrorubens' has dark-crimson berries and 'Red Cascade' is a beautiful weeping form with bright-red berries.

Euonymus europaea, common spindle tree: A deciduous shrub, 4m in height, with blunt square green twigs. Oval leaves, to 7cm long. Pink fruits with orange seeds. 'Atrorubens' has dark-crimson berries and 'Red Cascade' is a beautiful weeping form with bright-red berries.

Euonymus fortunei: Evergreen shrubs with long twigs, either recumbent (ground-cover) or climbing against walls. They develop self-clinging roots. Against a south-facing wall they may grow to as much as 5m. In the variety *vegata* the leaves are 3–6cm long, reversed oval, the veins very conspicuous. This species is very winter-hardy. There are numerous variegated cultivars, for example 'Coloratus', in which the foliage turns red in autumn; 'Emerald Gaiety' with a silvery-white margin along the leaves; 'Emerald 'n Gold', golden-yellow margins; 'Silver Gem', low growing, fine foliage with a silvery margin, not very winter-hardy. The variety *radicans* is a strongly rooting form with smaller leaves. Here, too, there are numerous cultivars, for instance 'Dart's Carpet', which makes excellent ground-cover. The variegated forms usually grow less rapidly and are not as winter-hardy as the green species.

Euonymus hamiltoniana var *hians* (syn *E. hians*): Deciduous shrub, up to 3m in height, with reversed oval to narrow elliptical leaves. Pink berries with red seeds.

Euonymus japonica: Evergreen, erect-growing shrub with green, non-rooting twigs. Height to 3m. Salmon-coloured berries with pink seeds. Some of the strains vary considerably in habit and leaf colour. Unfortunately their application is restricted because the species is not very winter-hardy. More useful as an indoor plant in cool rooms.

Euonymus planipes (syn *E. sachalinensis*): Deciduous shrub, to 3m tall, which starts into growth early in the year. Reddish autumn colouring. The red berries contain orange seeds. Erect-growing habit, with drooping twigs.

Euonymus fortunei var *vegeta* 'Emerald Gaiety'

Euonymus hamiltoniana var *hians*

Exochorda

Pearl Bush

Magnificent deciduous shrubs, unfortunately not entirely winter-hardy.

Situation Beautiful when grown singly, but also in combination with other shrubs. Sunny, preferably sheltered position. Particularly suitable for coastal regions.

Soil Rich soil. *Exochorda giraldii* requires a certain amount of lime; *E. racemosa* dislikes lime.

Propagation From seed, by grafting or from summer cuttings. *E. racemosa* develops basal shoots which may be detached and grown separately.

Exochorda giraldii: A shrub with arching branches and an abundance of white flowers April–May. The leaf-stalks and the main veins are red; the leaves are oval to oblong and fairly large. The variety *wilsonii* is more erect growing, to 3m tall and the same across.

Exochorda racemosa (syn *E. grandiflora*): A spreading shrub, 3m in height. In later life growth slows down. Large white flower umbels in May.

Exochorda giraldii var. *wilsonii*

Fagus sylvatica 'Fastigiata'

Fagus

Beech

Deciduous trees; older specimens have a majestic appearance. The trunk is smooth and grey; the leaves are well distributed and smooth-edged and in autumn the tree produces edible little nuts. Beeches provide a great deal of shade, so that few plants can grow underneath. Sun on the trunk may cause sunburn, as can be seen where trees are pruned at too early an age. Sunburn may also occur when a row of beeches is thinned out. Beeches have a fairly shallow root system and also suffer from drastic changes in the water table.

The beech genus comprises only a few species, the common beech being the one most often grown. The American beech (*Fagus grandiflora*) has larger leaves with a serrated to wavy edge.

Situation Beeches are often planted singly, but also make excellent hedging plants. Transplanting may create problems. This may be avoided to some extent by transplanting in the autumn and by covering the soil with dry beech leaves. Do not allow sun and wind to dry out the roots.

Soil Moist, loamy soil, rich in humus is ideal. The water table should not be too low and must be fairly constant.

Propagation From seed. Beeches do not produce seed every year, with the result that a particular size of tree is not always available. The seeds are sown in a frost-free spot immediately after they have ripened. Garden forms are increased by grafting on stock of *F. sylvatica*.

Fagus sylvatica, common beech: Height to 40m, 20m across. Smooth grey trunk and a broad crown. Spreading, elongated pointed buds. Fresh-green oval leaves to 10cm long, smooth edged. Initially they are slightly downy. Dead foliage is retained for a long time, often until the new buds start into growth. There are a number of fine cultivars, eg 'Asplenifolia', a 25m tall tree with deeply incised foliage, slow growing; 'Atropunicea', the brown beech, 40m in height, with a spreading crown and fairly large, dark brown-red leaves; 'Fastigiata', which has a columnar habit, to 20m in height and only 5m across; 'Pendula', the weeping beech, 20m tall, with a very broad crown, the branches drooping to the ground; 'Purpurea Pendula', the black weeping form.

Fagus sylvatica used as a hedge

Fallopia aubertii

Fallopia

Russian Vine

One of the fastest growing climbing shrubs, producing a profusion of flowers throughout the summer. The botanical name has been changed several times, so that in some books it may be found under *Polyganum* or *Bilderdykia*.

Situation If you want to cover a wall, pergola or shed quickly, the job may confidently be left to this climber. It flowers most profusely in full sun. Do not allow it to climb trees, for it will strangle them.

Soil Will grow in any garden soil, but for rapid progress it naturally requires adequate nutrients.

Propagation Cuttings with a heel attached are taken in summer. The plant can also be grafted on its own root, or be grown from seed.

Fallopia aubertii (syn *Polyganum aubertii, P. baldschuanicum, Bilderdykia aubertii*): The Russian vine may reach a height of as much as 15m. The initially brown-red leaves are 6–9cm long, oval to spear shaped, with a sharp point. White flowers in loose plumes from July to October. They often turn reddish after a time. In spring the plant may be drastically pruned.

Ficus carica

Ficus

Fig

This shrub has long been grown in warmer countries for the sake of its nutritious fruit, but its fine foliage also makes it an attractive plant for growing singly. Provided we choose the right strain and give the fig a sheltered position, we can eat figs from our own garden in this country as well. Here figs are usually trained. In an unheated greenhouse it is possible to have more than one harvest every year.

Situation Provide a sunny, and especially a sheltered, position, with minimum danger of frost and protected against severe north and east winds. The fig can be trained against a wall, but its naturally beautiful shape makes it suitable for planting singly.

Soil Nutritious soil.

Propagation From cuttings and by layering.

Ficus carica: Shrub or tree, up to 9m in height and 5m across, with a rounded crown and deeply incised foliage. Yellow-green flowers in May, followed by pear-shaped fruits.

Forsythia × intermedia 'Spectabilis'

Forsythia

Golden Bells

Deciduous spring-flowering shrubs, encountered in practically every garden. They flower on two-year-old or older wood and develop basal shoots which are left alone. Branches will keep well in water.

Situation The ornamental value of this shrub depends solely on its early and striking inflorescence. In summer, autumn and winter it is not very interesting and, unlike in the photograph, *Forsythia* plants are therefore rarely given a place of honour in the garden. *F. suspensa* can be trained against a wall. All *Forsythia* species will do well in sunny or partially shaded positions.

Soil Any standard garden soil.

Propagation From winter cuttings, basal shoots and by layering.

Forsythia × intermedia: Height to 2m. In April to May it produces an abundance of yellow flowers, especially in the case of the erect-growing form 'Spectabilis'. There are strains with arching or recumbent twigs and with surprisingly large flowers.

Forsythia suspensa: Height to 3m; soft twigs. Yellow flowers in April. 'Variegata' has yellow-blotched foliage.

Fothergilla

The foliage of these shrubs indicates that they belong to the witch hazel family. The fragrant white flowers appear in May and in the autumn the leaves turn a striking shade of orange red before they drop.

Situation *Fothergilla gardenii* is less than 1m tall, excellent for the rock garden. *F. major* (syn *F. monticola*) is a slow-growing shrub which may eventually grow to over 1.5m. It is beautiful planted singly in a small garden. Provide a position where it is sheltered against severe winds; the soil should be fairly moist. The autumn tints show to best advantage in full sun, but the shrubs will also thrive in partial shade.

Soil Nutritious, preferably lime-free soil, rich in humus.

Propagation By layering and from cuttings.

Fothergilla gardenii (syn *F. alnifolia*): The flowers appear before the foliage. Red autumn colouring.

Fothergilla major (syn *F. alnifolia* var *major*, *F. monticola*): Initially the foliage is bronze coloured; the creamy-white flowers appear at the same time. Orange-yellow to orange-red autumn colouring.

Fothergilla major

Fraxinus excelsior 'Aurea'

Fraxinus

Ash

Deciduous trees, occasionally shrubs, with leaves arranged in opposite pairs, usually composite pinnate. The fruits consist of winged nuts with one seed, and often remain on the tree throughout the winter. Some species flower profusely, but as a rule their ornamental value depends on the graceful foliage, in some strains unusually coloured. Young ash trees will tolerate a fair amount of shade, but older specimens prefer light.

Situation Because of their size, most ash trees are suitable only for very large gardens and for parks. In the long run they require a sunny position. They are resistant to strong winds. The species with unusual foliage colouring and rich inflorescence are particularly fine planted singly.

Soil Standard garden soil is very good, but deeply dug, loamy soil, rich in humus, is preferred.

Propagation The species from seed, garden forms by grafting.

Fraxinus excelsior 'Jaspidea'

Fraxinus americana, American ash: A dioecious tree, to 20m in height, with an oval crown. Smooth, olive-green-brown twigs, often somewhat bloomed. The black-brown buds are conspicuous in winter. A leaf consists of 5–9, but usually 7 leaflets, dark green and glossy on the upper surface, whitish underneath. Fine yellow and violet autumn colouring.

Fraxinus excelsior, common ash: Height to 40m, to 10m across; spreading crown. Pale-green to grey-green twigs with black buds. The leaves are usually composed of 9–13 leaflets with fine yellow autumn colouring. Flowers in April to May before the foliage appears. Among the beautiful autumn forms are: 'Aurea', to 15m, fairly slow growing, yellowish bark and golden-yellow foliage; 'Eureka', fast growing, to 20m, with an open, broad cone-shaped crown; 'Jaspida', the golden ash, 20m in height, with a broad pyramid-shaped crown and foliage which turns yellow in autumn, in winter the twigs are bronze yellow.

Fraxinus ornus: Bushy habit, a tree growing to 10m, tolerating drier soil than the common ash. Brown-grey twigs with grey or grey-brown buds. Fragrant white flower plumes in June. The leaves are composed of 7 leaflets. The bark remains smooth even at an advanced age, whereas in the common ash the bark cracks after a few decades and becomes reticulate.

Fuchsia magellanica

Fuchsia

Fuchsias are well known as indoor or balcony plants, but there are a number of practically winter-hardy species which may be planted in a sheltered position in the garden. Since they flower profusely throughout the summer, they deserve some extra care.

Situation Plant them singly or in groups, in borders or as small hedges, in a sunny or partially shaded position, preferably sheltered, for example against a south-facing wall. They should be cut back a little at the beginning of winter and must be covered with reeds or straw. In the following summer they will flower on the new wood.

Soil Light, humus rich and nutritious soil.

Propagation From cuttings.

Fuchsia magellanica (syn *F. macrostemma*): Erect-growing bush with single, pendent and slender flowers from May to September. There are a number of well known strains, for instance 'Gracilis', to 1m tall and as much across, with gracefully arching twigs and red flowers; 'Riccartonii', grows to 2m; red and violet flowers.

Gaultheria

Hardy, low-growing evergreen shrubs with red, blue or black berries; belonging to the heather family.

Situation Excellent as ground-cover; in damp soil, especially, they will develop into a fine dense carpet. Suitable for both small and large gardens as infilling; *Gaultheria shallon* is also good for planting singly. Give partial or deep shade.

Soil Acid, humus-rich peat soil or moorland soil.

Propagation By division, from seed or from cuttings.

Gaultheria procumbens: Height to 15cm, 20cm across, producing scattered, white or single pink flowers July–August. The red fruit is an edible pseudo-berry. The leathery leaves are dark green and glossy, 5cm long and 1.5cm broad, circular to oval, blunt, finely serrated along the edges. In autumn the foliage discolours to purple brown.

Gaultheria shallon: The hairy twigs may grow to about 50cm in length and bear brown-green leaves, 12cm long and 5cm broad, which are pointed oval, heart-shaped at the base. White or slightly pink flowers in pendent plumes; black berries.

Gaultheria procumbens

Genista lydia

Genista

Broom

Attractive little shrubs with predominantly yellow, butterfly-like flowers. Because of their dense green branches they are sometimes regarded as being evergreen. Leaves are distributed all along the twigs. They are difficult to transplant and are therefore grown in containers.

Situation The small species are very suitable for the rock garden, sometimes as ground-cover, and in small gardens. The taller growing species are used in heather gardens and wild gardens. The best species are beautiful planted singly.

Soil Standard garden soil, lime free.

Propagation The species from seed, cultivars by grafting.

Genista aetnensis: A 4m shrub, half as much across, with yellow flowers in July. The foliage borne by the reed-like twigs soon drops.

Genista lydia: Dense, broad shrub, to 60cm in height, with grey-green arching twigs, prickly at the tips. A profusion of yellow flowers May–June. An attractive shrub for growing over a low wall.

Gingko

Maidenhair Tree

This tree always fires the imagination. It existed in ancient times, but is remarkably resistant to an industrial climate, so that it may almost be regarded as a kind of living fossil. Gingko resembles an ordinary foliage tree, but actually it belongs to a division of gymnosperms – the conifers.

Situation   A fine specimen tree with a columnar habit; it may eventually grow to 20m in height, about 8m across.

Soil   Standard garden soil.

Propagation   From summer cuttings or from seed.

Gingko biloba (syn *Salisburia adiantifolia*): A dioecious tree with very fine, fan-shaped leaves on long stalks. Before they drop in autumn, they turn a magnificent yellow colour. The foliage spirals round the long shoots and is arranged in circles round the shorter shoots. The twigs are smooth, greyish in colour. The male flowers are pendulous catkins, the female consist of a small stalk ending in two seed buds. After a warm summer, whitish-yellow flowers with a disagreeable scent develop.

Ginkgo biloba

Gleditsia triacanthos 'Elegantissima'

Gleditsia

Honey Locust

Deciduous trees with treacherous thorns even on the old wood, and singly or doubly pinnate foliage. Clusters of fragrant, butterfly-like flowers are followed by seed pods. It is a lightwood tree, rarely suffering from insect infection. In a windy situation branches may snap. Can be pruned.

Situation   These 'armoured' trees are very suitable for creating impenetrable hedges, the more so as they tolerate pruning. Provide a sunny situation and protection against strong winds. The smaller garden forms, in particular, make attractive specimen trees. The yellow foliage of 'Sunburst' looks well in gardens with a colour scheme containing yellow elements. Because it can be pruned it is suitable for even the smallest gardens. When allowed to grow it is a real parkland tree.

Soil   Good garden soil, which may be on the dry side.

Propagation   The species from seed; garden cultivars are grafted.

Gleditsia aquatica: Height to 15m, 5m across, slow growing. The tree is characterised by its long, branching thorns and the lenticels on the young twigs. Greenish flowers June–July.

Gleditsia japonica (syn *G. horrida*): Height to 20m, 7m across. A tree with numerous, 5–8cm long thorns both on the trunk and on the twigs. Green flowers June–July, followed by sickle-shaped pods.

Gleditsia macrantha: A tree to 15m in height, with thick branches and grey bark. Numerous thorns on the trunk as well as on the branches. Green flowers June–July.

Gleditsia triacanthos: This is the best known species, a tree growing to 20m height and 7m across, with a spreading, loosely branching, umbrella-shaped crown. The glossy brown-grey twigs have numerous lenticels and grow in zigzags. The top buds sometimes develop into thorns. Both trunk and twigs are covered in tripartite thorns. The leaves are 8– to 15–lobed, usually double pinnate and fresh green, with yellow autumn colouring. Clusters of greenish flowers June–July, followed by sickle-shaped pods, up to 30cm long, which are retained for a long time. Among the useful garden forms are 'Elegantissima', a dense, thornless, columnar shrub; 'Inermis', resembling the species, but thornless; 'Pendula', graceful, with thornless branches; and 'Sunburst', thornless with foliage which is yellow in the early stages, but later turns yellow green.

Gleditsia triacanthos 'Sunburst'

Gymnocladus dioicus

Gymnocladus

Kentucky Coffee Tree

This deciduous, slow-growing tree belongs to the pea family. Beautiful foliage colouring in spring and autumn.

Situation   A fine specimen tree in a sunny situation. Unsuitable for small gardens.

Soil   Nutritious, porous garden soil.

Propagation   From seed or from root cuttings.

Gymnocladus dioicus (syn *G. canadensis*): A loosely branching tree, to 20m tall and 15m across, with smooth, thick, irregularly shaped twigs, pale grey in winter. The tree starts into growth late in the season (mid to late May), when the leaves are tinged with pink; these may grow to nearly 1m in length. The greenish-white flowers appearing in May to June are inconspicuous. Yellow autumn colouring. The leaves drop first, then the leaf-stalks and finally the elongated brown-red seed pods.

Halesia carolina

Halesia

Snowdrop Tree

Deciduous bush or tree with widely spreading branches bearing numerous bell-shaped white flowers in April. These are followed by winged green fruits. Fine yellow autumn colouring.

Situation Beautiful when planted singly in a sunny or partially shaded position. May also be used in groups or planted along paths edged by light trees.

Soil Standard lime-free garden soil.

Propagation From seed or by layering.

Halesia carolina (syn *H. tetraptera*): A tree or shrub, initially erect growing, later becoming umbrella shaped as a result of the spreading branches. Peeling bark. The pointed oval leaves are fresh green on the upper surface, hairy on the reverse; they are 5–15cm long and wavy edged. The white flowers appear in groups of 2–7. The pear-shaped fruits are four-winged. The species *monticola* may grow to a height of 6m, 7.5m across; *H. carolina* remains smaller in all its parts and the leaves are more hairy underneath.

Hamamelis × *intermedia* 'Orange Beauty'

Hamamelis

Witch Hazel

Deciduous shrubs with a striking inflorescence in winter. A few species flower in the autumn; occasionally there is fine yellow autumn colouring. The leaves are distributed along the twigs; they resemble those of alder and hazel. The fragrant flowers consist of linear, slightly crumpled petals. Because the bushes are usually leafless while they are in flower, a suitable background must be provided.

Situation Beautiful specimen plants for sunny or partially shaded positions. The autumn-flowering witch hazel enjoys partial shade. Winter-flowering shrubs should preferably be planted close to the house, so that they may be enjoyed from the living-room. Remember that the shrub is less interesting in summer, so place some summer-flowering plants nearby. *Hamamelis* is slow growing.

Soil Will do best in slightly acid sandy soil with an adequate humus content. In calciferous clay the witch hazel is definitely out of place.

Propagation The species from seed, by layering or from cuttings. Garden cultivars are grafted on stock of *Hamamelis virginiana*.

Hamamelis × *intermedia*: The result of crossing *H. japonica* and *H. mollis*. Among the beautiful cultivars are 'Jelena', to 3m tall and as much across, with orange flowers January–February; 'Orange Beauty', which has yellow to orange-yellow flowers; and 'Ruby Glow' with dark brown-red flowers.

Hamamelis mollis: A very well known shrub, to 4m in height, bearing large, golden-yellow and delightfully scented flowers from January to March. The twigs are densely haired and bear obovate leaves, to 15cm long, with dense grey hair on the reverse. The linear petals are sometimes red at the base. 'Brevipetala' has small orange-yellow flowers and grows to 3m. 'Pallida' has sulphur-coloured flowers.

Hamamelis virginiana: Differs from the above-mentioned species and cultivars in that it may grow somewhat taller, and especially because of its flowering season which occurs in the autumn, in September or October. The ornamental value of the flowers is less, since they are concealed by the foliage. The petals are not crumpled. The pale-green, obovate leaves, to 15cm long, turn a striking yellow colour in autumn.

Hamamelis mollis

Hebe Andersonii hybrid

Hebe

Small evergreen shrubs with small white, pink or violet-coloured flowers, not always very conspicuous. The leaves grow opposite and, when scale-shaped, give the shrub the appearance of a conifer. There are also species with round, spear-shaped or oval leaves. Unless otherwise described, the species mentioned below are reasonably winter-hardy; but in severe winters, without a covering of snow, some protection is desirable.

Situation *Hebe* should be planted in a sunny, warm spot, preferably somewhat sheltered, in porous, fairly dry soil. As a rule *Hebe* plants are used in the rock garden or along low walls, which they may overgrow. It is also possible to make them emerge from a very level, dense carpet of plants, for example from among thyme, pinks or similar growth.

In general, pruning is restricted to the removal of dead flower plumes and old branches which have grown bare at the base.

Soil Nutritious sandy soil. Lime is tolerated.

Propagation From cuttings taken in winter.

Hebe armstrongii

Hebe buxifolia

Hebe Andersonii hybrids (syn *Veronica × andersonii*): Flowering shrub, much loved because of its late flowering season of August to October. Purple flowers in dense spikes and corrugated, oblong to spear-shaped leaves. The bushes grow to 1m in height and as much across. Unfortunately not entirely winter-hardy, but worth trying in coastal areas. There are also hybrids in which the leaves are blotched and edged with a creamy colour, and forms in which the flowers are purple. 'Autumn Blue' produces violet-coloured flowers September–October; height 40cm, 50cm across.

Hebe anomala: A shrub to over 1m in height, with bare twigs and spear-shaped, 8–20cm long pointed leaves, dark green and glossy on the upper surface. The flowers are white to pale red-purple and appear June–July. Not very well known, but quite winter-hardy.

Hebe armstrongii: A densely branching shrub, to 60cm tall and 90cm across, with scale-shaped foliage which makes this *Hebe* look like a conifer. The leaves are golden green, in winter more bronze coloured. White flowers in groups of 3–8. Suitable for rock gardens and in a golden-yellow colour scheme.

Hebe buxifolia: Height to 30cm, with 8–12mm long, oblong to obovate leaves overlapping like roof tiles, densely arranged in four rows. Their colour is dark green and glossy. White flowers in 3cm long, dense spikes, June–August. Flat fruits.

Hebe cupressoides: The finely haired, erect-growing or oblique twigs with their 1mm long, scale-shaped leaves make this plant resemble a 25cm tall dwarf cypress. The pairs of leaves are so widely scattered that they leave the stalks partially bare. Little pale-blue to white flowers in groups of 3–8 in June.

Hebe glaucocaerulea (syn *H. pimeleoides* var *glaucocaerulea*): A strongly branching, somewhat creeping little shrub, to 30cm in height. Blue green in all its parts and in July to August bearing lavender-coloured little flowers in short, sparse spikes. The leaves overlap like roof tiles and are oblong to obovate, 8–11mm long.

Hebe ochracea: A shrub to 40cm tall. Strongly branching twigs covered with small, triangular, contiguous leaves – actually golden-green or bronze-coloured scales. Closely resembles *H. armstrongii* with which it is sometimes confused, but it has much greener foliage, and is not winter-hardy.

Hebe pinguifolia: A recumbent shrub, to 30cm in height, with dense, leathery foliage, round to oval, dull blue-green and arranged in four rows. Sometimes the leaves have a red margin or are slightly tinged with red. White flowers in 2cm long spikes, borne in the axils of the leaves from May to July.

Hebe salicifolia: Beautiful shrub, to 3m in height, with bare green twigs and elongated, spear-shaped leaves, grey green in colour. White-violet flower clusters June–July.

Hedera

Ivy

Evergreen shrub, often grown as a climber or as ground-cover. There are many varieties varying in shape and foliage colour. As a rule ivy develops aerial roots which enable it to climb high walls or trees without further support. The shrub has two kinds of leaves: those on the growing shoots differ in shape from the leaves borne on the flowering shoots. Plants grown from cuttings of flowering shoots will have lost the ability to climb, for example *Hedera helix* 'Arborescens'. Usually *Hedera* will climb for a long time without flowering. Once flowers develop, the plant ceases climbing and will flower at the top every year. The yellow-green flower umbels appear in September or October; they are followed by black or yellow berries, attractive to birds. In mild winters the foliage may be retained, but in a severe frost it will turn brown and drop. The branches usually remain alive, but when they grow on trees the cold may kill them. The variegated forms are less hardy than the species, something that should be taken into account when planting the shrubs.

Situation   A vigorous climber for covering walls, fences and pergolas. Stone walls do not greatly suffer, but be careful with woodwork. Mature trees are able to support the plant, but growing trees should be kept free of rampant ivy, for they might not survive. The plant may be severely cut back. *H. colchica* is less vigorous than *H. helix*; its variegated forms are frequently planted near front doors. It is somewhat less winter-hardy than the common ivy. In addition to being an excellent climber, ivy is also very suitable for ground-cover, especially in shady positions. The twigs will root at the nodes. Shrub forms may be planted singly. Smaller growing cultivars with unusual leaf shapes are attractive in the rock garden, while trailing twigs create a pleasant effect in window-boxes.

Soil   Not too dry, standard garden soil. The fastest growth will occur in humus-rich, nutritious soil.

Propagation   From cuttings. *Hedera* readily reverts to type, so that it is essential to choose characteristic shoots.

Hedera colchica, Persian ivy: The scaly yellow-brown twigs bear two kinds of leaves. Those on the growing shoots are triangular, rounded, or slightly heart-shaped at the base; those on the flowering shoots are elongated oval, wedge-shaped at the base. Yellow-green flower umbels in September, followed by black berries. 'Arborescens' is a 1m tall shrub form. 'Dentata' has strongly serrated foliage. 'Dentovariegata' is a green and white variety with large, leathery, grey-green leaves with a white margin. The foliage of 'Sulphur Heart' has irregularly shaped white blotches.

Hedera colchica 'Sulphur Heart'

Hedera helix

Hedera helix 'Sagittaefolia'

Hedera helix, common ivy: The leaves on the growing shoots are lobed, those on the flowering shoots are smooth edged. The yellow-green flowers appear in 5- to 8-stalked umbels; the berries are yellow or black. This ivy may grow to as much as 20m in height.

There are numerous cultivars of the common ivy, classified under the sub-species *poetarum*. 'Arborescens' is the shrub form already mentioned, not above 1.5m, freely flowering. 'Baltica', sometimes regarded as a variety, has somewhat smaller leaves and appears to be much more winter-hardy. 'Deltoidea' has somewhat triangular leaves, in winter fading to brown. 'Goldheart' has small green leaves with a striking yellow blotch in the centre. 'Sagittifolia' has small, arrow-shaped leaves.

Hedera hibernica, Irish ivy: Often regarded as a variety of the previous species. Glossy, less deeply lobed foliage with pale-green veins. Cultivated on a large scale.

Hibiscus syriacus 'Coelestis'

Hibiscus

Rose Mallow

This tropical plant genus includes evergreen as well as deciduous, and herbaceous as well as woody, plants. The leaves are evenly distributed, lobed. The large flowers usually grow singly in the axils of the leaves and consist of five petals and sepals. The only species suitable for use in the garden is *Hibiscus syriacus*. There are magnificent hybrids with pastel-coloured flowers, single as well as double. The flowers are particularly conspicuous because they appear late in the season.

Situation A beautiful specimen plant for a sheltered, sunny position. In view of its sensitivity to frost we must keep strictly to the rule that the worse the climate, the more sheltered the situation. Young plants, in particular, often need a covering of straw in winter. In spring only the branches damaged by frost are removed. The shrub starts into growth very late and there is therefore no need to worry unduly that it has died during the winter. Maximum flowering is achieved only in warm summers; it may continue until the onset of night frosts.

Soil Nutritious, preferably loamy soil.

Propagation From cuttings.

Hibiscus syriacus, rose of Sharon: A bare, erect-growing shrub, height between 2 and 3m, with grey twigs. The leaves, to 9cm long, are usually 3-lobed, but the shape may vary. Large, isolated, violet-coloured flowers in August and September. There are many beautiful garden cultivars; single-flowered forms are a little stronger than those with double flowers.

'Admiral Dewey', double white flowers.
'Ardens', double purple flowers.
'Coelestis', single violet-coloured flowers, darker in the centre; low growing.
'Lady Stanley', white flowers with red marking, double.
'Oiseau Bleu', an improved form of 'Coelestis', with large, deep-blue single flowers. Grows more vigorously. In bad weather the flowers will close up.
'Punicus Plenus' is red, semi-double. Flowers early in the season.
'Red Heart', single, pure-white flowers with red blotches.
'Rubis' has single, deep-red flowers.
'Speciosus' is semi-double, white, with red blotches.
'Totus Albus', low growing; pure-white single flowers. An improved form, with very large white flowers, is 'William R. Smith'.
'Woodbridge', vigorous growth; large, single red flowers.

Hibiscus syriacus 'William R. Smith'

Hippophaë rhamnoides

Hippophaë

Sea Buckthorn

Dioecious shrub with thorny twigs and striking orange berries which are a beautiful contrast to the greyish foliage. The sea buckthorn, and in particular the variety *maritima*, is very wind-resistant. It is indigenous in chalky dune-soil; in some countries it also grows in pebble beds in rivers.

Situation These hardy shrubs may be used successfully in many positions: in coastal gardens as soil-retainers, in window-boxes and in garden schemes based predominantly on silver-leaved shrubs and perennials. In a vase, cut branches give pleasure for a long time.

Soil Will grow in the poorest soil, but in that case will remain small. Prefer chalky soil.

Propagation From seed, cuttings or basal shoots.

Hippophaë rhamnoides: A tree to 3m in height and as much across, with green-yellow flowers March–April, before the appearance of the narrow grey leaves. After wind-pollination, bright orange berries will develop.

Holodiscus dumosus

Holodiscus

Little known deciduous shrubs, flowering profusely, and attractive in winter because of their shape and powdery fruits.
Situation Sunny and partially shaded positions; the soil should not be too dry. Beautiful planted singly, but also attractive in the shrub border.
Soil Standard garden soil.
Propagation From cuttings and by layering.

Holodiscus discolor: Height to 4m, 2.5m across, a shrub with an erect-growing habit and arching twigs. Serrated or slightly lobed leaves, to 9cm long, green on the upper surface, grey green underneath. Yellow-white flowers in large, arching plumes July–August. Var *discolor* grows a little broader; the leaves are felty and white on the reverse.
Holodiscus dumosus (syn *Spiraea dumosa*): A fairly rare species, growing to only 1m in height and 2m across. It has an almost recumbent habit. White, slightly more erect flower plumes July–August. Dark-green lobed foliage.

Hydrangea anomala ssp petiolaris

Hydrangea

Hortensia

Deciduous ornamental shrubs with a characteristic inflorescence and smooth-edged or lobed foliage. The leaves grow opposite. The inner corolla of an inflorescence consists of tiny fertile florets; they are surrounded by sterile florets with large sepals, coloured as if they were petals. In addition to the shrubs with beautiful foliage and flowers, there are a number of climbers.
Situation Most hortensias can be planted either singly or in groups. They require a sunny to partially shaded position; the climbing hortensia is a shrub for partial or deep shade and is excellent for covering a north-facing wall. It requires less moisture than the other, more water-loving hortensias. No garden is complete without a *Hydrangea paniculata*. Because of the variation in size, hortensias suit small as well as large gardens. Not all species are 100 per cent winter-hardy.
Soil Acid, damp soil, for example peaty soil.
Propagation Shrub forms from cuttings taken in winter, climbers from summer cuttings.

Hydrangea anomala ssp *petiolaris* (syn *H. petiolaris*, *H. scandens*), climbing hortensia: A climber growing to 7m in height, 5m across, with self-clinging roots developing on the bright-brown, peeling twigs. The large, fresh-green, cone-shaped terminal bud is a striking feature. Oval, serrated, pointed leaves to 12cm long. Very broad white flower umbels with single sterile florets. Winter-hardy. Initially it does not grow very fast and until the self-clinging roots develop it will need some support. Should be pruned as little as possible.

Hydrangea arborescens: Height to 3m, a shrub with erect-growing, peeling grey twigs. White flower umbels July–August; there are few if any sterile florets. The shrub is cut back drastically every year to restrict it to 1m in height. The form most often planted is 'Grandi-flora', which produces broad clusters of sterile white flowers. The largest flowers are achieved if the plant is cut back to the ground every year.

Hydrangea aspera ssp *sargentiana* (syn *H. sargentiana*): Height to 2m and as much across, a shrub producing violet-coloured fertile and white sterile florets July–August. The leaves, to 25cm long, are oval and covered in rust-coloured hairs. Winter-hardy. May be cut down in spring.

Hydrangea involucrata: Densely branching shrub, to 1m in height. The leaves are oblong to oval, to 25cm long, downy. Flowers in 15cm broad clusters; the fertile florets are white, the sterile purple. Flowering season July–August.

Hydrangea macrophylla: This is actually the indoor hortensia, but there are winter-hardy forms suitable for the garden. They flower on the previous year's wood. To prevent them growing bare at the base they are re-juvenated by pruning before they flower. New shoots will develop which will produce the flower buds for the following year. 'Blue Wave' will have blue flowers in acid soil; otherwise they are pink or lilac. 'Bouquet Rose' flowers profusely, pink or blue, and 'White Wave' has white sterile flowers. *Hydrangea macrophylla* ssp *serrata* (syn *H. serrata*) grows to 1m in height and as much across. The leaves are smaller and thinner than in the species and they are not glossy. The flat inflorescence has large pink or blue sterile florets. The best known strain is 'Acuminata', 1.5m tall with bluish sterile flowers.

Hydrangea paniculata: Height to 4m and as much across. Erect-growing, non-peeling twigs. White flowers in large, pyramid-shaped plumes July–August; they sub-sequently turn pale red. In 'Grandiflora' all the florets are sterile. 'Praecox' flowers six weeks earlier and remains more compact.

Hydrangea quercifolia: Height 1–2m, a shrub with foli-age resembling oak leaves. The reverse is often covered in thick, felty white down. Beautiful red autumn colour-ing. The inflorescence is plume shaped and consists of numerous fertile white florets. Every plume also usually contains one sterile flower, which later discolours to red. The flowering season is July to August.

Hydrangea macrophylla

Hydrangea paniculata 'Grandiflora'

Hypericum calycinum

Hypericum hookerianum 'Hidcote'

Hypericum

St John's Wort

Evergreen and deciduous shrubs and herbaceous plants, with a profusion of yellow flowers. They are characterised by the opposite growing leaves and the large number of stamens protruding from the corolla, greatly contributing to the beauty of the plant. In severe winters the shrubs may freeze, but as a rule they will start into growth again. They tolerate a fair amount of shade, but will also do well in sunny situations. Several species of this genus have become naturalised in western Europe, but these are rarely, if ever, cultivated.

Situation The shrubs are compact in habit and are therefore suitable for small gardens, either planted singly or in groups. *Hypericum calycinum* makes excellent ground-cover. Provide a sunny or partially shaded position. The soil should be dry rather than moist.

Soil Humus-rich soil. *H. inodorum* in particular requires adequate nutrients.

Propagation From summer or winter cuttings. *H. calycinum* develops a large number of runners and can be divided.

Hypericum androsaemum: Deciduous, scentless shrub, to 1m in height, with 10cm long leaves; larger than in any other species. The reverse of the leaves is whitish; young tip-leaves are often tinged with violet brown. Golden-yellow flowers in groups of three or more July–September. The glossy berries are initially red, later turning black.

Hypericum beanii: Semi-evergreen shrub, to 1m tall, with arching twigs. The oval leaves are arranged along the twigs in two rows. Flat, dark-yellow flowers July–September. The best known form is the cultivar 'Goldcup', in which the flowers are bright yellow.

Hypericum calycinum: Often used as ground-cover. Usually evergreen, but in the absence of snow cover it will lose its foliage in severe winters. This recumbent, vigorously spreading shrub grows to a maximum of 45cm in height. The bare, almost square twigs bear dark-green, oval to oblong, 8cm long leathery leaves. Large, usually isolated golden-yellow flowers July–September; they are followed by pale-green berries.

Hypericum hookerianum: The species is not cultivated in this country because it is not winter-hardy, but the strain 'Hidcote' is grown on a large scale. A shrub to 2m in height and as much across, with dark, blue-green leaves, to 7cm long, and large yellow flowers with orange stamens July–September. Adequately winter-hardy.

Hypericum inodorum (syn *H. elatum*): Height to 1m; angular twigs and oval, to 8cm long, leaves. The yellow flowers appear in July and August. After the flowering season the sepals are retained and curve back. The berries are elongated, oval and pointed, initially brown red, later black. 'Elstead' grows less vigorously; it is partially evergreen, with red-brown twigs. The flowers soon fade. Initially the berries are bright scarlet in colour. 'Goudelsje' is a dense, erect-growing shrub, to 2m across. Yellow flowers in July and August; brown-red berries discolouring to black.

Hypericum kalmianum: A narrow-leaved shrub, to 1m in height, with bare, angular twigs and clusters of small, lemon-yellow flowers with golden-yellow stamens July–September.

Hypericum kouytchense: Evergreen, sometimes deciduous shrub, to 1m in height, with arching twigs. The oval leaves are 4–6cm long, bluish on the reverse. The golden-yellow flowers, 6cm in diameter, appear July–September; recurved petals and very long stamens. Red berries.

Hypericum × moserianum: The result of crossing *H. calycinum* and *H. patulum*. A semi winter-hardy shrub, 60cm in height and 1.2m across, with arching, angular twigs. Broad-oval, to 6cm long leaves and large, golden-yellow flowers, growing singly or in groups of two or three, in July and August. Not entirely winter-hardy.

Hypericum inodorum 'Elstead'

Ilex × altaclarensis 'Camelliaefolia'

Ilex

Holly

Largely evergreen shrubs with alternate leaves and leathery, often spiny foliage, often very beautiful in colour. The flowers are hermaphrodite, but since in one plant only the stamens and in the other only the pistils develop, holly may be regarded as dioecious. To ensure berries, male and female specimens must therefore be planted together. Flies will see to the cross-pollination. Holly should be transplanted with a large soil-ball adhering, and only in the dormant season or when it has just started into growth.

Situation Holly species indigenous to this country are used for creating windbreaks and under trees, since they tolerate a great deal of shade. In sunny positions they will produce more berries. The ideal position is in partial shade, sheltered against strong sun in winter and against drying winds; the level of humidity in the air should be high. The root system must be kept out of the sun as must as possible, something that is easily achieved with ground-cover or low-growing plants. Hollies with variegated or unusually shaped foliage are often attractive growing singly, but they may also be planted in groups in the shrub border; smaller growing

Ilex × altaclarensis 'Golden King'

Ilex aquifolium 'J.C. van Tol'

species are suitable for window-boxes as well. Cut branches with an abundance of berries are very popular, especially at Christmas time. Finally, holly makes a beautiful hedge, impenetrable if the species selected is a spiny one. Unfortunately most species and strains grow very slowly.

Problems with holly are usually due to their lack of winter-hardiness. Even *Ilex aquifolium*, which is indigenous in western Europe, may be badly damaged in a severe winter, especially if it is not protected against strong east winds. The variegated forms are even more tender. *I. × altaclarensis* also gives up easily; *I. crenata* is a little hardier. The only truly hardy holly grown in this country is the deciduous *I. verticillata*. In the United States there are a number of other popular hardy species, for example *I. glabra, I. opaca* and *I. pedunculosa*, which originates in Japan. Oddly enough these hollies are rarely cultivated in Europe.

Soil. Holly makes few demands as regards soil, but prefers soil containing humus, since this is more moisture retaining.

Propagation The species from seed; garden forms are grown from cuttings or from improved seedlings of the common holly.

Ilex × altaclarensis: The result of crossing *I. aquifolium* and *I. perado*. Resembles the common holly, but has larger and more spiny leaves. Height to 10m. 'Belgica' has orange-red berries and 'Camelliaefolia', as the name implies, has leaves similar to those of the *Camellia*, ie spineless. It is a more or less pyramid-shaped shrub or tree, 7m in height and 4m across. 'Golden King' grows about a metre taller. It is a spreading shrub; the foliage has a golden margin. The species as well as the strains are attractive for cutting and can be used for hedges.

Ilex × aquifolium, common holly: Height to 15m, but usually much lower growing; a shrub or tree with smooth green branches. Oval, to 7cm long leaves with relatively few spines, often wavy edged. Flowers May–June, with brilliant red berries at a later stage. The following are a few of the cultivars:

'Argenteomarginata', height 7–8m, broad-pyramidal habit, very winter-hardy. The fairly sharply spined leaves have a beautiful silver margin. A multitude of berries. 'Argentea Longifolia', 8m tall, a tree or shrub with dentate, white-edged and fairly long leaves; red berries. 'Atlas' does not produce berries; it is 8m in height, very suitable for hedge making. 'Aureomarginata' has golden-yellow leaf margins; no berries; fast growing, height 6–8m. 'Bacciflava' has yellow berries. 'J.C. van Tol' is a very well known strain with few spines along the leaves and a profusion of large, orange-red berries. There is also a form with a golden-yellow margin to the foliage. In 'Madame Briot' the leaves are slightly larger than in the species; they have a golden-yellow margin or are entirely yellow; orange-red berries. 'Pyramidalis' is self-pollinating and does not need a companion tree to produce berries. Height 8–10m; glossy, almost smooth-edged foliage and red berries. 'Silver Queen', height 5–6m, has leaves with a broad, creamy-white margin and purplish twigs. It is a male plant and bears no berries.

Ilex bioritsensis (syn *I. pernyi* var *veitchii*): A dense shrub with striking, glossy green leaves, to 3cm long, with sharp spines projecting at either side. The berries are red.

Ilex crenata, Chinese or Japanese holly: Densely branching shrub, height to 3m, with oval to spear-shaped leaves, up to 3cm long, usually crenate along the entire edge. Black berries. 'Convexa' grows to 1.5m and has a bushy habit and unusually convex leaves. Ideal for broad hedges which do not have to grow too tall. 'Golden Gem' grows to 50–80cm and has golden-yellow foliage, a little smaller than that of the species.

Ilex verticillata: Densely branching, erect-growing shrub, height to 4m, with thin, pale-brown twigs. When the shrub starts into growth the leaves are purple, later green, to 7cm long, oval to reversed egg-shaped, singly or doubly serrated. The foliage turns yellow in autumn and drops in winter. A profusion of fine red berries.

Ilex verticillata

Indigofera

Indigo Plant

Fairly unfamiliar, pea-flowered shrubs of graceful appearance, flowering in summer.

Situation Indigo shrubs enjoy a sunny, sheltered position. They are beautiful planted singly, but also when planted in groups. At the end of winter dead wood is removed, or the plant is cut down to the ground. Planted in the shelter of a wall they are less endangered by frost and grow taller.

Soil Standard garden soil, also in dry positions.

Propagation From seed, cuttings or rooted runners.

Indigofera gerardiana (syn *I. dosua*): A flowering shrub, to 2m tall, with irregularly pinnate leaves and pale-red flowers in July and August. Not entirely winter-hardy; must be covered in winter.

Indigofera kirilowii: Height to 1m, 2m across, a dense shrub with lightly haired foliage and dense clusters of red-purple flowers in June. This shrub is quite winter-hardy and flowers on the current year's wood. Its dense habit makes it a valuable ground-covering plant.

Indigofera kirilowii

Jasminum

Jasmine, Mock Orange

The most winter-hardy species of this genus is the winter jasmine; an appropriate name, as the shrub produces its soft yellow, clearly jasmine-like little flowers throughout the winter. The translation of the botanical name is 'naked-flowering jasmine', which indicates that the foliage does not appear until the flowers have faded.

Situation In sunny and partially shaded positions, for example against a south- or west-facing wall, preferably near a window so that the flowers are easily enjoyed. In winter, protection against severe cold and strong wind is essential. The twigs are not self-clinging, but if they are tied here and there the shrub may grow to as much as 3m. Can also be used as ground-cover.

Soil Standard garden soil.

Propagation From cuttings, by layering or from seed sown under glass; it will germinate within a few weeks.

Jasminum nudiflorum: The soft, square, green twigs bear 3-fold, dark-green leaves; flowers in groups of 1–4 from December to February.

Jasminum nudiflorum

Juglans cinerea

Juglans

Walnut

Deciduous, monoecious trees or shrubs with large, pinnate, composite leaves, arranged alternately along the branches, smooth-edged or dentate. In autumn the shrub produces nuts with a hard husk.

Situation Some are planted for the sake of their graceful appearance, but the majority for the sake of their nuts. Provide a sunny or partially shaded position. A magnificent specimen tree for large gardens.

Soil Nutritious soil.

Propagation From seed and by grafting.

Juglans cinerea: A tree, height to 25m and almost as much across, with greenish catkins in May. The oblong nuts, covered in stiff hair, grow in groups of 2–5 on a hairy stalk. Does not grow as fast as *J. nigra*.

Juglans nigra: A tree to 45m in height, with a broad, open crown. More or less round nuts, growing singly or in groups. Used for medicinal purposes.

Juglans regia: May grow to about 25m and has a broad, dense crown. The nuts are easy to crack.

Juniperus

Juniper

A large genus, consisting of hardy, evergreen conifers. The juniper is indigenous in Europe, in cold, northern regions as well as in the south, in damp as well as in dry soil. There are two kinds of needles: juvenile and mature. Both may occur on the same plant. The juvenile foliage consists of small needles with sharp points, for example in the common juniper. In the adult foliage the needles are scale-shaped and are densely arranged round the twigs. Foliage colouring varies greatly: green, greyish, bluish, yellow or white variegated. Junipers are dioecious, therefore to obtain berries it is necessary to plant male and female specimens together. The fruits take two to three years to ripen, so that a shrub may bear flowers, unripe green and ripe blue berries at one and the same time. Ripe berries are eaten by birds or are made into gin or used in cooking. Both foliage and berries of *Juniperus* are very aromatic.

Situation   Provide a sunny or partially shaded position. Most species are fairly wind-resistant. Junipers with unusual foliage colouring and/or habit are beautiful planted singly, for instance in a heather garden. Slow-growing forms are frequently planted in rock gardens. The low-growing, creeping types make fine ground-cover, but the more erect-growing, spreading forms can also be used for this purpose. They are suitable for in-filling and require little maintenance. Tall, fast-growing types make an attractive background, and can also be planted in groups in the shrub border. The plants are poisonous and may cause skin irritations.

Soil   Junipers are not very choosy; they will grow in acid as well as in calciferous soil; most species will do fairly well even in poor, sandy soil. *Juniperus communis* 'Hibernica' requires adequately porous soil; *Juniperus virginiana* damper and better quality soil.

Propagation   The species from seed which may take as much as two years to germinate. Garden forms are increased from cuttings taken in winter.

Juniperus chinensis: A tree or shrub to 25m in height, with smooth twigs and predominantly or exclusively sharp, needle-shaped foliage grouped in twos or threes. The needles have two white streaks on the upper surface and contiguous small, blunt scales. Cone-shaped berries, size to 10mm, brown with a white tinge. Flowering season late April, early May. Male plants are more columnar in shape and have more needle-shaped leaves. The female plants have a somewhat broader habit and slightly arching twigs with more scale-shaped leaves. A large number of different strains are available.

Many writers now classify a large number of strains, but especially 'Pfitzeriana', under the hybrid *J. × media*, the result of crossing *J. sabina* and *J. spaerica*. The latter

Juniperus chinensis 'Blaauw'

Juniperus chinensis 'Hetzii'

105

Juniperus chinensis 'Pfitzeriana Aurea'

Juniperus communis 'Compressa'

name is thought to be a synonym for *J. chinensis*. Classification under *J. chinensis* is the practice adopted here. In time there will no doubt be changes in the nomenclature of the genus *Juniperus*.

'Blaauw' has grey-green foliage and is a compact dwarf form with plume-shaped twigs, slightly curved at the tips. Height approximately 1.5m.

'Blue Cloud' is a low-growing, broad shrub with grey-blue foliage.

'Blue and Gold' is an open, loose bush with golden-yellow and blue-green coloured scales and a few needle-shaped leaves. Height 2m and the same across.

'Blue Point' has a regular, pointed cone shape; the foliage is blue grey.

'Echiniformis' is a dwarf form, eventually a flattened sphere with very short twigs arranged closely together. The needles are very tiny.

'Fruitlandii' has a spreading habit with dense ramification; the foliage is bright green. Actually an improved form of 'Pfitzeriana Compacta'.

'Gold Coast' reaches a moderate height. Spreading habit; deep golden yellow.

'Hetzii' grows to 2m, but may be twice as much across. It is a vigorous grower with spreading branches and blue-grey-green foliage. Pruning is essential if dense ramification and a fine shape are to be achieved.

'Kaizuka' is an erratically shaped bush with irregularly placed, oblique branches. The scale-shaped foliage is fresh green. A very decorative specimen plant for a reasonably sized garden with a Japanese atmosphere.

'Keteleeri' develops a 5–10m tall, blue-grey-green column.

'Old Gold' grows to 1 or 1.5m and has bronze-coloured foliage even in winter. Also suitable for containers.

'Parsonii' has almost horizontal, widely spreading and fairly thick branches with scale-shaped green leaves. Height 1m, 3m across.

'Pfitzeriana' is a very well known and much cultivated strain growing to 2m in height and 5m across. This large shrub has green foliage and graceful habit, the foliage growing in horizontal layers, the ends of the twigs arching a little. Easy to prune. In 'Pfitzeriana Aurea' the young foliage and the twigs are golden yellow, later more greenish yellow, and bronze coloured in winter.

'Pfitzeriana Glauca' has grey-blue foliage.

'Plumosa' grows to 1m. It is a male form with spreading, plume-shaped branches; the tips of the twigs are blunt. Like 'Plumosa Aurea', the yellow-green form, it has an irregular shape.

'Plumosa Albovariegata' is slow growing and white-flecked.

'Stricta' is a small, cone-shaped conifer, very densely branched. Needle-shaped foliage of a beautiful blue-grey colour, steel blue in winter.

'Wilson Weeping', to 20m; an open tree with erect-growing branches and pendulous foliage, dense at the extremities of the twigs.

Juniperus communis, common juniper: A shrub to 5m in height, in good soil it has a more columnar habit than in poor soil, where the tree grows broader, with sharper needles. This erect-growing shrub has winged twigs and conspicuous axillary buds. The needles are awl-shaped, 1.5cm long, pointed; they grow in groups of three and have broad white streaks on the upper surface. The cones are covered in blue bloom. Flowers April–May.

'Compressa' is a slow-growing plant, eventually reaching 1m. It has permanent juvenile foliage and develops into a blue-grey column.

'Depressa Aurea' grows to the same height, but is vase shaped, up to 4m across at the top. In summer the foliage is golden yellow, in winter it is bronze coloured.

'Depressed Star' is the all-green form, usually referred to as var *depressa*.

'Dumosa' has a low-growing, broad habit, but the twigs grow to a height of about 1m. The green needles are 10mm long. This is a clone of the botanical variety *depressa*.

'Echiniformis' is a slow-growing dwarf form which develops as an irregular sphere, 30cm in height and 60cm across. The green-blue-green needles are fairly thick, opposite.

'Hibernica' is the Irish juniper, a well known specimen plant. It develops as a narrow column, to 6m in height, and has blue-green foliage. Accepts dry soil. Also suitable for hedges.

'Hornibrookii' does not grow beyond 1m; it has a low, creeping habit and green foliage, discolouring to a brownish shade in winter. Used mainly in rock gardens and on slopes.

'Meyer' develops a broad cone-shape, to 3m in height. The sharp needles are grey blue in colour.

'Minima' is an irregularly growing, recumbent dwarf form with triangular twigs and non-spiny, blue-streaked needles.

'Pyramidalis' has a broader and looser habit than 'Hibernica' and has multiple heads.

'Repanda', 30cm in height and sometimes as much as 1.5m across, has a creeping habit. The upper surface of the needles has a silvery streak, the reverse is green. The foliage is very soft to the touch.

'Suecica' resembles 'Hibernica', but is more grey blue and softer to the touch.

'Vase' actually has the shape of a vase or, if you prefer it, a nest. It is a *depressa* type, height to 1m, funnel-shaped habit. The needles are streaked with white on the upper surface and are dark green underneath. The foliage turns brown in winter.

Juniperus conferta (syn *J. litoralis*): Height to 60cm. This conifer grows very broad and has fresh-green foliage, spiny to the touch. Suitable for the rock garden, as ground-cover and as an edging plant in a position where it can droop over some object such as a low wall, or disguise a bare area of ground.

Juniperus horizontalis (syn *J. prostrata*): Not a vigorous

Juniperus communis 'Hibernica'

Juniperus horizontalis

Juniperus recurva var *coxii*

Juniperus sabina 'Tamariscifolia'

grower; a recumbent shrub, to 30cm in height, with fairly long shoots up to 3m across. Accepts dry soil and is an attractive plant for covering slopes.

'Douglasii' is a fairly vigorous grower, a little taller and broader than the species. The foliage is blue green in summer, violet blue in winter.

'Glauca' has intensely bluish, exclusively needle-shaped foliage. It has a creeping habit and forms a fine carpet. 'Bar Harbor' has even more compact growth.

'Jade Spreader' has foliage of a beautiful sea-green colour, reminiscent of jade.

'Plumosa' is a spreading, creeping grey-green shrub, more purple coloured in winter. The twigs have plume-shaped ramification and point obliquely upwards. All the foliage is needle-shaped.

'Prostrata' reaches the same height as the species, but is more spreading. Develops a fine carpet; the tips of the twigs curve upwards a little. Blue-grey-green foliage.

'Viridis' has a striking, fresh-green colour; it grows a little taller than the other strains, to 60cm.

'Wapiti' is the fastest grower of all the *horizontalis* forms. Height about 30cm.

'Wiltonii' is extremely slow growing, very low. Very fine silvery-blue foliage; the colour is maintained in winter. Excellent for rock gardens and troughs.

Juniperus procumbens: A recumbent shrub, to 50cm in height; at the top the twigs grow slightly erect. Exclusively needle-shaped foliage, in circles of three, blue green and dense. Two white blotches at the base of the upper surface. 'Nana' remains a little lower, but spreads to 3m.

Juniperus recurva: A tall, pyramidal tree or shrub with arching twigs. The variety *coxii* has a narrow-pyramid shape, gracefully arching branches and dark, greyish-purple cones. Unfortunately this species and its variety are not very winter-hardy.

Juniperus sabina: Strong, low-growing, sometimes erect-growing shrubs with bushy habit and foliage which has a disagreeable scent when rubbed. Brushy branches and almost square twigs with blue-green foliage. The needles are small, sometimes lacking entirely; the small scales are densely arranged. Flowering season April–May. The small cones are covered in blue bloom.

'Arcadia' remains low and has widely spreading branches with pale-green foliage, predominantly scale-shaped.

'Blue Danube' grows taller, with spreading branches and greyish-blue, scale-shaped foliage.

'Erecta' is one of the best known strains, an erect-growing, spreading form with a number of columnar and broom-shaped branches.

'Hicksii' is a vigorous grower with oblique branches which at a later stage may arch a little. The grey-blue foliage turns purplish in winter and is almost entirely needle-shaped.

'Musgrave' has juvenile as well as mature foliage, coloured green. Low, spreading habit, height to 60cm.

'Tamariscifolia' is a densely branching low shrub with overlapping twigs and sharp, bluish-green needles. Few adult leaves. Height 50cm, to 4m across.

Juniperus scopulorum: A tree up to 10m in height, often with multiple trunks. The foliage is almost exclusively scale-shaped and lies close to the twigs. The species is not in cultivation, only a number of cultivars such as 'Blue Heaven', cone-shaped habit, grey-blue foliage, numerous fruits; 'Grey Gleam', columnar habit, very delicate silver-grey foliage; 'Springbank', narrow cone shape, height to 2m, silvery-blue foliage, graceful and quite winter-hardy; 'Wichita Blue', a broad cone shape, with fine blue-green foliage throughout the year.

Juniperus squamata: A recumbent shrub, to 25cm tall, sometimes with a number of erect-growing twigs. The needles are arranged in threes and are blue-white on the upper surface, green underneath. Flowering season April–May; black cones.

'Blue Star' is a particularly beautiful strain, to 1m in height and 1.5m across; spherical shape and deep blue-grey needles.

'Boulevard' grows to twice the size of the previous form; compact habit, blue-green foliage with two bluish-white streaks on the reverse. Approximately 1m across.

'Loden' develops into a narrow column, to 3m in height. The foliage at the ends of the twigs has the juvenile shape; the remainder is adult.

A very well known form is 'Meyeri', a broad, erect-growing, bushy shrub, 3–5m in height. The needles are of a striking bluish-green colour. Should be drastically pruned to prevent it becoming bare with age.

'Wilsonii' has a broad-pyramidal, compact habit, height 2m. Curved, awl-shaped tips to the twigs; blue-grey foliage.

Juniperus virginiana, red cedar: A shrub or tree to 30m tall, with thin, usually only slightly branched twigs. Short, pointed, often sharp needles, blue white on the upper surface. The pointed scales stand away slightly from the tips of the twigs. Flowering season April–May. Small cones, covered in blue bloom; they ripen within one season.

'Burkii' forms a narrow, blue-green cone. Predominantly needle-shaped foliage, turning purplish in winter.

'Canaertii' is a densely branching, fairly vigorously growing cone-shaped tree with dark-green foliage and numerous long, unbranched lateral twigs.

'Glauca' has an open columnar shape, to 5m tall. Practically all scale-shaped foliage, of a striking bluish-white colour.

'Grey Owl' has broadly spreading branches and a beautiful silver-grey colour.

'Hillii' forms a dense, grey-green pillar. The foliage is exclusively needle-shaped and in winter turns a striking brownish-red colour.

'Reptans' has stiff, slightly erect branches. Height to 60cm, 2m across. The pale-green foliage is needle- or scale-shaped and feels rough to the touch.

Juniperus squamata 'Meyeri'

Juniperus squamata 'Wilsonii'

'Skyrocket' is a particularly beautiful specimen shrub with a very narrow columnar shape. Grows to 4m in height, but only 60cm across. The fine adult foliage is dark blue-grey.

Juniperus virginiana 'Skyrocket'

Kalmia angustifolia

Kalmia

Calico Bush

Evergreen shrubs, flowering in spring or summer. They belong to the heather family.

Situation Calico bushes enjoy a sheltered position in partial shade and slightly damp soil. Where the soil remains very damp they may be planted in the sun and they are therefore very suitable for the rock garden. Because of their size they may be used in small gardens; they are beautiful planted singly.

Soil Humus-rich, peaty soil. Sandy soil should be mixed with a large quantity of peat.

Propagation From runners, cuttings or seed sown under glass.

Kalmia angustifolia: A shrub to 1m in height and almost as much across, with axillary red-purple flowers June–July. Usually opposite leaves, spear-shaped and flat. Slow growing.

Kalmia latifolia: About 2m in height; bare twigs. The leathery leaves are dark green on the upper surface, slightly paler on the reverse. The pale-red flower clusters appear in May and June.

Kerria

Jew's Mallow

Deciduous shrubs which are nevertheless conspicuous in winter because of their fresh-green wood.

Situation Suitable for planting singly or in groups in a sunny or partially shaded position. They will grow in dry as well as in damp soil. In severe winters they may freeze down to the ground, especially when they have only recently been transplanted. Don't worry – they will start into growth again and will flower late in the year. Pruning, though rarely necessary, should be done immediately after the flowering season.

Soil Porous, not too heavy, soil.

Propagation From cuttings and from rooted basal shoots.

Kerria japonica: A shrub up to 2m in height and as much across, with smooth green, arching twigs. The leaves are pointed and doubly serrated. The isolated, orange-yellow double flowers appear April–May. The var *simplex* has single flowers. This form is sometimes referred to as the 'common' species, while the double-flowered form is called 'Pleniflora'. The variegated form 'Picta' is particularly attractive.

Kerria japonica

Koelreuteria

Koelreuteria paniculata

Not very well known. A small tree or bush with beautifully shaped foliage turning yellow in the autumn.

Situation A magnificent specimen plant; its diameter makes it unsuitable for very small gardens. It grows slowly and drops its foliage in the autumn. Prefers a position in full sun. Preferably provide some shelter, for the plant is not entirely winter-hardy.

Soil Calcareous, nutritious soil is preferred. Clay soil is therefore very suitable.

Propagation Seeds are sown in pots, under glass, unheated, immediately they have ripened.

Koelreuteria paniculata: A smooth tree with greyish twigs. Height about 6m, 3m across. As the tree grows older a loose, almost spherical crown develops. The grey twigs bear composite foliage, to 40cm in size. The 7–15 leaflets are 3–5cm long, oval, serrated, sometimes deeply incised, stalkless. Yellow flowers in plume-shaped clusters July–August, followed by green, bladder-shaped fruits.

Kolkwitzia

An attractive flowering shrub with dense ramification and a loose habit. A profusion of flowers May–June.

Situation Can be used in any position, since it is beautiful not only during the flowering season, but, because of its habit and the shape of its foliage, afterwards as well. Attractive planted singly, even in a small garden. Also suitable for planting in groups. Provide a sunny position, preferably sheltered against strong winds.

Soil Standard garden soil.

Propagation In spring, from seed or cuttings, but also from cuttings taken in summer.

Kolkwitzia amabilis: A dense shrub, to 2.5m in height and 2m across, with arching, peeling twigs. The bluish-green leaves are 3–7cm long, oval and pointed, and are borne on hairy leaf-stalks, 2–3cm long. Large plumes of pale-red flowers May–June; they are bell-shaped and have yellow-orange blotches inside. They fade to practically white. There are beautiful cultivars: 'Rosea' has dark-pink flowers, 'Pink Cloud' – the name speaks for itself.

Kolkwitzia amabilis

Laburnum × watereri 'Vossii'

Laburnum

Golden Chain

Well known deciduous shrubs belonging to the pea family, with large clusters of yellow flowers in late spring. They are poisonous in all their parts, but particularly the seeds.

Situation Provide a sunny to partially shaded position. Their size makes them suitable even for small gardens. In this connection *L. anagyroides* 'Pendulum' deserves special mention; it grows to 4m in height and 3.5m across. Occasionally golden chain finds it difficult to start into growth after having been transplanted.

Soil Standard garden soil.

Propagation The species are sown out of doors in spring. Garden forms are grafted.

Laburnum anagyroides (syn *L. vulgare*), common laburnum: Height to 8m, 4m across. The twigs and the reverse of the leaves are hairy. Scentless yellow, pendulous flower clusters May–June, two weeks before *L. alpinum*, which has fragrant flowers.

Laburnum × watereri is the result of crossing *L. alpinum* and *L. anagyroides*. 'Vossii' is the finest strain and has the longest flower clusters.

Larix

Larch

Deciduous conifers, attractive throughout the year and therefore very suitable for planting singly, especially against a background of dark, evergreen conifers. In spring the foliage is fresh green; at that time some larches produce red, others green-white, flowers. In autumn the foliage turns yellow and in winter the tree's silhouette, with its numerous small cones, is worth a second glance. Larches grow very rapidly.

Situation In view of their size they are suitable only for parks and large gardens. An exception is *Larix kaempferi*, provided it is pruned as a hedge. In Japan it is used for bonsai cultivation. The photograph shows a garden bonsai, a hundred years old! Provide a sunny situation with porous soil. Plant singly or in groups. A *Larix* plantation has a very special attraction.

Soil Humus-rich soil.

Propagation From seed.

Larix decidua (syn *L. europaea*), European larch: A cone-shaped tree, to 25m in height and 7m across, with smooth, yellowish arching twigs and small buds containing resin. Bright-green needles, 2–3cm long, are arranged in groups of 30–40, like a kind of shaving brush. The female flowers are green and red, the cones 4cm long. Yellow autumn colouring. The dead-straight trunk produces hard-wearing wood.

Larix gmelinii (syn *L. dahurica*), Asian larch: A pyramid-shaped tree with smooth, red-brown twigs without bloom, and yellow-brown buds with scales. The fairly thick needles are initially yellowish, later dark green and are retained for a fairly long time in autumn. Normally about 20m in height, but in unfavourable circumstances it becomes a low-growing or spreading tree. Oval to cylinder-shaped, 3.5cm long cones.

Larix kaempferi (syn *L. leptolepis*), Japanese larch: A tree up to 25m in height, broad cone-shaped, with initially hairy red-brown twigs and pointed red buds. The 3.5cm long needles, blue green, are arranged in bundles of at least 40 and have two clear white stripes on the reverse. The cones are up to 4cm long. 'Pendula' with its arching twigs is a very beautiful garden form and is grafted on tall stock.

Larix laricina (syn *L. americana*), American larch: A tree to 30m in height and 8m in diameter, with a reddish trunk and narrow pyramidal habit. Smooth, orange-red, later brown, twigs, often covered in bloom and bearing dark-red buds. Bright blue-green needles, to 2.5cm long, turning yellow when they drop. Oval cones, to 2cm long.

Larix gmelinii

Larix kaempferi

113

Lavandula

Lavender

Although lavender is often combined with perennials, it is a true shrub. The fine grey-green foliage and the delightful scent of the small flowers are sufficient reason for planting a few clumps in the garden. Lavender is not 100 per cent winter-hardy.

Situation Lavender requires a position in full sun and is very suitable for use as an edging plant or a low hedge. In a border it is attractive in combination with *Gypsophila* or surrounded by *Acaena* or thyme. Many a linen cupboard is perfumed by the dried flowers. Also suitable for dried-flower arrangements and in scented gardens or herb gardens.

Soil Porous soil which need not be very nutritious. Lavender is a lime-loving plant.

Propagation From non-woody summer cuttings.

Lavandula angustifolia ssp *angustifolia* (syn *L. officinalis*), common lavender: A 30–60cm tall dwarf bush with purple-violet flowers June–July. If the shrubs are cut back after flowering they will not grow bare at the base. Fine strains are 'Hidcote Blue', dark violet, and 'Blue Dwarf', 25cm.

Lavandula angustifolia ssp *angustifolia*

Lavatera olbia

Lavatera

Not very winter-hardy; a semi-shrub with a prolonged flowering season and magnificent large flowers.

Situation *Lavatera* is an excellent and very popular border plant, especially because of its long flowering season. In view of its height it looks best at the back of a border or in the centre of a bed. It is also possible to cultivate standard trees which are kept frost free in winter, in a pot. *Lavatera* is attractive in combination with *Gypsophila*, dark-purple larkspur or asters in matching colours. Cut branches will keep for two weeks in water; nearly all the buds will come out.

Soil Porous, nutritious, somewhat calciferous soil.

Propagation In spring cuttings are taken from plants which have not been damaged by winter frost.

Lavatera olbia: A semi-shrub, up to 2m tall and 1m across, with pale-red, mallow-like flowers from July to October. The branches are woody at the base. Dense ramification.

Lespedeza

Little known, but very graceful pea-flowered bush, not entirely winter-hardy. It flowers in late summer and autumn.

Situation Beautiful planted singly in sunny or partially shaded positions, even in small gardens or window-boxes. It prefers a sheltered situation. Every spring the stalks should be cut back to the ground; new shoots will bear flowers in the same year.

Soil Dry, humus-rich soil.

Propagation Cuttings of half-ripe wood are taken early in summer.

Lespedeza bicolor: An erect-growing shrub, to 1.5m in height, with angular red-brown twigs. The leaves are grey green and densely haired underneath. Red-purple flower plumes in August and September.

Lespedeza thunbergii (syn *L. formosa*): To 2m tall and as much across; the grooved, lightly haired twigs arch. Trifoliate dark-green leaves. Red-purple flower plumes September–October.

Lespedeza thunbergii

Leycesteria formosa

Leycesteria

Little known, deciduous shrub which nevertheless looks attractive throughout the year because of its bamboo-like stalks. The flowers are followed by berries adored by birds, especially pheasants.

Situation Free-standing, but also in groups, in a sunny or partially shaded position, even in fairly dry soil. In view of their size they are suitable even for fairly small gardens. In cold winters the stalks may be damaged by frost; in the following spring they should be cut back to the base.

Soil Nutritious, preferably loamy soil.

Propagation Sow early in spring, in an unheated frame. The seed germinates readily. After a year the seedlings may be moved to their permanent position.

Leycesteria formosa: A shrub to 2m in height and over 1m across, with smooth, hollow, green twigs, initially covered in bloom. The leaves are 4–15cm long, oval, smooth edged; those borne by the infertile twigs are often deeply incised. The white flowers, arranged in pseudo 'ears' are surrounded by striking red bracts and are followed by purple berries.

Ligustrum ovalifolium 'Aureomarginata'

Ligustrum sinense var *stauntonii*

Ligustrum

Privet

Very well known (semi-) evergreen or deciduous shrubs, easily pruned and therefore frequently used for hedges. Leaves opposite, smooth edged; the white flowers contain a lot of nectar and are therefore attractive to insects. There are fine variegated forms.

Situation Privet is one of the least expensive hedging plants; this is probably why it is found everywhere. Nevertheless there are more beautiful hedges, especially in winter, for privet soon drops its foliage in wind and frost and then looks rather unattractive. If you have an old hedge, bare at the base, it can be rejuvenated by cutting it back to just above the ground, after which it will start into growth again. Empty spaces can be filled with young plants. Shrubs should be pruned to a pyramidal shape, hedges tapered at the top, otherwise the plants will grow bare again at the base.

Privet plants will grow both in full sun and in partial shade. If they are not pruned, or only tidied up a little, they will produce a multitude of flowers in summer. Not all species are 100 per cent winter-hardy. The common privet can be used in shrubberies and windbreaks. Occasionally, attractive standard trees with fine foliage are available.

Soil Standard garden soil. The roots must not dry out when the plants are moved.

Propagation From cuttings.

Ligustrum amurense: A very winter-hardy shrub, to 2.5m in height with oval, evergreen foliage. Creamy-white flower plumes June–July.

Ligustrum obtusifolium: Spreading habit; height to 3m. The up to 6cm long leaves drop in winter. White flowers July–August.

Ligustrum ovalifolium, hedge privet: Height over 2m; a semi-evergreen shrub with white flower plumes in July. 'Aureum' has yellow or yellow-blotched foliage, in 'Argenteum' the leaves have a white margin, in 'Aureomarginata' the margin is yellow.

Ligustrum quihoui: A broad shrub with little ramification; height to 2m. The elliptical leaves are fresh green in colour and drop very late in the year. The most beautiful feature is the white flower plumes which do not appear until September. Prefers a slightly sheltered position.

Ligustrum sinense var *stauntonii*: A shrub to 2m in height and 3m across, with densely haired twigs and large, loose white flower plumes July–August.

Ligustrum vulgare, common privet: Deciduous shrub with small white flower plumes June–July. Height 3–4m. 'Aureum' has yellow foliage. 'Lodense' is a dwarf form with brown winter foliage.

Liquidambar

Liquid Amber

The liquid amber tree belongs to the witch hazel family. At a first glance the tree resembles a maple, which also often has incised leaves. However, in the liquid amber tree the leaves are alternate, in the maple they are opposite. Amber trees have a broad habit and magnificent autumn colouring.

Situation It is a lightwood tree and therefore requires a free-standing, sunny position. Provide shelter in view of possible frost damage.

Soil Nutritious, damp soil.

Propagation Sow in autumn. Sometimes the seeds take a long time before they germinate. Can also be increased from offsets.

Liquidambar styraciflua: A tree to 15m in height and as much across, pyramid shaped, with smooth twigs with, from the second year onwards, corky ridges and a grey colour. The green leaves are 10–20cm long, palmate, with serrated, pointed lobes. They turn dark red in autumn. In winter the branches may be damaged by frost; they should be removed, preferably when the buds begin to fill out.

Liquidambar styraciflua

Liriodendron tulipifera

Liriodendron

Tulip-tree

A large, deciduous tree belonging to the *Magnolia* family. The *Magnolia* is often referred to as the tulip-tree, but this is incorrect. There are several reasons for planting a tulip-tree: its stately silhouette with dead-straight trunk; the large, tulip-shaped flowers in early summer; and the unusually shaped foliage which turns a magnificent yellow in autumn. They are fast growing and are resistant to air pollution, not very prone to disease and fairly drought-resistant, although they prefer soil with an adequate moisture content.

Situation The tulip-tree is a fine specimen tree, popular for use in parks and large gardens, and very beautiful planted singly in a large lawn. Provide a sunny situation.

Soil Prefers humus-rich and if possible loamy soil.

Propagation From seed and by layering. Sow in autumn, in pots with sandy soil. Only a small percentage will germinate.

Liriodendron tulipifera: A tree to 20m tall and 8–10m across, with smooth twigs and typically flat, dark buds, covered in blue bloom, which clearly characterise the

Liriodendron tulipifera 'Fastigiatum'

tree in winter. The leaves are 7–12cm across, 4-lobed, typically incised at the tip. From spring until autumn the foliage is fresh green; before it drops it turns soft yellow. The large, yellow-green flowers with orange marking inside appear June–July, usually high in the tree and no problem to the bees which they attract. As is the case with all members of the *Magnolia* family, the fleshy roots are somewhat vulnerable. To avoid root-rot the trees are planted in spring, when the buds begin to fill out. Large trees are difficult to transplant. The buds are not self-splitting and contain a winged, 1- or 2-seed nut. There are a number of fine, usable strains, such as 'Fastigiatum', to 15m in height and 5m across and therefore suitable for smaller gardens. The crown of this tree has a narrow pyramid shape and it has erect-growing branches. In 'Obtusilobum' the tip of the foliage is not incised. In 'Integrifolium', too, the leaf-tip is hardly, if at all, incised and the foliage is not lobed. 'Aureomarginatum' has leaves with a greenish-yellow margin and blotches.

Lithodora diffusa

Lithodora

Gromwell

Evergreen, not entirely winter-hardy little shrub with a creeping habit and magnificent blue flowers.

Situation Its long flowering season and the gentian-blue colour of the flowers make gromwell much in demand for rock gardens. Also attractive in a greenhouse collection of alpine plants. Provide a sunny, warm sheltered situation and well-drained soil; and possibly cover in winter in periods of severe frost and drying winds.

Soil Sandy garden soil is excellent.

Propagation From seed, cuttings and by layering. Young plants are cultivated in a cold frame. Give ventilation whenever possible, but keep covered in bad weather in spring, autumn and winter.

Lithodora diffusa (syn *Lithospermum diffusum, L. prostratum*): Grows to a height of 15cm, but its creeping habit makes it reach a spread of 80cm. Recumbent, roughly hairy twigs, with narrow, 1–2cm long leaves. Deep-blue flowers May–July, sometimes a little later. 'Heavenly Blue' is particularly beautiful.

Lonicera

Honeysuckle

A very varied genus, consisting of bushes and climbing shrubs, sometimes winter-hardy, sometimes deciduous. Leaves alternate, usually undivided. The colour, shape and fragrance of the flowers may be very attractive, but in some cases the flowers are insignificant. Not all species are 100 per cent winter-hardy.

Situation The evergreen shrubs *Lonicera nitida* and *L. pileata* tolerate a great deal of shade. Late winter sun in combination with frost may cause a lot of damage. Shrubs planted in full sun should then be covered with fir branches. These two species are fairly low-growing and can be used as ground-cover, but also in containers, as infilling, and even as small hedges. The finest of the deciduous species can be planted singly, but most species are planted as undergrowth, since they are so tolerant of shade. Can also be used in groups in the shrub border. Climbing honeysuckle plants may be planted to grow against walls or pergolas or in trees. They require some support. In a draught they are prone to aphis infection. The base of the plants often grows bare with age and they must therefore be rejuvenated by pruning at regular intervals, or a small evergreen bush is planted in front to hide the bare foot. Climbing honeysuckles enjoy full sun or partial shade.

Soil Standard garden soil. When planting climbers make a large planting-hole and add manure and humus.

Propagation From cuttings taken in summer or winter.

Evergreen shrubs:

Lonicera nitida (syn *L. yunnanensis*): Height to 1.5m, a shrub with erect-growing twigs covered in short hairs, and thin, leathery, oval leaves. Greenish flowers, 1cm in size, in May; they have a very light fragrance and are followed by violet-coloured berries. 'Hohenheimer Findling' has proved to be less likely to be damaged in a severe winter. This strain has smaller leaves than the species. 'Baggeser's Gold' is particularly beautiful.

Lonicera pileata: Almost horizontal twigs, covered in short hairs; oblong leaves, to 3cm long, with pale-green reverse. Usually does not grow beyond 50cm. Fragrant white flowers in May, followed by violet-coloured berries. More winter-hardy than *L. nitida*.

Deciduous shrubs:

Lonicera × amoena: The result of crossing *L. korolkowii* and *L. tatarica*. A robust, broad shrub, to 2m in height, flowering more profusely than its parent plants. 'Arnoldiana' in particular can be recommended; it has large, white flowers, lightly tinged with red purple, May–June.

Lonicera × bella: A cross between *L. morrowii* and *L. tatarica*. Erect-growing, a form midway between its

Lonicera nitida 'Baggesen's Gold'

Lonicera maackii

Lonicera × brownii 'Dropmore Scarlet'

Lonicera × heckrottii 'Goldflame'

parents. The flowers appearing May–June are white or reddish, later more yellow. The finest strain is 'Polyantha', profusely flowering, with bright red-purple flowers.

Lonicera caerulea: Dense ramification; height to 1m. White-yellow flowers April–May, followed by berries covered in blue bloom. Numerous varieties and garden forms.

Lonicera fragrantissima: Height to 2m, a partially evergreen shrub which in mild winters may produce fragrant, creamy-white flowers December–March. Oval, pointed leaves, to 7cm long, bluish underneath. Dark-red berries.

Lonicera korolkowii: Fast growing, to 2.5m in height and as much across. The hollow twigs arch gracefully and bear egg-shaped to oval, pointed grey-green leaves. Pink, sometimes white flowers in June, followed by red berries. Since the overall impression of the shrub is greyish, it looks attractive in a grey-purple-blue-pink flower scheme. 'Aurora' has larger flowers, always pinkish in colour, and broader foliage.

Lonicera maackii: Height to 3m and as much across; a dense, bushy shrub with hairy twigs and egg-shaped to oval, pointed green leaves, to 8cm long. Fragrant white flowers in June, fading to yellow.

Lonicera morrowii: A 3m tall shrub with spreading habit, soft downy twigs and 5cm long leaves, oval to oblong, pointed. The initially white flowers which appear May–June later fade to yellow. Red berries.

Lonicera × purpusii: The product of crossing *L. fragrantissima* and *L. standishii*. It is conspicuous for its fragrant creamy-white flowers which appear as early as February or March. In May it already bears red berries. The leathery foliage is retained for a long time.

Lonicera tatarica: A shrub to 3m in height, with rose-red flowers May–June, followed by red berries. The oval leaves, 5cm long, are green on the upper surface, blue green underneath. 'Alba' has white, 'Zabelii' dark-pink, flowers.

Climbing shrubs:

Lonicera × brownii: The result of crossing *L. hirsuta* and *L. sempervirens*. Moderately fast growing, to 4.5m, with dull-green foliage, bluish green on the reverse. From May to August it bears striking purple-red flowers arranged in whorls. 'Punicea' has orange-red flowers. 'Dropmore Scarlet' and 'Fuchsioides' are two other popular strains.

Lonicera caprifolium, perfoliate honeysuckle: A twining plant with hollow twigs and blunt, oval leaves, blue green underneath. Delightfully fragrant, yellow-white flowers May–June. This climber is not freely available.

Lonicera × heckrottii: A cross between *L. americana* and *L. sempervirens*. A deciduous climber, to 2m in height, sometimes more shrub-shaped. The foliage is dark green on the upper surface, blue green on the reverse. The flowers which appear from June to September are arranged in whorls and are purple on the outside, pale yellow inside.

Lonicera japonica: A semi-hardy plant producing white flowers, fading to yellow, June–September. 'Reticulata', less hardy but with very beautiful yellow-veined foliage, belongs to the variety *repens*.

Lonicera periclymenum, common honeysuckle: A climber to 10m tall, with bare, hollow twigs and pointed oval leaves, to 6cm long, bluish on the reverse. Flowers May–June, occasionally for a second time in September; yellowish, fragrant flowers in terminal clusters. Well known strains are 'Belgica', in which the corolla is red purple on the outside and white yellow inside, and 'Serotina' which flowers a little later and has thinner foliage.

Lonicera × tellmanniana: The product of crossing *L. sempervirens* and *L. tragophylla*. A beautiful twining plant, to 5m in height, not entirely winter-hardy but excellent for a south-west facing wall. Vigorous growth; orange-red flowers in June. The reverse of the leaves is somewhat bluish.

Lonicera periclymenum

Magnolia liliiflora 'Nigra'

Magnolia

Deciduous or evergreen trees or shrubs with alternate, smooth edged foliage and large, decorative flowers, often enclosed in two hairy scales when in bud. The fruit is a little like a fir cone. A number of species flower before the foliage appears; in some cases the flowers are white, in others red purple. Often the *Magnolia* is incorrectly taken for a tulip-tree, whose botanical name is *Liriodendron*.

Situation Shrubs for sunny or partially shaded, sheltered positions. The early flowering forms, in particular, may be damaged by night frost if they are planted in an unfavourable spot. *Magnolia grandiflora* is suitable only for coastal regions and even there it has to be given a very sheltered situation. The wood of the other species mentioned is definitely hardy. Where there is little shelter in the garden it is necessary to select later flowering species. *Magnolia*'s occur in all sizes. *M. stellata* is very suitable for small gardens. Tree forms may be considered for parks and large gardens.

Soil Humus-rich, with adequate moisture and nutrients

Magnolia × soulangiana 'Lennei'

Magnolia stellata

Propagation The species from seed, which remains viable for a short time only. Garden forms by layering or grafting under glass.

Magnolia denudata: A tree with numerous branches; height to 4m. The branches are curved, the leaves oblong, 8–15cm long. The many, erect-growing, fragrant white flowers appear April–May. Not very well known, but recommended.

Magnolia grandiflora: A winter-hardy tree, to 20m in height and 8m across, with red-brown buds and twigs. Leathery, glossy green oblong leaves, to 20cm long, with rust-coloured down on the reverse. Saucer-shaped, fragrant white flowers June–August.

Magnolia kobus (syn *M. tomentosa*): A tall shrub or tree; the crumpled bark has an aromatic scent. The buds are covered in short hairs. The leaves, which drop in autumn, are obovate, to 14cm long. White flowers appear April–May, just before the foliage.

Magnolia liliiflora (syn *M. purpurea*, *M. quinquepeta*): A spreading bush with grey buds covered in short hairs and reversed oval leaves. Fragrant, deep-pink and white flowers with greenish sepals in May. 'Nigra' has smaller, dark-purple flowers. Its flowering season is somewhat later and is often repeated in summer. Height to 3m; glossy dark-green leaves.

Magnolia × loebneri: The result of crossing *M. kobus* and *M. stellata*. A particularly attractive addition to a small garden. Maximum height 6m, often smaller; a compact shape can be maintained by pruning after the flowering season. Best known by its cultivars: 'Merrill', which has large, pure white flowers even at an early age, and 'Leonard Messel', in which the large flowers are red purple outside.

Magnolia × soulangiana: The result of crossing *M. denudata* and *M. liliiflora*. Height to 7m, 4m across. The foliage is often hairy on the reverse; the flowers vary in shape and colour – in the parent form they are white tinged with a little pink. Flowering season April–May. The following Soulangiana hybrids are recommended: 'Alba Superba', pure white, medium early; 'Alexandrina', very early, the flowers are rose red on the outside; 'Brozzonii', very large flowers, white with a hint of purple, late flowering; 'Lennii', broad, bell-shaped flowers, purple on the outside, late flowering; 'Speciosa', the flowers are purple at the base, the outer petals are slightly curved, late flowering season.

Magnolia stellata (syn *M. kobus* var *stellata*): Slow growing, to 2m; very suitable for small gardens. The star-shaped white flowers appear as early as March or April and may therefore be damaged by late night-frost. The shrub itself is quite hardy. Spear-shaped leaves, to 10cm long, practically bare underneath. In 'Rosea' the flowers are tinged with pink.

Mahonia

Oregon Grape

Beautiful evergreen shrubs with attractive flowers and fruits and often fine autumn colouring. Alternate leaves, irregularly pinnate, sometimes with a spiny edge. The flowers appear in terminal plumes and are followed by blue berries, covered in bloom. Few of the eighty species are cultivated in our part of the world, but those few are very popular, probably due partly to the fact that they tolerate a great deal of shade.

Situation *Mahonia* bushes will thrive both in sun and in shade, but should preferably not be planted in dry soil. Draught is fatal and causes the foliage to drop. Fine autumn colouring will occur only in sunny situations; in the shade the plants will remain green. The beautiful autumn leaves are frequently incorporated in flower arrangements. Because of their dense growth *Mahonia* shrubs can be used as infilling, and also as low hedges or for edging borders. The best species can be planted singly, even in small gardens, and in large containers. In the shrub border they may be combined with other ornamental shrubs. Since they tolerate a great deal of shade they will also do well planted under other growth.

Soil Humus-rich, damp soil is preferred.

Propagation The species from seed or by layering. *Mahonia aquifolium* may possibly be increased from basal shoots.

Mahonia aquifolium (syn *Berberis aquifolium*): Erect-growing bush, to 2m in height and a little more across, with glossy green, oval, sharply dentate foliage. Slow growing. The yellow flowers appear April–May and have a delightful fragrance. They are followed by blue berries. In autumn the foliage is bronze coloured. The bush should be kept compact by removing lanky shoots after the flowering season. If necessary the plant may be cut back severely. It also develops basal shoots. Plants grown from seed are somewhat variable.

Mahonia bealei (syn *Berberis japonica* var *bealei*): A shrub to 1m in height and as much across, with sharply toothed, blue-green foliage. Yellow flowers in erect-growing clusters, 10cm long, February–May. They are followed by blue berries.

Mahonia japonica (syn *Berberis japonica*): Height to 1m; pale- to yellow-green foliage. Arching, sulphur-yellow flower clusters February–May.

Mahonia × media: A cross between M. *japonica* and M. *lomariifolia*. The best known form is 'Charity', a very fine shrub with 50cm long leaves composed of 21 narrow oval leaflets, each of which may reach a length of 10cm. The inflorescence may be as much as 40cm long; the florets are yellow. In mild winters it may flower as early as January Unfortunately not very winter-hardy, so that it must be given the most sheltered position possible.

Mahonia aquifolium

Mahonia bealei

123

Malus 'Adams'

Malus baccata 'Gracilis'

Malus

Crab Apple

Deciduous trees and shrubs with beautiful flowers and attractive fruit, just like ordinary apple trees. However, the crab apple is grown for the ornamental value of its flowers and for its fruit which is excellent for jelly making rather than for eating raw. Nevertheless the (small) apples of some strains are quite edible.

In crab apples the leaves are alternate and usually have a serrated edge. The colour of the flowers is liable to fade; it varies from white to deep red-purple. The berries vary from yellow to purple. The flowering season only lasts about ten days, but if several species and strains are planted together the blossom may be enjoyed for at least a month.

Situation Crab apples may be planted in any reasonable sized garden. Many strains are sold as standard trees, so that they take up little ground-space. It is important that the crown should be carefully shaped, so that the branches are well distributed. Once the correct shape has been achieved, pruning is restricted to the removal of infertile shoots or surplus branches. The flower buds develop on short shoots ending in a fat bud. Few of the original species are now available. The accent lies more and more on hybrids, the origin of which is not always clear. For that reason the strains are usually mentioned in alphabetical order, without reference to the species.

Unfortunately many species and strains are sensitive to scab and must be sprayed at an early stage. If you prefer not to do this, you are advised to restrict yourself to the more scab-resistant forms. Crab apples are quite winter hardy and are rarely damaged by frost.

Soil Standard garden soil, preferably well drained, with a water level at least 1m, preferably 2m, down. Sandy soil must be manured every year; in clay this is rarely necessary.

Propagation Only botanical species are grown from seed. Garden forms are grafted on stock or budded.

Malus 'Adams'. Height to 10m, 8m across; a tree with dense growth and single, red-purple flowers in May. The fruit is red purple as well.
Malus 'Aldenhamensis'. Height to 3m, a tree with grey-purple foliage and a profusion of red-purple flowers, sometimes semi double. The fruit is grey purple, small, inconspicuous.
Malus 'Almey'. An erect-growing tree, to 6m in height; grey-purple foliage, later turning grey green. Single, red-purple flowers early in the season. They are followed by small red fruits.
Malus 'American Beauty'. Vigorously growing bush. The young leaves are reddish, later turning more green.

Red-purple, almost double flowers. Very few fruits. Scab-resistant.

Malus × *atrosanguinea*. The result of crossing *M. halliana* and *M. sieboldii*. A tree growing to 5m, with arching branches. Green foliage, red-purple flowers fading at a later stage. Small greenish-yellow fruits tinged with a little red.

Malus baccata. A tree to 8m in height with a dense habit and white flowers April–May. These are followed by orange-red fruit. The form usually supplied under this name is *Malus* 'Red Siberian'.

Malus 'Butterball'. A small tree with green foliage and red-purple flowers tinged with white. The round, golden-yellow fruits which later turn orange, are particularly beautiful.

Malus coronaria. A tree to 6m tall, with large green leaves and in May white flowers, slightly tinged with red purple and smelling of violets. This is a thorny species. Fine red-orange autumn colouring. The fruit has little ornamental value. The best strain is 'Charlotte'. The tree does not flower until it is a few years old.

Malus 'Crittenden'. A small tree with very pale red-purple flowers. The red fruits grow in large clusters and are retained for a long time.

Malus 'Dorothea'. Low to medium-sized bush with thin branches and green foliage. The flowers are semi-double, initially red purple, later turning paler. Even young specimens flower profusely. The small fruits are yellow.

Malus 'Eleyi'. A densely branched bush or small tree, with large, grey-purple leaves later turning more brown green. The large, red-purple flowers are single and are followed by the dark red-purple fruit which is retained until November.

Malus floribunda. A purely botanical species which usually (after pruning) grows into an erratically shaped tree, to 6m in height. The twigs arch gracefully and bear a profusion of pale red-purple flowers, white inside. The small, yellow-green fruits are inconspicuous. Scab-resistant.

Malus 'Golden Hornet'. A broad tree, to 6m in height, with green foliage and pale red-purple flower-buds. The flowers are white inside. The yellow fruits are retained for a long time. Not sensitive to scab.

Malus 'Gorgeous'. A tree growing to 5m, with green foliage. The flowers are initially pale red-purple, later white. The large, glossy red fruit is very striking and is retained for a long time.

Malus 'Hillieri'. A small but vigorous bush with green foliage. Single, sometimes more double, red-purple flowers; yellow and orange fruit. Not sensitive to scab. Frequently used for forcing.

Malus 'Hopa'. A small tree with a broad habit, height to 5m, and spreading branches. The foliage is initially grey purple, later green. Early, single, red-purple flowers are followed by red fruit with an orange tinge.

Malus floribunda

Malus 'Golden Hornet'

Malus 'Mary Potter'

Malus 'Zita'

Malus 'John Downie'. A large bush or tree, to 6m, with dark-green foliage. The flower-buds are pale red purple, white inside. The egg-shaped orange-red little apples which are produced in great abundance are particularly beautiful.

Malus 'Lemoinei'. A large tree with grey-purple foliage and single, dark red-purple flowers in May. The fruit is very dark in colour and not very conspicuous. The richest flowering occurs in mature trees.

Malus 'Liset'. A densely branched tree, to 6m in height, with grey-purple foliage. The red-purple flowers appear even while the tree is still young. Dark red-purple fruit. Not very sensitive to scab.

Malus 'Makamik'. A tree to 5m tall, with a round crown. The foliage is reddish when it starts into growth, later bronze green. Dark red-purple flowers, fading at a later stage; a white star in the centre. The spherical fruits are orange red. Very sensitive to scab.

Malus 'Mary Potter'. A low, spreading shrub with green foliage and flowers which are pale red-purple when in bud, white inside. Small red fruits which drop early in the season.

Malus × *micromalus*. The result of crossing *M. baccata* and *M. spectabilis*. A small, multi-branched tree, to 4m in height, green foliage. The flowers are bright red-purple and are followed by small yellow apples.

Malus 'Neville Copeman'. A large tree with a broad crown; pale grey-purple foliage later turning green and pale red-purple flowers. The bright-orange apples in autumn are its best feature.

Malus 'Prof Sprenger'. A tree to 6m in height, green foliage. Pale red-purple flowers, fading at a later stage. Golden-yellow foliage colouring and orange apples in autumn. Scab-resistant.

Malus 'Profusion'. A good-sized shrub or small tree, height to 4m. The leaves are reddish when they start into growth, later brown green. The dark red-purple flowers turn paler at a later stage. Dark-purple apples.

Malus 'Radiant'. A small tree with foliage which is reddish when it starts into growth. The flowers are red purple while in bud, later paler. The red apples are retained for a long time.

Malus toringo (syn *Malus sieboldii*): A tree growing to a height of 5m, with arching branches and glossy green foliage, turning yellow in autumn. White flowers in May, followed by yellow fruit. The variety *sargentii* (syn *M. sargentii*) is a spreading, 2m tall bush with fragrant white flowers in May. The branches are spiny. Both forms are scab-resistant.

Malus tschonoskii. A large tree, to 8m in height; red-purple and white flowers. Of all crab apples this species has the finest autumn colouring of yellow, orange and red, all at the same time.

Malus 'Zita'. A weeping form which is grafted on tall stock and may grow to a height of 5m. Pale red-purple flowers in May and a multitude of orange-red apples.

Metasequoia

Dawn Redwood

One of the few conifers which does not remain green in winter. Fast growing; the fresh-green foliage discolours in autumn. Very hardy. Prior to 1941 the tree was known only in the form of fossil remains, but then it was discovered in China and a large number of young trees have meanwhile been grown from seed.

Situation A magnificent specimen tree, suitable for parks and large gardens. Provide a sunny situation, sheltered from strong winds, and adequately moist soil.

Soil Nutritious soil. From time to time apply some dung.

Propagation From seed, and from summer or winter cuttings.

Metasequoia glyptostroboides (syn *Sequoia glyptostroboides, M. disticha*): A tree to 35m in height and 12m across, with a pyramidal habit and rapid growth, especially in the early years. The needles are 1–3cm long and turn yellow in autumn, after which they drop, together with the opposite short shoots. The bark is dark grey and in mature trees peels off in thin strips. The isolated spherical cones grow on long stalks.

Metasequoia glyptostroboides

Morus alba 'Pendula'

Morus

Mulberry

At one time the mulberry was very popular: the foliage served to nourish silkworms and the delicious fruit was enjoyed in the middle of summer. The beautifully shaped foliage has a brilliant yellow colour in autumn.

Situation The common species are not very suitable for small gardens, but the weeping form *Morus alba* 'Pendula' is still in demand. The black mulberry may reach a great age and is an ornament in any garden. To encourage fruit formation, some people apply a quantity of dried blood every year. Provide a sunny to partially shaded position, and give some shelter.

Soil Light, sandy soil is best to encourage ripening. Mulberries love lime.

Propagation From cuttings and by grafting.

Morus alba, white mulberry: yellow-green flowers in May, followed by white or pale-purple pseudo-fruits, edible in July or August. 'Pendula' has drooping branches.

Morus nigra, black mulberry: The pseudo-fruits are dark red.

Nothofagus antarctica

Nothofagus

Southern Beech

Deciduous shrub or tree with unusual, herringbone-like ramification and a large number of obvious lenticels, in mature trees showing up as white streaks on the trunk. These features make the tree very attractive even in winter. In spring and early summer the foliage has a delightful fragrance. In autumn the foliage turns golden yellow.

Situation Beautiful when planted singly in a sunny or partially shaded position. Often used in large containers. Its slow growth makes it suitable for small gardens.

Soil Humus-rich, fairly acid soil.

Propagation From seed or by layering.

Nothofagus antarctica: In our part of the world a southern beech rarely exceeds 10m; usually pyramid shaped, especially when it is planted as a tree. The leaves grow close together; they are somewhat leathery and, especially in spring, feel a little greasy or oily to the touch. Green flowers in May, followed by minute pseudo-nuts.

Nyssa sylvatica

Nyssa

Tupele

A little known, large, deciduous tree with striking autumn colouring. The wood of the roots swells considerably in water.

Situation Beautiful when planted singly in sunny or partially shaded, very sheltered spots. Damp soil. Dislikes being transplanted. Not very hardy in our part of the world.

Soil Humus-rich, lime-free soil.

Propagation From seed.

Nyssa sylvatica: In parts of Canada, Mexico and the United States, where the tree originates, it will grow to a height of 30m and develop a dense round crown. Here it will not reach more than 20m in height, 12m across. Sometimes the branches droop to the ground, so that the foliage entirely hides the trunk, but sometimes its habit resembles that of an oak. The leaves are 5–12cm long, obovate, smooth edged, leathery, glossy dark green and grey green underneath; in autumn they turn orange to scarlet. Greenish flowers in May, followed by fleshy dark-blue fruits.

Osmanthus

Fragrant Olive, Holly-leaved Olive

Dense, evergreen shrubs with foliage resembling that of holly, but in *Osmanthus* the leaves are opposite, in holly they are alternate. The white or creamy flowers appear in spring or autumn and usually have a soft, sweet fragrance. Not all species are winter-hardy; *Osmanthus yunnanensis* is an example.

Situation Most species are particularly suitable for use in small gardens, but *O. yunnanensis* is definitely out of place there. Provide a sunny or shady position. The general rule is the damper the soil, the more sun will be tolerated. Plant them singly, in groups, in window-boxes or as a hedge, depending on the species.

Soil Not very demanding, but humus-retaining soil is preferred.

Propagation From seed, cuttings and by layering.

Osmanthus × burkwoodii (syn × *Osmarea burkwoodii*): This little bush is the result of crossing *O. delavayi* and *O. decorus*. It is a very slow-growing, but beautifully compact shrub with oval, 2–4cm long, glossy dark-green and crenate to serrated leaves, almost sessile. The white flowers appear in terminal and axillary clusters April–May; they have a delightful fragrance. As a rule this *Osmanthus* grows to a height of 1m and approximately the same across.

Osmanthus decorus (syn *Phillyrea decora*, *P. vilmoriniana*): A broad, almost spherical shrub, 3m in diameter. The bare twigs carry fairly large, leathery dark-green leaves, smooth edged and with a yellow-green reverse. The white flowers grow in axillary clusters and appear in May. They are conspicuous for their scent and are followed by dark berries.

Osmanthus heterophyllus (syn *Olea aquifolium*, *Osmanthus ilicifolius*): Oval, dark-green, leathery foliage, initially spiny, but smooth edged in older specimens. White flowers in axillary clusters September–October, followed by dark-blue berries.

There are a number of deviant varieties and strains of this species. 'Aureomarginatus' has yellow-edged foliage; 'Gulftide' has a squat habit and lobed, sharply serrated foliage, olive green in colour; 'Myrtifolius' produces small, blunt leaves, like those of myrtle; 'Rotundifolius' is a slow-growing cultivar with thick, black-green round leaves.

Osmanthus yunnanensis (syn *O. forrestii*): A shrub to 8m in height, 9m across, with fragrant white-yellow flowers in May, followed by oval, dark-blue fruits.

Osmanthus × burkwoodii

Osmanthus yunnanensis

Ostrya

Hop Hornbeam

Deciduous trees, belonging to the birch family. The catkins resemble those of the hop-plant, hence the name hop hornbeam. Flowers and foliage appear together in spring. The foliage turns a fine shade of yellow in autumn.

Situation Attractive when grown singly. An easy plant; will thrive both in full sun and in partial shade.

Soil Standard garden soil.

Propagation From seed.

Ostrya carpinifolia, European hop hornbeam: Height to 20m, a tree with a round crown and smooth, spreading branches. The egg-shaped leaves are 5–10cm long, pointed, doubly serrated and rounded at the base. The colour is dark green, in the autumn turning bright yellow; the reverse is slightly downy. The pendent catkins are about 5cm long.

Ostrya virginiana: Height to 20m, 15m across, a tree with a round to pyramidal habit. This hop hornbeam's branches droop more than in the previous species. The leaves are 6–12cm long, pointed, somewhat heart-shaped at the base. Spindle-shaped nuts in autumn.

Ostrya virginiana

Pachysandra terminalis

Pachysandra

A very hardy, evergreen ground-covering plant for shady sites. It is a semi-shrub, but is often sold as a hardy perennial.

Situation Excellent ground-cover, in damp soil may develop a dense carpet even under trees. Also suitable for window-boxes or other containers, to hide an ugly pond-edge or as an edging plant. Before it starts into growth the tips should be lightly pruned to encourage the development of a dense carpet.

Soil Nutritious soil, rich in humus, not too calcareous.

Propagation From winter cuttings or by division.

Pachysandra procumbens: Unfortunately not easily available; a partially evergreen plant, to 25cm in height, with beautiful green foliage and fragrant white flowers March–April.

Pachysandra terminalis: A creeping semi-shrub, 30cm in height and as much across, with smooth green, erect-growing stalks. The leaves are 5–8cm long, diamond- to spatula-shaped, coarsely serrated and leathery, yellowish in the sun, dark green in shade. Clusters of small flowers in April.

Paeonia

Peony

This genus includes shrubs as well as perennials, in
general producing magnificent flowers. The shrubs as a
rule require greater care, are more difficult to grow and
often prove not to be winter-hardy.
Situation Suitable for planting singly in a sunny, but
particularly sheltered and well-drained position.
Paeonia delavayi tolerates a little more shade, is winter-
hardy and is easier to grow than the tree peony in the
photograph.
Soil Nutritious soil, for example clay.
Propagation By division, from cuttings or by layering.
They take a long time to root.

Paeonia delavayi: This plant develops runners; it has
smooth twigs and trifoliate leaves. Height to 1m. Dark
purple-red flowers, 5cm in diameter, in July.
Paeonia suffruticosa (syn *P. arborea, P. moutan*),
common tree peony: A shrub to 1.5m in height and as
much across, with thick twigs and trifoliate leaves, blue
green underneath. In May–June it bears white-pink
often double flowers, to 30cm in diameter. Hybrids
occur in many colours.

Paeonia Suffruticosa hybrid

Parthenocissus tricuspidata

Parthenocissus

Virginia Creeper

Deciduous climbers with beautiful autumn colouring.
Most species are self-clinging.
Situation A climber for sunny or partially shaded positions. Fast growing; it may cover an entire building. The
best situation is against a south- or west-facing wall,
where it will suffer least from frost. May also be used as
ground-cover, although it will generally not develop a
dense, compact carpet.
Soil Nutritious, humus-rich soil. If it is placed near a
wall it is necessary to dig a large planting-hole and fill it
with leafmould, rotted manure etc.
Propagation From seed, cuttings or by layering.

Parthenocissus inserta (syn *P. vitacea var typica*):
Height to 10m, 4m across. It is not self-clinging and
must therefore be trained. Greenish flowers June–July,
followed by blue-black berries.
Parthenocissus tricuspidata: May grow to as much as
20m. The suckers are self-clinging. 'Veitchii' is a very
fine strain.

Paulownia

Large deciduous trees with enormous leaves. The flower-buds are present in rudimentary form in autumn and unfold in spring before the foliage starts into growth. Unfortunately they are injured by frost.
Situation A magnificent specimen tree for a sheltered position, as far as possible out of the wind. The soil must be well drained.
Soil Nutritious, calcareous soil.
Propagation From summer cuttings or seed sown in spring.

Paulownia tomentosa (syn *P. imperialis*): Height to 15m; a tree with a broad, umbrella-shaped crown and thick, stiff spreading branches. The oval, sometimes 3-lobed leaves are 12–30cm long and are borne on densely haired twigs ending in a brown plume of overwintering flower-buds. If they live through the winter without injury the buds will open April–May. The flowers are a little like those of the foxglove, but they are pale violet with yellow streaks. The pointed oval capsules contain winged seeds.

Paulownia tomentosa

Pernettya mucronata

Pernettya

Small evergreen shrub belonging to the heather family. In autumn and winter it bears brightly coloured berries, but unfortunately it is not 100 per cent winter-hardy.
Situation A shrub for sunny or partially shaded spots, where the soil is adequately moist. Suitable for small gardens, especially in coastal areas. The plants should be placed in groups, male and female plants, for *Pernettya* is dioecious. Easy to prune. Branches with or without berries are used in flower arrangements.
Soil Lime-free, humus-rich soil.
Propagation The species from seed, strains only from cuttings taken in winter.

Pernettya mucronata: An evergreen bush with red-brown twigs; height to 1m and as much across. The glossy dark-green leaves are 5–15cm long, oval and with a spiny point. The insignificant white flowers which appear in May are followed by pink-white berries. 'Crimsonia', 'Mother of Pearl', 'Signal' and 'Snow White' are beautiful garden forms with fairly large berries.

Perovskia

Russian Sage

Semi-shrubs, frequently sold as hardy perennials. A greyish appearance and violet-blue lipped flowers. Quite winter-hardy. Mature plants dislike being moved.
Situation Provide a sunny, well-drained position. *Perovskia* looks beautiful planted singly among low ground-covering plants, for example thyme, *Acaena*, or cat's foot. Also attractive in borders with a violet-blue and grey colour scheme, possibly also including white and pink.
Soil Fairly dry soil; the plants like lime.
Propagation Ripe shoots are cut in autumn and rooted under glass. As a rule it is easier to grow the plants from seed.

Perovskia atriplicifolia: A semi-shrub, height to 1.5m, erect-growing habit. The shoots growing from the woody base are covered in felty down; the leaves are initially grey and felty, later smooth, fragrant when rubbed. Elongated spikes of violet-blue flowers August-September. 'Blue Haze' and 'Blue Spire' are beautiful strains.

Perovskia atriplicifolia 'Blue Spire'

Phellodendron amurense

Phellodendron

Cork Tree

Medium-sized deciduous trees. Mature trees are covered in a corky layer.
Situation A fine specimen tree for parks and large gardens. Provide a sunny or partially shaded position.
Soil Standard garden soil, preferably containing some lime.
Propagation From seed and cuttings.

Phellodendron amurense: Height to 15m, 10m across; a tree with a broad, open crown and widely spreading branches. The pinnate leaves are composed of 5–13 leaflets, each 5–11cm long, oval with a long point and pointed, sometimes slightly oblique, at the base. They are smooth edged, glossy green on the upper surface, bluish on the reverse. In autumn the foliage turns golden yellow. The powdery clusters of green-yellow flowers appear in July and are followed by glossy black berries. In young trees the bark is silvery grey; older trees may have a corky layer as much as 6cm thick. The flowers smell of turpentine, as do bruised leaves.

133

Philadelphus coronarius

Philadelphus Lemoinei hybrid

Philadelphus

Mock Orange

Strong, deciduous shrubs found in practically every garden. From May until well into July the various species and strains produce delightfully scented white flowers. A large number of hybrids with beautiful flowers have been developed; unfortunately some of them are no longer fragrant.

The mock orange has erect-growing, sometimes arching twigs and opposite-growing leaves. Pruning and thinning should take place immediately after the flowering season. Older specimens tend to grow bare at the base and should be rejuvenated by pruning in good time.

Situation The mock orange will do well and flower profusely in a sunny or partially shaded position. Forms with variegated or yellow foliage should be grown in full sun. The plant occurs in several sizes and can therefore be used in a small garden as well as in a park. Beautiful when planted singly, but also in groups in a shrub border.

Soil Standard, slightly damp garden soil.

Propagation From cuttings.

Philadelphus coronarius, sweet mock orange: An erect-growing shrub, 3–4m tall, producing an abundance of very fragrant white flowers May–June. Fast growing, it has peeling twigs and oval, widely toothed leaves.

Philadelphus hybrids: The results of crossing various species. Usually shrubs with peeling twigs and large, often double flowers. The following are a number of beautiful cultivars:

'Albâtre', scented double flowers, to 4cm across, and non-peeling twigs; 'Dame Blanche', a low, slow-growing bush with milk-white fringed flowers, semi-double, with little or no fragrance; 'Innocence', a low-growing bush with yellow-blotched foliage and semi-double flowers; 'Lemoinei', is fragrant with single white flowers, height over 1m; 'Manteau d'Hermine' produces large, pure white, double flowers and reaches a height of about 1m; 'Virginal' is a large shrub with semi-double, fragrant flowers.

Philadelphus Lemoinei hybrids: Shrubs to 2m in height and 1.5m across, with thin twigs and small leaves. Cruciform single white flowers with a strong fragrance June–July. The centre of the flowers is slightly tinged with red.

Philadelphus microphyllus: A bush to 1m in height, with fragrant white flowers June–July. This is the least hardy species; it requires some cover in winter.

Philadelphus Purpureomaculatus hybrids (syn *P. × purpureomaculatus*): Height to 1m; the twigs peel late in the season. Smooth-edged oval leaves. Isolated flowers, 2–3cm in diameter, with a wine-red blotch at the base of the petals.

Photinia

Chinese Hawthorn

Deciduous shrubs or small trees with hawthorn-like flower umbels, red fruits and fine autumn colouring.
Situation An attractive shrub for sunny or partially shaded, sheltered spots, planted singly but also at the back of a shrub border. They rarely need pruning.
Soil Standard garden soil, preferably lime-free and well drained.
Propagation From seed, by layering or from cuttings of soft, semi-ripe or hard wood.

Photinia villosa: A shrub growing to 5m in height and almost as much across, with erect-growing, thin, smooth twigs, arching at a later stage. The green, almost leathery leaves are 5–8cm long, obovate, abruptly pointed and sharply serrated, hairy on the reverse. In autumn they discolour to a flaming orange to deep-red shade. The white flowers appear in June and are followed by 8mm long, glossy red fruits.

Photinia villosa

Picea abies 'Wartburg'

Picea

Spruce

Well known evergreen conifers growing on a large scale especially in northern countries. They resemble the silver fir, *Abies*, but the difference becomes obvious if we pull off a needle: in the case of *Picea* a small piece of bark will come off with the needle, not so in the case of the *Abies*. In technical terminology this bark section is referred to as a 'leaf-cushion'. In addition the cones are erect growing in the case of the silver fir, pendent in the spruce. There are innumerable garden forms, all very hardy, with a large variety of foliage shapes and colours.
Situation *Picea* will thrive in sunny or partially shaded positions. The smaller types are very attractive in the rock garden. The common spruce and the white spruce are used as hedges or as windbreaks. The white spruce and the oriental spruce are particularly wind resistant. Since most species grow fairly tall they can serve as hedges or windbreaks only in very large gardens. Species with an unusual habit or colouring, such as the very well known Colorado spruce, are often planted singly. If we want to grow the smaller types in window-boxes it is essential to plant them out of a draught, since otherwise they may be attacked by red spider, or the needles may

Picea breweriana

Picea glauca 'Conica'

discolour. Pruning is restricted to the removal of dead branches; in the case of cultivars the odd wild shoot might be removed. *Picea abies* supplies deal, which is used on a large scale.

Soil Most species will do well in any, not too poor, garden soil. Calcareous soil is less suitable. Humus-rich soil is preferred.

Propagation The species from seed, cultivars by grafting or from cuttings.

Diseases In addition to red spider, this genus may be attacked by the green spruce aphis which may be combated by spraying in winter with creosote, or the aphids may be sprayed in April to May with a general insecticide.

Picea abies (syn *P. excelsa*), common spruce, Norway spruce, Christmas tree: A broad-columnar to pyramid-shaped tree, up to 20m in height and 5–7m across, a native of Europe. Smooth red-brown twigs and resin-free buds. Pointed, to 2.5cm long, glossy dark-green needles with an attractive scent. The needles are clearly arranged in two rows on the underside of the twigs. The scales of the cones are slightly curved. There are many more low-growing than tall strains.
'Acrocona' grows to 6–8m and as much across, provided it is not pruned when young. It develops very unusual cones at an early stage. 'Cranbrassiliana' is a squat, cone-shaped conifer, to 2m in height and 3m across, with red-brown buds and hard needles. 'Inversa' is densely branched, the branches are contiguous to the trunk and later spread along the ground. This is a very unusual weeping form. 'Nidiformis' grows to 1–2m in height, 3m across. It is slow growing and, except when it grows very old, has a nest-shaped hollow in the centre. 'Procumbens', 1m tall and a little more across, has horizontally layered branches. 'Repens' has a spreading and creeping habit; height to 50cm, sometimes 1.5m across. Short, radial needles. Suitable for covering slopes. 'Wartburg' is a very fine weeping form with a leaning trunk, from which the branches hang almost vertically. Dense ramification; height to 4m, 2m across.
Picea breweriana: A very graceful tree, 30m tall and 6m across, with partially raised, horizontal branches from which hairy, red-brown twigs depend. Blunt, somewhat radially spreading needles, 2–3cm long. Large cones. A beautiful specimen tree.
Picea engelmannii: Little known, cone-shaped tree, with grey-blue needles, to 2.5cm long. They point forwards and, when rubbed, have a disagreeable scent. Red-green, later pale-brown cones. The strain 'Glauca' has steel-blue needles.
Picea glauca (syn *P. alba*), white spruce: A pyramidal tree with dense ramification, to 25m in height and 5m across, with bare, red-brown, slightly bloomed twigs. Blue-green, 2cm long needles, pointing upwards a little and, when rubbed, smelling of blackcurrants. 'Albertiana' is a cone-shaped dwarf conifer, to 3m tall

and 1m across, compact and regular in habit, with thin needles. 'Conica', slow growing, reaches approximately the same dimensions and is densely covered in soft pale-green needles. 'Echiniformis' does not grow beyond 80cm in height but is almost double as much across. Spherical habit, flattened at the top.

Picea jezoensis: A large tree, to 40m in height; its habit resembles that of *P. abies*. The form most often cultivated is the variety *hondoensis*, a fine spruce, not very fast growing. The twigs are brown, the mature branches even darker in colour. The short needles are dark green on the upper surface, almost white underneath.

Picea mariana (syn *P. nigra*), black spruce: A narrow-pyramid shaped tree, to 15m tall, with initially hairy brown twigs and small, pointed, resin-free buds. Pointed, somewhat spiny needles, to 1.5cm long, blue green. The oval brown-purple cones have smooth-edged or dentate scales. This is the tree that supplies the paper industry. 'Nana' is an important garden form, 30–40cm in height, spherical, grey blue. Slow growing, suitable for the rock garden.

Picea omorika (syn *Pinus omorika*), Serbian spruce: A fast-growing conifer, to 20m in height, with a narrow-pyramidal to columnar habit which restricts its diameter to a maximum of 5m. The twigs are covered in dense brown hair; dark-brown, resin-free buds. The blunt, to 2cm long needles have two white streaks on the reverse. The violet-blue cones appear at an early age. 'Nana' is a beautiful dwarf form, to 1.5m tall, with a broad-cone shape and radially arranged needles.

Picea orientalis, Oriental spruce: A large tree with a cone-shaped crown. The young shoots are pale brown to yellow. Dark-green needles, 6–8mm long, square in section. A beautiful tree for parks. There are several cultivars with variously coloured needles, as well as dwarf forms suitable for small gardens.

Picea pungens: Height to 30m, pyramidal habit. A tree with bare, glossy orange-brown twigs bearing red-brown, resin-free buds. Spiny, dark blue-green needles, to 3cm long. The strain 'Glauca', also referred to as the Colorado spruce, is very well known. It is a cone-shaped tree with grey-blue needles radially arranged round the twigs and quite sharp. 'Glauca globosa' is slow growing, to 1m in height. It maintains its fine blue-green colour all the year round. 'Koster' may reach 10m and has magnificent blue needles and glossy cones, pale brown when ripe. 'Moerheim' resembles the previous form, but has longer needles.

Picea omorika

Picea pungens 'Koster'

Pieris

Beautiful evergreen shrubs, previously called *Andromeda* and still found under that name in the catalogues. The simple leaves alternate along the twigs. Sometimes the young foliage is red or bronze coloured, giving the bush a striking appearance. The terminal flower clusters are developed in autumn and may be damaged by severe frost and cold wind.

Situation From the above it may be deduced that *Pieris* should always be given a sheltered position, especially in the case of *P. formosa* and *P. japonica*. They enjoy a partially shaded situation in fresh, slightly damp soil. Like all other members of the heather family they look attractive in the heather garden. *P. japonica*, in particular, is very suitable for a free-standing position; this is the finest species. *Pieris* is also not out of place in window-boxes.

Soil Acid, humus-rich soil. If the soil does not meet these requirements it should be mixed with conifer-needle compost, peat or chopped turves.

Propagation From seed sown under glass, unheated, or from summer cuttings.

Pieris floribunda (syn *Andromeda floribunda*): A compact, spherical shrub to 2m tall. In the shade it may grow taller and more open. The erect-growing twigs bear oval, very finely serrated leathery leaves, to 8cm long, with black spots underneath. Bell-shaped white flowers in erect-growing plumes, 6–10cm long, April–May. This species is fairly hardy.

Pieris formosa (syn *P. forrestii*): Fairly sensitive to frost, even if it is covered in winter. May grow to a height of 3m, in this country it usually remains lower. The oval to oblong leaves, to 14cm long, are red when they start into growth. Fragrant white flowers in arching plumes April–May. 'Forest Flame' is a well known strain with beautiful autumn colouring, reasonably hardy in coastal regions.

Pieris japonica (syn *Andromeda japonica*): Height to 3m and as much across, a shrub with spreading to arching twigs and obovate leaves, finely crenated, especially along the upper part. Initially the foliage is brown red. White flowers in pendent plumes March–May. 'Flamingo' is a cultivar with darker, red-purple flowers, appearing in abundance even in young plants. 'Purity' is a Japanese cultivar with pure white flowers in large clusters. It flowers a little later in the season. 'Select' appears to be the most winter-hardy form. White flowers. 'Valley Rose' has pale red-purple flowers. In 'Variegata' the foliage has a white margin.

Pieris floribunda

Pieris japonica

Pinus

Pine, Fir

Evergreen conifers, easily recognised by their long needles which are arranged in bundles of 2, 3 or 5. They may be 3cm or as much as 20cm long. In the northern hemisphere, these trees are grown on a large scale for their wood. In young trees the crown is often a broad cone, but at a later stage it grows round or flattened. In an open situation the branches will frequently reach to the ground. In these circumstances they will cast so much shade that practically nothing will grow underneath, so that the springy brown needle carpet remains intact. Pines have an inconspicuous inflorescence. The cones ripen after two or three years and may then ornament the tree for a number of years.

Situation Fir trees have a graceful habit and are therefore attractive in a free-standing position. Provide a site in full sun. They are very drought-resistant and may thrive in the most unfavourable spots. In poor soil they make an effective screen or windbreak. The smaller garden forms may be considered for the rock garden, where they provide an evergreen feature.

Soil Many species will do well in poor soil, as may be seen in coastal regions. They prefer moderately acid soil, but the mountain pine and the shore pine tolerate lime.

Propagation Species from seed, garden forms by grafting or from cuttings.

Pinus nigra ssp *nigra*

Pinus pumila

Pinus cembra, Alpine pine: Wind-resistant pine which in its native habitat may grow to as much as 30m, but in this country does not reach more than 10–15m. The young twigs are felty, orange brown, the buds are pointed and resinous. Dark blue-green needles, to 12cm long, with blue-white streaks; 5 to a bundle. Does best in loamy, not too heavy soil with an adequate moisture content. 'Compacta Glauca' is a slender dwarf form, to 2m tall. Dense habit, blue-green needles, with blue-white streaks on the reverse.

Pinus contorta (syn *P. inops*): It owes its name to the fact that young needles are often strangely contorted. They are arranged in pairs and are dark green. Yellow-brown cones, to 5cm long. Height 5–6m, 4m across.

Pinus densiflora, Japanese red pine: Height 25–30m, a tree with an umbrella-shaped crown and bare twigs with slightly resinous buds. Limp, blue-green needles, not sharp. 'Umbraculifera' does not grow beyond 3m, as much across. Slow growing.

Pinus heldreichii: This conifer grows to 20m in height and 8m across, very vigorous. Cone-shaped dark-green needles and blue cones.

Pinus leucodermis: Sometimes considered to be a variety of *P. heldreichii*. Height to 20m, grey bark, leaving yellow patches when peeling. The needles are arranged

Pinus strobus 'Radiata'

Pinus sylvestris

in pairs, very close together. They are 6cm long, practically black when young. There are several cultivars, very suitable for use in the garden. 'Aureospicata' has yellow-pointed needles; slow growing. 'Compact Gem' is a particularly small dwarf form with very dark needles. In the course of ten years it does not grow above 25cm. 'Satellite' has a narrow cone shape, with open ramification. The needles are 8–12cm long, contiguous to the twigs, bright green.

Pinus mugo (syn *P. montana*), mountain pine: Height to 10m; bare brown twigs and red-brown, resinous buds. Dark-green needles, to 8cm long, growing in pairs, and glossy, obliquely hanging cones. Usually grown in bush form, especially the low-growing specimens which are often used in plantations. The ssp *mugo* and *pumilio* both have a recumbent habit.

Pinus nigra (syn *P. austriaca*), Austrian pine: Height to 40m, 8m across, a tree with bare, yellow-brown twigs and pale-brown, resinous buds. Spiny dark-green needles, to 16cm long, arranged in pairs. The ssp *nigra* (syn var *austriaca*) has an oval crown, later umbel-shaped and is very resistant to sea wind. The variety *maritima* has a more open habit. 'Pygmea' is a slow-growing dwarf form, to 3m in height, with dark, dull-green needles turning a fine shade of yellow in winter.

Pinus parviflora: Height to 15m, 6m across. Bare or finely haired twigs and pointed, somewhat resinous buds. Blue-green needles, to 7cm long, in bundles of 5, strongly contorted and assembled at the tips of the twigs. 'Glauca' is a beautiful specimen tree with deep-blue foliage and erect-growing squat-oval cones.

Pinus ponderosa, Western yellow pine: Fast growing, to 40m. The short, heavy branches are arranged fairly regularly round the trunk. Up to 26cm long needles in bundles of 3, dark green.

Pinus pumila, dwarf pine: Shrub up to 3m in height, 5m across, with blue-green, to 7cm long needles arranged in bundles of 5. Initially purple-violet cones, later turning red brown. Very tolerant of drought and wind and suitable for rock and heather gardens. 'Glauca' is very slow growing. It is less spreading than the species and has blue-grey needles.

Pinus radiata (syn *P. insignis*): A fast-growing pine, to 35m in height, with a decorative, very rough trunk and bright-green needles in bundles of 3; they drop in the third year. Elongated cones.

Pinus strobus, Weymouth pine: Height to 40m. Horizontal ramification and bare or slightly hairy twigs. Pointed, somewhat resinous buds and glossy, dark blue-green, often drooping needles, thin and limp, in bundles of 5. The cones are up to 15cm long and have flattened scales. The Weymouth pine is resistant to smoke and dust and is fast growing. It likes slightly damp soil. 'Radiata' is a spherical dwarf conifer with a squat habit, to 2m in height and as much across. The upper surface of the needles is green, the underside bluish. The needles do not droop.

Pinus sylvestris, Scots pine: Height to 35m, 8–10m across. A tree with an umbrella-shaped crown, filtering the light in an attractive manner. Bare, yellow-grey twigs and pointed, resinless buds. The blue-green needles, to 6cm long, grow in pairs. They are slightly spiny. 'Aurea' is slow growing, to 6m, and in summer has greenish, in winter golden-yellow, needles. 'Beuvronensis' grows to 1m in height and twice as much across. Its habit is initially compact, later more open; dark-green needles. The brown-red buds in winter are a striking feature.

Pinus wallichiana (syn *P. griffithii*): A pine tree up to 30m in height, with up to 18cm long pendent, blue-grey needles. The elongated pendulous cones are covered in white resin. Bare branches, covered in blue bloom, and pointed, resinous buds. Ensure a sheltered position and not too dry soil.

Pinus wallichiana

Platanus × hispanica

Platanus

Plane Tree

Well known in parks and streets, a tree whose peeling bark makes the trunk look blotched. The palmate leaves alternate along the branches and are thus easily distinguished from plane-leaved *Acer* species. Another characteristic is the spherical, long-stalked fruits.

Situation Because of their size they are suitable only for parks or very large gardens and as street trees. Provide a sunny or partially shaded position. Very beautiful planted singly.

Soil Standard garden soil, preferably containing clay or loam.

Propagation By layering, from winter cuttings or from seeds of which few are viable.

Platanus × hispanica (syn *P. × acerifolia*), common plane tree: The result of crossing the western and the oriental plane tree. Height to 30m, 12–18m across; a tree with smooth twigs and red buds. The leaves have pointed lobes with 3–5 teeth. The bark peels in thin sections.

Platanus orientalis, Oriental plane tree: The foliage is more deeply incised than in the previous species.

141

Poncirus

Beautiful, deciduous shrubs with fragrant blossom in spring and yellow fruits in autumn. Their strong thorns may create an impenetrable barrier.

Situation They should be planted singly or in groups in sunny or partially shaded positions and in well-drained soil. Keep them out of strong wind. Pruning is rarely necessary, although it encourages dense growth. It should take place immediately after the flowering season.

Soil Nutritious soil.

Propagation From seed or cuttings of partially ripened shoots.

Poncirus trifoliata (syn *Citrus trifoliata*): A fairly slow-growing shrub, to 3m tall and almost as much across. The green twigs are flattened, twined and strongly thorned and are used in flower arrangements. The trifoliate leaves are oval, 2–5cm long with a lightly crenate margin and a wedge-shaped base. The fragrant, single white flowers appear April–May. The fruit is a fragrant, but bitter, little orange.

Poncirus trifoliata

Populus alba

Populus

Poplar

Very fast-growing, deciduous trees with a great variety of foliage colouring and form. Our choice should be determined by such considerations as the time when they start into growth, the colour of the foliage at that time, the sensitivity to wind, and the susceptibility to certain foliage diseases and canker. Balsam poplars spread a delightful fragrance, while aspens appeal to a different sense, namely our hearing.

Situation The poplar is a pioneer tree, able to clothe empty new landscapes within a short time. Columnar black poplars can create a striking accent in large gardens, but they are more frequently planted as a wind-break or to hide an unsightly building. Some poplars are suitable for lining avenues, while most species produce useful wood.

Soil Not very critical, but some poplars require damp soil.

Propagation Poplars are easily increased from cuttings. These are usually taken in winter, but sawn trunks will root if inserted in soil.

Populus alba, white poplar: A tree growing to 30m in height and 15m across, sometimes cultivated as a shrub. Felty twigs and buds. The leaves are green on the upper surface, white and felty underneath. Greenish-yellow flowers March–April. Often found in dunes.

Populus balsamifera (syn *P. tacamahacca*), balsam poplar: A tree which may grow to 25–40m, but not in our part of the world. Purple-brown, practically cylindrical, hairy twigs with large, sticky buds from which balsam oil is produced. 'Aurora' is a variegated form, 10m tall and 3m across, which in winter is cut back severely in order to encourage variegated foliage.

Populus Canadensis hybrids: The results of crossing *P. deltoides* and *P. nigra*. Euramerican or Canadian poplars; they grow vigorously, to 20–25m, and have sticky buds in winter. 'Dorskamp' is the fastest growing, but is slightly sensitive to wind. The trunk is slender. 'Robusta' has a straighter trunk and a slightly narrower crown. This tree is very wind resistant, but is susceptible to rust, leaf-blotching and late-winter frost.

Populus nigra, black poplar: The pillar-shaped strain 'Italica' is particularly well known. Its angular twigs bear diamond-shaped leaves. 'Vereecken' grows a little broader. Both strains are very resistant to sea wind and create excellent windbreaks.

Populus Canadensis hybrid

Potentilla fruticosa

Potentilla

Cinquefoil

Hardy perennials or strong, deciduous little shrubs with a prolonged flowering season and therefore very popular. There are garden forms with variously coloured foliage and flowers; height also varies.

Situation Will thrive in sunny or partially shaded positions. They are planted singly, as edging plants, in groups in the shrub border and as low hedges. A number of species make suitable ground-cover.

Soil Standard garden soil.

Propagation From cuttings taken in winter.

Potentilla fruticosa: A bush to 1m in height and as much across, with peeling twigs. The leaves are composed of 5 leaflets, 15–40mm long, oblong to spatula-shaped, pointed and smooth edged. The underside of the leaves is slightly hairy. Yellow flowers May–August. The following are a few beautiful garden forms: 'Abbotswood', 70–100cm, large white flowers and blue-green foliage; 'Klondike', the same size, green foliage and golden-yellow flowers; 'Maanelys', a little taller; lemon-yellow flowers and blue-green foliage.

Prunus

Prunus × amygdalopersica

Prunus laurocerasus 'Rotundifolia'

This extensive genus belongs to the rose family and chiefly comprises deciduous shrubs and trees, including not only the well known stone-fruit trees such as cherries and plums, but also a selection of ornamental shrubs. Their common characteristics are the alternate foliage, the 5-fold flowers and the stone-fruits. Nearly every garden contains a *Prunus* species. Cherry laurels are often used for the sake of their evergreen foliage, their rapid growth and because they are extremely hardy. If it is a question of beautiful flowers we plant a Japanese cherry which has a supremely beautiful, if not very long, flowering season. The cherry plum produces more modest flowers, but includes forms with red foliage, beautiful and very striking for at least five months of the year. The autumn colouring of a *Prunus* can also be a feast to the eye; for instance *P. sargentii*. The trunks of *Prunus* trees, too, are often very attractive – the smooth, glossy, mahogany-brown bark of *P. serrula* is a good example.

Situation Deciduous ornamental cherries require a sunny position. The evergreen cherry laurels tolerate a great deal of shade. They will grow in the most unfavourable circumstances such as poor soil and in the drip of other trees; they are also fairly wind resistant. They are often used in shrubberies, in broad hedges, the low-growing species also to cover slopes.

Many of the deciduous shrubs are attractive throughout the year and are therefore suitable for a free-standing position. Others look well in groups in the shrub border. The sloe is found in informal plantations and windbreaks. *P. × gondovinii* 'Snow' deserves special mention; it is a standard tree with a round crown, very attractive, for example when it marks the start of a garden path. In general *Prunus* species require little pruning, except in the case of *P. triloba* and *P. glandulosa*, where the branches are cut back very low after flowering. Cherry laurels maintain a more compact shape if they are pruned, and it is also possible to cut back oversized specimens to such an extent that they almost have to start from scratch.

Starting from scratch is also necessary after a severe winter, when cherry laurels are frequently badly damaged by frost and sometimes die altogether. A strong, freezing wind, in particular, is fatal. Ornamental cherries also have serious problems in temperatures below −20°C. In a severe winter a 12-year-old *P. × yedoensis*, for example, had all the flower buds as well as some of the outer branches frozen. A *P. subhirtilla* 'Autumnalis' of the same age lost more than half its branches. Remarkably enough the odd flower appeared on young wood. Undoubtedly there are other ornamental cherries which dislike extremely low temperatures. In many books these shrubs are classified under zone 5 (temperature to −24°C), but this appears to be too optimistic.

Soil Provide nutritious, humus-rich soil, containing some lime, for deciduous species. Evergreen types are less choosy. Very cold and damp soil is unsuitable.

Propagation The species from seed, garden forms from cuttings. Cherry laurels from cuttings taken in winter. Standard forms are grafted or budded, usually on *P. avium*, the black cherry. Wild shoots must be removed as soon as possible.

Prunus × amygdalopersica, almond: The result of crossing *P. dulcis* and *P. persica*. A tree or shrub to 6m in height, sometimes with thorny twigs. Pink flowers March–April, followed by dry fruits with furrowed stones. Spear-shaped, finely serrated leaves, to 12cm long.

Prunus avium (syn *Cerasus avium*), black cherry, sweet cherry: A tree to 15m in height, with a fine pyramid shape. Oval to oblong, pointed leaves, to 15cm long, and white flowers in leafless bundles April–May. Dark, very sweet fruit. 'Decumana' has very large leaves with beautiful autumn colouring, white flowers and sweet fruit. The variety *duracina* has pale-coloured fruit with firm flesh. 'Plena' is a magnificent ornamental form with pendulous double flowers. Height to 18m, a tree with a broad pyramid-shaped crown.

Prunus cerasifera, cherry plum: Height to 10m; a tree or bush with green, sometimes thorny twigs. Isolated white flowers in April. The yellow fruit resembles a small plum. To 6cm long, oval, serrated and pointed leaves. There are numerous cultivars. 'Pendula' is a weeping form with green foliage. 'Atropurpurea' is a 6m tall tree or bush with a round crown and red-brown foliage. White flowers March–April, followed by sweet red fruit, provided the blossom has not been damaged by frost. 'Hollywood' (syn 'Trailblazer') has initially green, later brown-red foliage and white flowers in April. Large, red, edible plums in autumn. 'Nigra' resembles 'Woodii', but has larger leaves. 'Rosea' has salmon-red flowers and bronze-red-brown foliage, discolouring to dark green. It is a spreading, erect-growing shrub. 'Woodii' has purple-coloured foliage and pink flowers.

Prunus glandulosa, dwarf flowering cherry: A shrub to 1.5m tall, or a small standard tree with dark-brown twigs and up to 7cm long, oval-spear-shaped, sharply double-serrated leaves. White flowers in May. In 'Alboplena', the white almond, they are double and white, in 'Sinensis', the red almond, the double flowers are pink.

Prunus × gondouinii: The result of crossing *P. avium* and *P. cerasus*. A tree with predominantly thin twigs; the foliage resembling that of *P. avium*. Large, acid fruit. The best known strain is 'Snow', usually grafted, with a dense, spherical crown. A profusion of white flowers late April–early May.

Prunus laurocerasus (syn *Laurocerasus officinalis*,

Prunus padus

Prunus serrula

145

Prunus serrulata 'Kiku-Shidare-Sakura'

Prunus subhirtella 'Pendula'

Cerasus laurocerasus), cherry laurel: Evergreen, vigorously growing shrub with green twigs and oblong, glossy green leaves, to 25cm long. Height 4–6m. Dense white flower clusters, the same length as, or shorter than, the leaves, in May. There are many beautiful strains. 'Caucasia', to 3m tall, erect growing, is very hardy. 'Reynvaanii', too, is quite frost-resistant; height nearly 2m. 'Rotundifolia' is somewhat sensitive to frost, but is very fast growing. 'Zabeliana' is slow growing, to 1m in height and, in the course of time, 3m across.

Prunus lusitanica (syn *Cerasus lusitanica*), Portugal laurel: Height 3m; slightly sensitive to frost; a shrub with red-brown twigs and oval, to 12cm long leaves, retained in winter. White flowers in June. The flower clusters are longer than the leaves. Must be kept out of the morning sun in winter.

Prunus maackii, ornamental cherry: A vigorously growing tree, height to 10m, with oblong oval leaves. The white flowers appear before the foliage, in April, and are followed by black fruit. The magnificent reddish trunk is a striking feature.

Prunus padus (syn *Cerasus padus*, *Padus avium*), European bird cherry: A broad, 9m tall shrub without root shoots and with elliptic to obovate leaves, to 12cm long. White flowers in pendent clusters in May, followed by black fruit. Tolerates partial shade. 'Colorata' has red-brown foliage and pink flowers, remains a little lower. 'Pendula' is the weeping form.

Prunus sargentii (syn *P. serrulata* var *sachalinensis*), ornamental cherry: A tree or shrub to 10m in height, with initially brown foliage. Pink flowers in groups of 2–4 in May. The oval, to 12cm long leaves turn orange red in autumn.

Prunus serrula, ornamental cherry: Height to 7m; a tree with spear-shaped leaves turning red in autumn. White flowers April–May, followed by red fruit. The glossy red-brown trunk is strikingly decorative throughout the year.

Prunus serrulata, Japanese flowering cherry: One of the best known *Prunus* species, with initially red foliage and usually double flowers. They rarely produce fruit. There are an enormous number of magnificent strains. 'Amanogawa' develops a column to 9m tall, with pink flowers, fragrant and sometimes double, April–May. 'Hokusai' has a very spreading habit and has pink flowers late April–early May. 'Kiku-Shidare-Sakura' is a 3m tall weeping form with widely arching branches. In April it is covered in deep-pink, entirely double flowers. 'Kwanzan' grows to 12m, very vigorous, vase shaped. A profusion of dark-pink double flowers in May. Often used to line avenues. 'Shirofugen' is one of the latest flowering forms. The double flowers which appear in mid-May are initially white, later pink. A very broad shrub, 5–6m in height.

Prunus subhirtella, Japanese flowering cherry: The original form is rare. A very well known strain is 'Autumnalis', a 6m tall tree or shrub with 8cm long oval leaves. It sometimes flowers as early as November; the flowers are white, semi-double. Depending on the temperature there may be a second flowering in early spring. 'Autumnalis Rosea' has pink flowers. 'Pendula' is the 3m tall weeping form, with numerous arching branches and a cloud of small pink flowers in April.

Prunus triloba, Chinese flowering almond: A well-known shrub, whose flowering branches are sold in florists' shops in winter. It is a bush or small standard tree, 2m tall, with obovate, to 10cm long leaves. Pink, semi-double flowers March–April.

Prunus × yedoensis: Probably the result of crossing *P. speciosa* and *P. subhirtella*. Height 15m; a tree with a fairly flat, broad crown and smooth bark. A profusion of fragrant, single white flowers in April, followed by black fruit.

Prunus × yedoensis

Pseudosasa japonica

Pseudosasa

Magnificent evergreen bamboos which may develop into an enormous thicket. They rarely flower. Often they die after flowering.

Situation Since they are not entirely winter-hardy they must be planted in a sheltered site protected against strong wind, and should possibly be covered in severe winters. Provide a sunny or partially shaded position. Their size makes these bamboos suitable only for parks or large gardens. In smaller gardens their spread must be artificially restricted. Bamboos look very good in 'Japanese' gardens and near water.

Soil Humus-rich, adequately moisture-retaining soil.

Propagation By division.

Pseudosasa japonica (syn *Arundinaria japonica*, *Bambusa metake*): Height to 4m. Brown stalks covered in bristly hair, and dark-green, to 24cm long and 4cm wide leaves, blue green underneath.

Pseudotsuga menziesii

Pseudotsuga

Douglas Fir

Fast-growing evergreen conifer, used on a large scale in forestry. When rubbed the needles have a pleasant fragrance.

Situation   The species grows so large that it is used only in parks and very large gardens, often for the purpose of creating a restful background. They are beautiful planted singly, but also in groups. There are a number of dwarf forms which can be planted in the rock garden or in small gardens.

Soil   Standard garden soil.

Propagation   From seed, garden forms from cuttings.

Pseudotsuga menziesii (syn *P. douglassii, P. taxifolia*), green Douglas fir: In our part of the world it grows to 30m as a tree with a conical shape, straight trunk and smooth, resinous brown bark. Narrow pendent cones. When branches are cut the fairly thin, to 3cm long needles will not immediately drop. Excellent for decoration. The variety *glauca* has blue-green needles. 'Fletcheri' and 'Tempelhof Compacta' are dwarf forms, height to 2m.

Pterocarya rhoifolia

Pterocarya

Healthy, vigorous, fast-growing and very attractive deciduous trees with large feathery leaves. In summer, strings of nuts dangle from the branches.

Situation   A fine specimen tree for parks and large gardens. Provide a position in full sun or in partial shade in damp, deeply dug soil.

Soil   Nutritious soil.

Propagation   From seed or by layering.

Pterocarya fraxinifolia (syn *P. caucasia*): Height to 20m, a tree with a broad, fairly round crown. The bare buds are a characteristic winter feature. The leaves are composed of 11–12 leaflets, each 8–12cm long, spear-shaped and practically bare. The nuts hang in elongated catkins and have semicircular wings, approximately as long as they are broad. Brown buds.

Pterocarya rhoifolia: Height to 25m, 15m across. This tree differs from the previous species in that it has 2–3 involucral scales, which drop at an early stage leaving the foliage buds, covered in white down, bare.

Pyracantha

Firethorn

An extremely well known espalier shrub, decorating many a house-wall. Somewhat prone to scab. In May it produces thorny flowers, followed in autumn by a profusion of berries.
Situation It can serve as undergrowth, as a hedging plant or as an espalier, planted singly or in groups. Because of its thorns it can create an effective barrier. Provide a sunny to partially shaded position. The less sun, the fewer berries.
Soil Porous, nutritious soil, slightly on the dry side.
Propagation From cuttings and from seed.

Pyracantha coccinea (syn *Cotoneaster pyracantha*): A firethorn which is sensitive to scab and has been crossed with scab-resistant, but less hardy species, producing valuable hybrids such as 'Orange Charmer', 2–3m in height and 4m across with deep-orange berries. 'Golden Charmer' has large orange-yellow berries.

Pyracantha coccinea 'Orange Charmer'

Pyrus salicifolia

Pyrus

Pear

Deciduous shrubs or trees with single, serrated, sometimes lobed leaves and white flowers in spring. The fruits are round or pear-shaped.
Situation Provide a sunny position. Pears are beautiful planted singly and are used as avenue trees, in orchards and as ornamental trees in large and small gardens. The pear in the photograph would also thrive in a large container.
Soil Nutritious garden soil.
Propagation From seed or by grafting.

Pyrus communis (syn *Pyrus domestica*): The well known fruit tree which in April to May is clothed in white flowers and in late summer or in autumn produces pears, variously shaped depending on the strain.
Pyrus elaeagrifolia, ornamental pear: Height to 6m, 5m across; a small tree with felty young twigs and thorns. White flowers April–May. Round green fruit.
Pyrus salicifolia: Greyish, arching twigs with thorns. Flowers in the same period as the previous species, but more profusely. Pear-shaped fruit. 'Pendula' is a magnificent weeping form.

149

Quercus coccinea 'Splendens'

Quercus robur

Quercus

Oak

Deciduous or evergreen trees with single, alternating leaves and producing the well known acorns.

Situation Oaks are used on a large scale in forestry, but are also very beautiful in the landscape, lining streets or in parks; some of the smaller species can be planted in medium-sized gardens. Its imposing appearance and frequently attractive autumn colouring makes it a beautiful specimen tree. Provide a sunny or partially shaded position, except for the evergreen oaks and the cork-oak which prefer to be out of the sun. Oaks may live to a great age; keep posterity in mind and choose a situation where they can remain for 200 years!

Soil Standard garden soil, adequately moist.

Propagation The species from seed, garden forms are grafted.

Quercus cerris, Turkey oak: Height to 25m, a tree with a broad, pyramid-shaped crown. The dark-green, leathery foliage varies in shape and has brown autumn colouring. The cup of the acorn is covered in mossy down. The twigs, too, are initially downy. 'Pendula' is a fine weeping form with deeply incised leaves. In 'Argenteovariegata' the foliage has creamy blotches or margins.

Quercus coccinea, scarlet oak: A fast-growing oak, to 25m in height and 7m across, with oval, to 15cm long leaves, deeply incised and with magnificent red autumn colouring. Greenish flowers in May: single, short-stalked fruits. 'Splendens' is the best known strain.

Quercus ilex, holm oak: Height to 30m; an evergreen tree, but in this country merely a large shrub. The leathery leaves are initially dentate, later smoother edged.

Quercus robur (syn *Q. pedunculata*): A tree to 30m in height, with a broad, irregularly shaped crown, lobed leaves and acorns hanging in pairs from long stalks. 'Concordia' remains smaller and has golden-yellow foliage. 'Fastigiata' is pillar shaped, to 15m, and 'Pendula' is the weeping form.

Quercus rubra (syn *Q. borealis*): Height to 25m; a tree with a broad, open crown and leaves which vary in shape, but are never incised to further than halfway. When the foliage has achieved its magnificent autumn colouring, cut branches are sold in florists' shops.

Quercus × *turneri*: 'Pseudoturneri' has leathery, deeply lobed leaves and is partially evergreen. Height to 10m with a compact, cone-shaped crown.

Rhododendron

Of all the genera belonging to the heather family, the *Rhododendron* is the most extensive. It includes azaleas. Rhododendrons are predominantly evergreen shrubs, sometimes even trees, with alternate, smooth-edged, simple, leathery leaves, often grouped more densely at the tip of a twig. The flowers usually occur in terminal clusters; occasionally they are borne in the axils of the leaves or are isolated. The corolla consists of 5 or 10 distorted petals and is often funnel-shaped. The fruits contain very fine seed. Innumerable hybrids have been created by crossing the hundreds of species, many of which originate in Asia. As rhododendrons make specific demands as regards climate and soil, there are a number of specialist growers. With the aid of constantly improved techniques new strains are created for special conditions. For example, the Repens hybrids are low-growing bushes, ideal for owners of small gardens who like to plant rhododendrons but have no room for the larger forms. There is great variation in winter-hardiness. The finest colours, for example soft yellow, are the least frost resistant. See also under hybrids.

Situation Plant rhododendrons in a spot where morning sun and glaring midday sun cannot reach them. A draughty place is definitely unsuitable and they also dislike drying winds. They do best in a damp atmosphere. Although rhododendrons tolerate a great deal of shade, a position under dense trees is not very suitable, since the trees absorb too much moisture. Moisture is essential for good growth. They may be planted in a kind of hollow, so that water will run down to the root-clump. Dwarf forms are used in rock gardens, large containers and small gardens. The larger specimens are suitable only for parks and large gardens or as informal hedges. Rhododendrons look well when incorporated in oriental-type gardens.

Rhododendrons need little pruning. It is advisable to remove faded flowers, but on country estates with large tracts of these shrubs this is naturally impossible and is restricted to the more sensitive forms. It encourages bud formation. Chafed or too long branches should be removed. If this is done at the start of the flowering season they may be kept in a vase and still give pleasure. Overgrown – incorrectly planted – specimens can be drastically reduced.

Rhododendrons are frequently planted too close together. Large-flowered and fast-growing forms should be planted at least 2m apart. If they are planted more closely they will have to be thinned out as soon as the leaves of neighbouring specimens touch each other. However, the best method is to give them sufficient space from the start and to be patient at first. This is not all that difficult, for the areas in between may be filled

Rhododendron augustinii 'Blue Tit Major'

Rhododendron hybrid 'Hollandia'

Rhododendron hybrid 'Koster's Cream'

Rhododendron × *praecox*

with all kinds of low-growing flowering forest plants. Fertiliser should be applied not too late in the year, for this would affect flower formation in the following year. Use lime-free fertiliser. Sulphate of ammonia is excellent.

Soil Provide humus-rich, acid soil with adequate moisture content. If the soil does not meet these requirements it is necessary to make a large planting-hole and to fill it with improved soil. A good recipe is: 3 parts woodland soil or peat-litter, 1 part leafmould, 2 parts garden soil, 1 part rotted cow manure. When buying rhododendron plants it is important to note where they have been grown. If they are to be planted in sandy soil it is advisable to choose shrubs grown in humus-rich sandy soil. A shrub grown in peat-soil will develop few if any roots outside its clump.

Propagation The species from seed, garden forms from cuttings or by grafting on seedlings. This is a job for the expert. Layering is an excellent method for amateurs, but rooting will take a long time.

Rhododendron species:

Rhododendron augustinii: A shrub to 1m tall, with oblong leaves, scaled on the reverse and covered in bristly hairs along the main vein. Broad funnel-shaped flowers in groups of 3–4, lavender blue or blue violet, with a yellow or green blotch. 'Blue Diamond' is a beautiful strain with deep-purple flowers, fading to violet blue, from mid April to early May. 'Blue Tit' is cultivated on a large scale; violet-blue flowers in the second half of April. It develops into a compact round bush and bears numerous, though not very large, flowers. 'Blue Tit Major' has particularly large flowers.

Rhododendron catawbiense, hollow-leaved rhododendron: Height to 3m, very strong. The progenitor of numerous hybrids. Lilac flowers dotted with olive green, May–June. Tolerates a fair amount of shade.

Rhododendron dauricum: A 2m tall shrub with fairly small pink flowers, funnel shaped, February–March, depending on the weather. The leaves are up to 4cm long. Very hardy.

Rhododendron ferrugineum: A compact shrub; it may grow to a height of 1m. Small, rose-red flowers in July. Attractive in the rock garden. There is also a strain with white flowers. A well known alpine plant which tolerates some lime in the soil.

Rhododendron hybrids: Spreading shrubs, 2–3m in height. They are arranged on the basis of their flowering season and hardiness.

The following strains are quite winter-hardy. Early flowering, March–April: 'Cosmopolitan', pink; 'Hollandia', carmine red; 'Peter Koster', pale red. Flowering season May–June: 'America', red; 'Belle Heller', white; 'Catawbiense Boursault', lilac pink; 'Catawbiense Grandiflorum', lilac; 'Dr V.H. Rutgers', deep red; 'English Roseum', pink to lilac; 'Koster's

Cream', one of the most hardy yellow strains; 'Nova Zembla', bright red; 'Scintillation', pale pink; 'Van Weerden Poelman', red. Late flowering, June–July: 'General Eisenhower', dark carmine red; 'Gomer Waterer', white to pale lilac.

A little less hardy, but worth growing are the following. For early flowering: 'Furnival's Daughter', pale pink with a red blotch; 'Jean Marie Montague', scarlet; 'Marcia', yellow; 'Mrs Betty Robertson', pale yellow with a little pink. Medium early: 'Dr Arnold W. Endtz', carmine red; 'Earl of Donoughmore', bright red; 'Marinus Koster', deep pink; 'Pink Pearl', pale pink. 'Kluis Sensation' is scarlet, late flowering.

Reputable growers have numerous other strains in their catalogues.

Rhododendron impeditum: A small shrub, to 30cm in height, with small foliage and pale purple-blue flowers in May.

Rhododendron luteum (syn *R. flavum*): A well known, hardy species, the progenitor of numerous strains. It is a deciduous azalea, to 2m tall, with dense ramification. The spear-shaped, initially downy leaves turn yellow red in autumn. Fragrant golden-yellow flowers in May, just before the leaves develop.

Rhododendron minus (syn *R. punctatum*): A dense shrub with fairly thick leaves, to 10cm long; the underside is densely covered in red-brown scales. Purple-pink flowers with green markings in June.

Rhododendron mucronulatum: A small, deciduous shrub with a very early flowering season – in mild winters it may start in January. The flowers have a broad funnel-shape and are purple pink. Frost will injure the flowers.

Rhododendron ponticum: Resembles *R. catawbiense*, but has flat, pointed leaves, pale green underneath. Lilac flowers with orange dots May–June. This species is sensitive to frost. In 'Imbricatum' the leaves overlap like roof-tiles. It is a low, slow-growing strain with purple flowers.

Rhododendron × praecox: A product of crossing *R. ciliatum* and *R. dauricum*. Height 1.5–2m, this shrub flowers as early as March or April. Night frost may damage the dark-red flowers. Fits into a small garden and is therefore planted fairly often.

Rhododendron racemosum: A 1m tall shrub with regularly distributed foliage. The leaves are dull green on the upper surface, silvery grey with brown scales underneath. Pale-pink flowers in April. This shrub may die back in frosty weather, but will always start into growth again.

Rhododendron Repens hybrids: Low-growing shrubs, about 1.5m tall, flowering profusely and often very early. Provide a sheltered situation. 'Elizabeth' is somewhat sensitive to frost; red flowers in late March or early April. 'Gertrude de Schäle' is bright red and quite hardy. The following flower a little later: 'Baden Baden', scarlet; 'Carmen', dark red; 'Elizabeth Hobbie', bright

Rhododendron Repens hybrid 'Elizabeth Hobbie'

Rhododendron Williamsianum hybrid

Rhododendron 'Golden Eagle' (Knapp Hill-Exbury)

Rhododendron Occidentale hybrid 'Irene Koster'

red; 'Frühlingszauber', dark red; 'Jewel', deep scarlet; 'Salute', red; 'Scarlet Wonder', luminous red; all are quite winter-hardy.

Rhododendron viscosum (syn *Azalea viscosa*): Height 1.5–2m, a deciduous azalea with dark-green oval leaves, blue green on the reverse. White flowers with a touch of pink, April.

Rhododendron Williamsianum hybrids: Height to 1m, sometimes double as much across. Shrubs with a semispherical shape and horizontally spreading branches. Broad-oval, bright-green leaves, to 4cm long, initially bronze green, blue green underneath. The bell-shaped, pale-pink flowers appear in clusters of 2–5 in late April. A sheltered position is essential. Crossing has resulted in beautiful strains, including 'April Glow', with rose-red flowers very early in the season. 'Bow Bells' has soft coral-pink flowers May–June. 'Karin' flowers earlier, deep pink. 'Oudijk's Sensation' dark red, flowers in mid May, very winter-hardy. 'Wilbrit' flowers at the same time, pink. 'Tibet' has pink flower buds and white flowers; it does not flower until May or June.

Rhododendron yakushimanum: A spherical shrub, to 1m tall, with side shoots covered in silvery, felty down. Firm, leathery leaves, to 10cm long and in May a great profusion of pale-pink flowers, fading to white.

Rhododendron yedoense: Height to 1m; a deciduous shrub with oval to spear-shaped leaves, slightly hairy on the upper surface, densely so underneath. Double lilac-pink flowers with purple dots April–May.

Japanese azaleas: This group includes semi-evergreen, low-growing shrubs, 50–150cm, which may be divided into early and late flowering forms, with small or large flowers. An exact division is not feasible.

Early flowering forms (first half of May) with large flowers are: 'Favourite', deep pink; 'Fedora', deep pink; 'Kathleen', dark pink; 'Lilac Time', deep lilac; 'Vuyk's Scarlet', deep scarlet. The following flower in the second half of May: 'Beethoven', blue purple; 'Moederkensdag', double carmine flowers; 'Palestrina', ivory white. Early flowering strains with small flowers are: 'Addy Wery', deep vermilion red; 'Adonis', white; 'Aladdin', geranium red; 'Campfire', deep red; 'Hino-Crimson', deep carmine red; 'Polar Bear', white; 'Purple Splendour', purple; 'Stewartstonian', deep orange red; 'Victorine Hefting', deep pink. Later flowering forms are: 'Blaauw's Pink', salmon pink; 'Florida', pale red; 'Hardijzer Beauty', pink.

Knap Hill–Exbury azaleas: Height to 2m; deciduous, erect-growing shrubs, flowering in the second half of May or in June, depending on the strain. Flowers in beautiful pastel shades, for example soft yellow, pale orange, rose red; also white. Often very fragrant. The strains mentioned are quite hardy.

The following flower in the second half of May: 'Ballerina', white; 'Balzac', deep orange red; 'Gibraltar', deep orange; 'Gold Dust', golden yellow and apricot; 'Golden Eagle', bright orange; 'Golden Flare', golden yellow with a bronze-coloured blotch; 'Persil', white with a yellow blotch; 'Pink Delight', deep pink with a yellow blotch; 'Strawberry Ice', pale pink; 'Sylphides', very soft pink. A little later flowering are: 'Basilisk', pale yellow; 'Gallipoli', carmine red; 'Hotspur Red', vermilion; 'Klondyke', golden yellow. Later still: 'Cecile', deep pink; 'Fireball', deep orange; 'Golden Sunset', deep yellow; 'Royal Command', vermilion; 'Satan', deep red; 'Sun Chariot', golden yellow.

Occidentale hybrids: These shrubs are descended from *Rhododendron occidentale*, a low-growing shrub with fragrant white or pink flowers with a yellow blotch. They may be larger than their progenitor; they flower in the second half of May or a little later and are quite hardy. Well known forms are: 'Exquisita', pale pink with a yellow blotch; 'Irene Koster', pink with a yellow blotch; 'Magnifica', creamy to yellow; 'Pink Cloud', pink.

Pontica hybrids: Also called Ghent azaleas. They flower in the second half of May or a little earlier. The fragrant flowers are not very large. 'Coccinea Speciosa', orange; 'Corneille', double pink flowers; 'Narcissiflora', double yellow flowers.

Rustica hybrids: Shrubs with double flowers in the second half of May. The following are some beautiful strains: 'Aida', pink with a little lilac; 'Freya', salmon yellow; 'Norma', rose red; 'Velasquez', creamy white with a touch of pink.

Garden azaleas: Also called *Rhododendron molle* (syn *Azalea mollis, A. sinensis*). The flowering season is April–May; the flowers are slightly fragrant. A number of well known strains are: 'Adriaan Koster', dark yellow; 'Apple Blossom', pink as the name implies; 'Christopher Wren', orange yellow; 'Dr M. Oosthoek', deep orange red; 'Frans van der Bom', salmon orange; 'Hortulanus H. Witte', bright orange yellow; 'Queen Emma', orange; 'Koster's Brilliant Red', orange red; 'Prominent', pale orange red; 'Salmon Queen', yellow to salmon pink; 'Samuel T. Coleridge', pink; 'Saturnus', orange red; 'William Hardijzer', deep red.

Rhododendron Pontica hybrid 'Narcissiflora'

Rhododendron 'Samuel T. Coleridge' (garden azalea)

Rhus typhina 'Laciniata'

Rhus

Sumach

Deciduous small trees or shrubs with fine foliage, strikingly coloured in autumn, and attractive fruits.

Situation Plant them in full sun, in well-drained, possibly dry soil. They are beautiful planted singly, even in small gardens. As a rule the sumach is dioecious, so that male and female specimens have to be planted together in order to produce the fruit plumes, which are retained until well into winter.

Soil Standard garden soil.

Propagation The easiest method is to increase them from rooted runners. Layering and taking cuttings is also possible.

Rhus glabra: Height 2–3m, 4m across; a shrub with bare branches; scarlet autumn colouring. The dense fruit plumes are dark red.

Rhus typhina, staghorn sumach: Height to 5m, the same across. A shrub or tree with green twigs, subsequently red and finally covered in brown down. In 'Laciniata' the foliage is deeply incised.

Ribes sanguineum 'Carneum'

Ribes

Deciduous, fructiferous, ornamental shrubs which flower early in the year. The foliage is aromatic.

Situation The red flowering *Ribes* is planted singly or in groups and will thrive in full sun. The alpine currant, the golden currant and the American black currant are grown in groups, as cover for other plants, or as undergrowth.

Soil Standard garden soil.

Propagation From cuttings.

Ribes alpinum, alpine currant: Height nearly 2m; greenish-yellow flowers and red fruit. The foliage is retained for a long time.

Ribes americanum (syn *R. floridum*), American black currant: Height nearly 2m, brown-red autumn colouring and black berries.

Ribes odoratum (syn *R. aureum*), golden currant: Fast-growing, to 2m; golden-yellow flowers and black berries. Tolerates shade.

Ribes sanguineum, flowering *Ribes*: A shrub to 3m tall, with a profusion of dense red flower-clusters April–May. 'Carneum' and 'King Edward VII' are beautiful garden forms.

Robinia

False Acacia

Deciduous shrubs or trees with pinnate leaves alternating along the, often angular, twigs. The fragrant white or pink, butterfly-like flowers are grouped in pendulous clusters and produce excellent honey. In all species the branches break off very easily. Pruning is rarely, if ever, necessary.

Situation The false acacia is a true lightwood species and therefore requires a sunny position. These plants will do well even in dry soil. As the branches are so fragile, a sheltered spot is desirable. *Robinia hispida* and *R. kelseyi* are particularly prone to branches breaking off and it is therefore advisable to grow them as espaliers. The trees are beautiful planted singly, as is *R. hispida*. The shrubs may also be used in groups in the shrub border.

Soil Standard garden soil.

Propagation The species from seed, by layering and from basal shoots. Garden forms as well as *R. viscosa* are usually grafted on *R. pseudoacacia* stock.

Robinia hispida, rose acacia: Height to 3m; a shrub with spine-less twigs, first red and covered in stiff hairs, later olive green with red tips. The 7–13 leaflets are round to broad-oval, bare, awned and with a blunt tip. Dense clusters of pink flowers in June; often flowering for a second time in late summer.

Robinia kelseyi: A 2–3m tall shrub with bare twigs and small spines; 9–11 pointed, oblong, bare leaflets. Pink flower-clusters May–June.

Robinia pseudoacacia, false acacia: A tree to 25m in height with an umbrella-shaped crown and bare, usually very spiny, twigs and branches. The buds are invisible in winter. The foliage consists of 9–11 bare, oval, awned leaflets. Fragrant white or pink flowers with a greenish-yellow blotch on the upper petal. The flower-clusters are about 20cm long and are followed by bare seed-pods. Several parts of this acacia are poisonous. There are a number of good strains, including 'Appalachia' which has a dead straight trunk and pyramidal crown, and is reasonably wind-resistant. 'Bessoniana' has a graceful, oval crown, is practically thornless and is sensitive to wind. 'Frisia' is smaller, about 10m in height, with yellow foliage, red thorns and fan-shaped crown with spreading branches. 'Semperflorens' flowers June–September, but most profusely in June; it is fairly wind-resistant, with an open crown. 'Tortuosa' grows shrub-shaped and has freakishly contorted branches; the pendulous leaves are also somewhat contorted.

Robinia viscosa: Height to 15m; a tree with lightly spined, sticky, olive-green twigs, 13–15 bare leaflets and pale-pink flowers in June.

Robinia hispida

Robinia pseudoacacia 'Frisia'

Rosa 'Chicago Peace'

Rosa 'Betty Prior'

Rosa

Rose

A garden without this much-loved flowering shrub is unthinkable. The rose is deciduous (except for a few species which retain their foliage in winter), erect growing or climbing; the twigs are usually thorny. The alternate leaves are, as a rule, pinnate. The flowers appear singly or in clusters and have 5 sepals and 5 petals; often they are delightfully fragrant. They are followed by the well known pseudo-fruits – the rose-hips. The forms now available are derived from a number of botanical species; new hybrids are constantly being added to the long list. On the other hand the old-fashioned roses and somewhat lesser known botanical species today enjoy growing popularity.

Situation Roses are planted not only for the sake of their beautiful colours and shapes, and the delightful fragrance of their flowers, but also because of the attractive rose-hips and the beautiful foliage, which may achieve striking autumn colouring. Large-flowered roses and floribunda roses are usually grown in beds, preferably with ground-covering plants in between; this looks better than bare earth. In the case of pink or red roses, in particular, it is advisable to include some blue-purple or blue-violet in the colour scheme, for example lavender, catmint or perennial violas. Periwinkle and various forms of veronica might also be considered. Mulching with tree-bark or grass clippings is a good alternative, but less imaginative.

Large-flowered roses and floribundas can also be grown as standards or in combination with other shrubs and perennials in a mixed border. They are beautiful in combination with grasses. Climbing roses may be used to cover walls, fences, pergolas and other partitions, or as ground-cover. Very vigorous growers can climb old fruit trees and create a cascade of flowers. Dwarf and miniature roses are suitable for window-boxes, pots on the terrace or balcony, the rock garden or among ground-cover. Botanical roses and park roses are planted in large shrub borders, but also look well as informal hedges or in semi-wild plantations.

The number of ways to use roses is legion, but it should always be kept in mind that these plants require a suitable position. In the shade or in a draughty situation they will be prone to all sorts of pests and diseases and they will flower very much less profusely. Roses should always be planted in full sun, preferably late in the year, say after 1 November; only when the soil is very damp should they be planted in spring. The junction of stock and scion should always be about 3cm below the surface. Place roses in a bucket of water immediately they arrive; possibly add some cow manure. Plant them after about an hour; the roots must be kept out of the sun. Water freely and in a dry spring always be ready with the watering can or the hose. Rooting will be encouraged if the plants are cut back severely. It may be painful to do this to a much-desired shrub, but the result will definitely be better than if you leave all the shoots on the plant. Roots which have been damaged in transit should be removed cleanly.

Roses are not always entirely winter-hardy. Shrub roses are easily protected by being earthed up. A layer of dead foliage round the base of the plant gives further protection. To prevent the leaves blowing away, cover them with soil or coarse manure.

Climbing roses are not so easily protected and in a severe frost most branches will be damaged, except in a very sheltered position, ie against a south- or west-facing wall, in a patio etc. As a rule they will start into growth again from the base: these are not suckers. The plant will bear few flowers that year, but if the next winter is milder you will have flowers again the following year.

Standard roses, in which the graft is situated well above ground, are even more tender. In mild winters a plastic bag or reed matting may provide some protection, but in temperatures below −15°C even this will be insufficient and you will probably have to write off the plants. The stock is probably still viable, but is of no use.

Many old-fashioned shrub roses and species roses are quite hardy and do not have to be protected. Miniature roses are treated like shrub roses: they must be earthed up and this cover has to be removed in good time in spring.

Soil Roses require soil dug to a depth of at least 60–80cm, friable, humus rich, nutritious and containing a certain amount of lime. Every winter, surround them with cow dung, and in spring carefully work this into the soil. At the same time, add bone-meal to encourage the plants to flower for a second time. In winter the water table should preferably be at 80 to 100cm.

When replacing old roses by new specimens, the soil must be treated to counteract rose disease caused by eelworms. The soil should be removed to a depth of 60–80cm and replaced by fresh garden soil. African marigolds secrete a substance which destroys eelworms and it is therefore possible to plant the bed with African marigolds for a year or two, after which the bed is dug to a depth of two spits, incorporating the foliage of the marigolds. Now the new roses can be planted, but be sure to dig in a fair amount of cow dung.

Pruning In spring when there is no longer a danger of frost, shrub roses are pruned in such a way that 3–5 eyes are left on each branch. The top eye has to point outwards. In the case of vigorous plants, leave more eyes than in their weaker brethren. Three to four strong branches are left on each bush after first removing spindly and dead branches. When cutting roses for indoors we must leave at least one complete (usually 5-fold) leaf to each branch. Faded roses are removed just above the topmost complete leaf. Species roses are

Rosa 'Climbing Sarabande'

Rosa 'Yellow Doll'

159

Rosa centifolia

Rosa gallica 'Versicolor'

thinned out a little in spring. In the case of climbing roses leave a number of well-developed long shoots, pruning the side-shoots to 3–5 eyes. Every 3–4 years old branches are replaced by young shoots, which develop in the course of the summer and have to be tied in. Take care; they break easily.

Propagation Botanical species are grown from seed or cuttings. Cultivars are bud-grafted.

The following are the main groups of roses.

Large-flowered roses or hybrid tea roses: Shrubs growing to a height of 1.5m, between June and October producing large, beautifully shaped, single-growing double flowers, often fragrant and occurring in a complete range of colours, with the exception of pure blue. Among the well known strains are: 'Blessings', pink, lightly scented, 90cm; 'Chicago Peace', the same height, salmon pink and yellow; 'Dame de Coeur', bright red, 80cm; 'Eden Rose', fragrant, deep pink, 80cm; 'Ernest Henry Morse', cherry red, with an attractive scent; 'Ena Harkness', warm red, slightly pendulous flowers, fragrant, 80cm; 'Grandpa Dickson', soft yellow, 90cm; 'Duke of Windsor', orange red, pleasant scent; 'Michèle Meilland', soft pink and salmon coloured, 90cm; 'Papa Meilland', velvety blood-red, delightful scent, 90cm; 'Pascali', pure white, 90cm; 'Peace', soft yellow with pink margins, faint scent, 90cm; 'Piccadilly', yellow with red, 70cm; 'Pink Peace', pink but not resembling 'Peace', delightful fragrance; 'Prima Ballerina', cherry red, unusual fragrance, height 110cm; 'Silver Lining', pink and silver, very fragrant, 80cm; 'Super Star', one of the best known forms, excellent for cutting, salmon orange and delightfully scented; 'Sutters Gold', golden yellow with red margins, fragrant, 80cm; 'Virgo', pure white but unfortunately not very vigorous, 70cm; 'Wendy Cussons', carmine red, pleasant scent, 75cm; 'White Wings', single, white, faintly scented flowers, 100cm.

Floribunda roses: Height to 2m; clusters of single or double flowers, sometimes with a delightful scent, between June and October. As a rule they flower more profusely and over a longer period than hybrid tea roses. There is a distinction between polyantha roses, somewhat lower growing; floribunda roses, taller and with fairly large single or semi-double flowers; and floribunda-grandiflora roses, with double flowers resembling hybrid teas. The finest effect is achieved by planting several specimens of the same strain together. Floribunda roses are generally very strong and require little attention; this is why they are used on a large scale in public gardens. The following are reliable strains: 'Allgold', yellow, semi-double, 70cm; 'Betty Prior', red purple, single, 100–150cm; 'Chinatown', yellow, double, fragrant, 170cm; 'Duftwolke', rose red, double, delightful scent, 90cm; 'Diablotin', orange, semi-double, 60cm; 'Europeana', blood red, semi-double, 90cm; 'Fresco', orange and yellow, double, 70cm;

'Friesia', yellow, double, fragrant, 50cm; 'Georgette', pale pink, double, fragrant, with dark foliage, 60cm; 'Lili Marlene', velvety red, single, 80cm; 'Maria Mathilde', white, double, 70cm; 'Olala', blood red, double, 80cm; 'Paprika', bright stone-red, semi-double, 70cm; 'Pernille Poulsen', salmon pink, double, with a long flowering season, 70cm; 'Queen Elizabeth', a well known bright-pink, double rose, 150cm; 'Sarabande', orange red, single, 70cm; 'Saratoga', creamy white, double, 80cm; 'Scarlet Queen Elizabeth', coral red, double, 130cm; 'Snow White', pure white, double, 90cm, also available under the name 'Iceberg'; 'Sunday Times', cherry red, double, 60cm.

Climbing roses: Shrubs varying in origin, with shoots which may reach 6m in length. They usually flower from June to August. Some strains have large, double flowers (climbing hybrid teas); others have single or semi-double, smaller flowers. Modern climbers usually have a slightly longer flowering season and are brighter in colour than the old-fashioned strains, which flower mainly in July. Good strains are 'American Pillar', 4–6m tall, not continuous flowering, with single, red-purple flowers with a white centre, in clusters; 'Bantry Bay', pink, semi-double flowers with a delightful scent, to 3m; 'Climbing Sarabande', red, semi-double, faint scent, 4m; 'Compassion', pale apricot, double, fragrant, with a continuing flowering season, 3m; 'Constance Spry', a well known old-fashioned rose with fragrant, double, fairly flat pink flowers, 2.5m; 'Danse des Sylphes', geranium red, double, 3m; 'Dortmund', single, red, 2.5m; 'Golden Showers', a very well known yellow, semi-double rose, flowering continuously, 3m; 'Handel', pale pink with white, double, flowering continuously, 3.5m; 'Leverkusen', pale yellow, double, 3m; 'New Dawn', a very well known, pale-red, delightfully fragrant rose, double, 2.5m; 'Parkdirektor Riggers', blood red, single, very strong, 4.5m in height; 'Paul's Scarlet Climber', well known, double red rose, 3m; 'Violet-blue', an old-fashioned climbing rose with violet-blue, initially more red-purple, semi-double flowers, faintly scented, 4–6m; 'Zepherine Drouhin', an old rose, delightfully fragrant, semi-double, flowering continuously, thornless.

Miniature or dwarf roses: Bushes to 50cm tall which flower continuously from June to September. They are actually miniature versions of the two preceding groups. 'Amourette' produces double white flowers, height 30cm; 'Elegant Pearl' has a great profusion of white flowers, 40cm; 'Finnstar' has pale-orange, double flowers, 35cm; 'Machana' is pure yellow, double, 35cm; 'Minerette', pale-pink, semi-double flowers, 35cm; 'The Fairy', small, double, pink flowers in compact clusters, 30cm, flowers continuously; 'Yellow Doll', yellow, double, fading flowers, 30cm; 'Zwergkönigin', dark-red, semi-double flowers, 35cm.

Standards: Roses from the first two groups which have been grafted on stock and look like small trees. If a

Rosa glutinosa

Rosa laevigata

Rosa macrantha 'Raubritter'

Rosa moyesii 'Nevada'

climber is grafted on stock, the result will be a weeping standard. The most sensitive area of a rose, the junction between scion and stock, is thus well above ground. In winter we ensure that this spot cannot freeze by covering it with fir branches or straw. In principle any of the roses mentioned above can be grafted on stock, but in practice the choice is fairly restricted. Buy one with a regular crown and three grafts.

Botanical (old-fashioned) roses: Shrubs to 3m in height, many of them flowering in June, some in May, others a little later. The flowers are usually single, sometimes delightfully scented. Many species produce magnificent, brightly coloured rose-hips in autumn. They often develop into spreading bushes and take up a lot of space. Among well known species are:

Rosa blanda (syn *R. fraxinifolia*), maple-leaved rose: A shrub to 2m in height and 3m across, with oval to obovate leaves, usually 7 in number, smooth flower-stalks and single, pale-pink flowers and round hips.

Rosa canina, dog rose: Height to 3m, a shrub with hooked thorns and oval leaves. Single, pink or white flowers June–July, in groups of two or more. Oval red hips.

Rosa centifolia, cabbage rose: Height 2m, the same across. A strongly thorned bush with an open habit. Bright-green twigs with fairly round leaves and somewhat pendulous, double pink flowers, the outer petals longer than the inner. Flowering season June to July. In 'Muscosa', the moss rose, sepals and stalks are covered in mossy down. 'Blanche Moreau' is the white, 'Red Moss' the red, moss rose. 'Fantin-Latour' is a bushy shrub with fragrant, flat pink flowers and large dark leaves. In 'La Noblesse' the flowers are soft red. 'Petite de Hollande' has pale-pink, pompon-shaped flowers.

Rosa × damascena, damask rose: Height 3m, a shrub with hooked thorns and often bristles as well. Oval to oblong leaves, spiny leaf-stalks and large red or bluish flowers in groups of 5–10, June–July. Red hips.

Rosa gallica, French rose: A large bush with grey-green twigs; it develops runners. The thorns and the bristles drop easily. Fairly thick leaves, hairy on the reverse. Isolated, rose-red flowers in June, orange hips. 'Officinalis' is a well known form, 2.5m tall, with fragrant, double pink flowers. It flowers profusely and sometimes produces hips. 'Versicolor' ('Rosa Mundi') has striking white and rose-red striped flowers and dull-green foliage.

Rosa glauca (syn *R. ferruginea*, *R. rubrifolia*): Height 2m, a bush with arching twigs covered in reddish bloom. Few, almost straight, thorns and conspicuously blue-green foliage, sometimes tinged with red. Pink flowers June–July, followed by red hips. Very decorative.

Rosa glutinosa: Develops into a 30–70cm tall, dense spiny bush with oval leaves, densely covered in glands. Small single pink flowers in June, followed by orange hips.

Rosa laevigata, Cherokee rose: Height 6m, fresh green foliage and fragrant, single white flowers in June. Large, oval, bristly hips.

Rosa macrantha: Height 1.5m, a bush with spreading, arching branches and pale-pink, single or semi-double flowers in the last two weeks of June, red hips. 'Raubritter' grows to 1m in height and 2m across with clusters of spherical, pink, semi-double flowers June–August.

Rosa moschata, musk rose: Height 1–4m, the leaves composed of 5–7 pointed oval leaflets. White flowers in clusters of up to 10, musk scented; brownish hips.

Rosa moyesii: Height 2–3m, a bush with arching twigs and numerous short, straight thorns. Pointed oval leaves and dark-red flowers in June, followed by oval hips, pinched in close to the tip. 'Geranium' has scarlet flowers, a compact shape to 2m, and orange hips. 'Nevada' produces an abundance of large white flowers June–July. 'Sealing Wax' has pale-pink flowers.

Rosa multiflora (syn *R. polyantha*), multiflorous rose: Partially evergreen, with few spines, obovate leaves and profuse clusters of small white flowers June–July. Small, brownish hips.

Rosa pimpinellifolia (syn *R. spinosissima*), Scotch rose, burnet rose: A dense shrub, 2m tall, with underground runners and stiff, thorny, bristly twigs. White, pink or yellow flowers May–June, black hips. One of the best known strains is 'Frühlingsmorgen', with large, single, pink with pale-yellow flowers, often flowering for the second time in late summer.

Rosa rubiginosa (syn *R. eglanteria*), sweet briar: A vigorous shrub, 2.5m in height, with very thorny branches and single pink flowers; fine orange hips. Even when not in flower the bush is apple scented.

Rosa rugosa, Japanese rose: Height 1–1.5m, fresh green foliage and numerous thorns. Large red or white, delightfully fragrant flowers and edible, fairly large, orange hips.

Rosa pimpinellifolia 'Frühlingsmorgen'

Rosa rubiginosa

Rubus

Bramble

A large genus of predominantly deciduous shrubs, some grown for their fruit, others for their ornamental value.
Situation The *Rubus* in the photograph is a little known ground-covering plant. A much better known species is *R. tricolor*, which tolerates a great deal of shade. The species with bloomed twigs are particularly ornamental in winter. Most species will grow both in sun and in partial shade, even in very poor soil.
Soil Standard garden soil.
Propagation By division and from cuttings.

Rubus calycinoides (syn *R. fockeanus*): An evergreen, ground-covering plant, to 10cm tall, suitable for partially shaded, sheltered spots and damp soil. It is a creeping shrub with self-rooting twigs, a few small spines and white flowers May–June, followed by red fruit. Cover in winter.
Rubus leucodermis: Height to 2.5m, a bush with spiny twigs covered in blue bloom. Scant clusters of flowers May–June, followed by good tasting, bloomed berries.

Rubus calycinoides

Salix alba 'Tristis'

Salix

Willow

Deciduous shrubs or tall trees, and a common feature in the landscape, for instance the pollard willow, usually *Salix alba*, and the large weeping willow, *S. alba* 'Tristis', with its striking yellow twigs in spring. Newly established gardens frequently contain standard willows, producing attractive catkins in spring. Willows with twisted branches are also very popular, but they frequently grow too large for gardens. Willows are dioecious, and the male catkins are particularly attractive. The simple alternate leaves are usually long and narrow. Many willows are vigorous and fast-growing.
Situation The trees and large shrubs are suitable only for parks and large gardens. Those with unusual habit or fine foliage colouring are often beautiful planted singly. For the smaller garden there are numerous small shrubs and grafted (weeping) standards. Some species will grow both in damp and in very dry soil, but as a rule willows prefer moist soil. They may, among other things, be used as soil-retainers, as edging plants, as low hedges, to cover slopes, in rock gardens and in large containers. Provide a sunny or partially shaded position.

Soil Willows are fairly undemanding, but they enjoy loamy soil.
Propagation From winter cuttings. Sawn-off stumps will start into growth if planted in earth.

Salix alba, bat willow: A tree to 25m in height, 10–12m across. Downy, olive-brown-yellow twigs, often slightly pendulous. The leaves are spear shaped and downy on both surfaces; catkins April–May. 'Tristis', the yellow weeping form, 15m in height, has a broad crown and twigs drooping to the ground.

Salix caprea, goat willow: A tree or shrub to 6m in height, with grey-green wood and oblong to oval, dull-glossy dark-green leaves, blue green and felty underneath. 'Pendula' is a well known standard form. The correct name of the male weeping form is 'Kilmarnock'; it has large silvery-white catkins and the stamens later turn golden yellow. Its female counterpart is called 'Weeping Sally', but this cultivar is grown far less often. Naturally it has no stamens.

Salix daphnoides: A vigorous, erect-growing shrub which can be pruned in the shape of a tree. Limp, very brittle branches. Spear-shaped green leaves and very beautiful blue-bloomed twigs. A particularly decorative willow. Provide good support.

Salix hastata (syn *S. wehrhahnii*): A bush to 80cm in height, with oval leaves and large, silvery-white catkins March–April. 'Wehrhahnii' is the best known garden form.

Salix irrorata: A bush to 2m tall, with purple-bloomed twigs, very beautiful.

Salix matsudana: Bare, yellow-green twigs and narrow, spear-shaped leaves, yellow green underneath. 'Tortuosa', the corkscrew willow, is a well known form, 9m in height, fast growing and with spirally twisted branches, twigs and leaves. Very popular among florists and flower arrangers.

Salix purpurea, purple willow: A shrub to 4m in height and as much across, with red to yellow twigs and spatula-shaped, often opposite, foliage. The reverse of the leaves is pale- or blue-green. Will thrive in dry soil. 'Gracilis' is a low-growing form, 0.5–1.5m, sometimes used as ground-cover. The foliage is silver grey, brown red in autumn. This strain is also sold as a standard.

Salix repens, creeping willow: Height to 1m and at least as much across; a shrub with oval to spear-shaped leaves, blue green on the underside. Will grow in dry as well as in damp soil. 'Nitida', 50cm, has foliage covered in silvery down.

Salix sachalinensis: 'Sekka' is the garden form most often cultivated; height 4.5m, 3m across. These willows are conspicious because of their flattened brown branches, often used in flower arrangements. A profusion of fairly large catkins.

Salix hastata 'Wehrhahnii'

Salix matsudana 'Tortuosa'

Sambucus canadensis 'Maxima'

Sambucus racemosa 'Plumosa Aurea'

Sambucus

Elder

Fast-growing, deciduous shrubs with delightfully scented flowers which can be made into wine or lemonade. They are characterised by their thick, pithy twigs and their opposite, pinnate foliage. The flower umbels are followed by berry-like fruits, which can be made into jam.

Situation   The elder is a veritable pioneer. Initially the trees can serve as windbreaks for other plants and provide a large patch of green in an otherwise bare garden. Once the other plants are established, the elders may be pulled up. Perhaps it would be sensible to leave one specimen, for they are thought to keep out evil spirits. Provide a sunny or partially shaded position. Most species will even tolerate deep shade.

As a rule, elders are at their finest if they are cut back to about 20–30cm every year. This may be done in the autumn. They will rapidly start into growth in spring and will every year reach a height of 2–3m:

Soil   Elders will grow in any type of soil and even improve it. Old specimens are found in friable, nutritious soil, on the acid side.

Propagation   Very easily increased from cuttings taken in winter.

Sambucus canadensis, American elder: Height to 4m and as much across; young shoots grow from buds on the roots. The twigs are often covered in bloom and contain few lenticels. The foliage consists of 7–9 spear-shaped, pointed leaflets. Flattened white flower umbels June–July, followed by dark-purple berries. The foliage turns purple red in autumn. In 'Maxima' both foliage and inflorescence are larger than in the species. 'Aurea' has yellow foliage and cherry-red berries.

Sambuca nigra, European elder: A shrub or small tree, to 6m in height, without root runners. Grey twigs and numerous lenticels. The foliage usually consists of 5 pointed oval leaflets, pale green underneath. Yellow-white flowers June–July, followed by black berries. 'Aurea' has golden-yellow foliage. In 'Laciniata' the foliage is regular, and deeply incised. This form is resistant to sea wind and tolerates a great deal of shade.

Sambucus racemosa, red elder: Height about 4m and as much across, a shrub with bare, pale-brown twigs. The foliage is composed of 5–7 oval to spear-shaped, pointed leaflets. Yellow-green flowers in pendulous, spherical clusters as early as April or May. The berries are red. 'Plumosa' has deeply incised leaflets, initially bronze to brown in colour. 'Plumosa Aurea' also has deeply incised foliage, initially brownish, but later golden yellow. The autumn colouring is particularly fine. 'Tenuifolia' has very finely divided foliage.

Sarcococca

This dwarf shrub retains its foliage in winter. Shoots from the tree stool may develop into saplings. Inconspicuous, but delightfully scented flowers early in the year.

Situation Very suitable for gardens containing tall trees, for *Sarcococca* tolerates a great deal of shade. A partially shaded position is also satisfactory, but the shrub should definitely not be planted in full sun. In small gardens it is attractive planted singly, in larger gardens it may be planted in groups.

Soil Nutritious, humus-rich soil. Lime is tolerated.

Propagation From seed, cuttings or rooted runners.

Sarcococca humilis (syn *S. hookeriana* var *humilis*): An erect-growing, evergreen bush with dense ramification, to 50cm tall and the same across. The leaves are 3–8cm long, dark green and glossy, wedge shaped at the base. Small white flowers in axillary racemes January–March, followed by black berries.

Sarcococca humilis

Sciadopitys verticillata

Sciadopitys

Umbrella Fir

Slow-growing, evergreen conifers, with needles arranged in an unusual manner. It will eventually attain a perfectly spherical shape. In its native country, Japan, it reaches a height of 30m, here only 10–20m.

Situation It will show to best advantage free-standing in a lawn or surrounded by low-growing bushes. Provide a spot in full sun, somewhat sheltered against wind. The tree is entirely winter-hardy.

Soil Will do best in nutritious, neutral to slightly acid soil with an adequate moisture content.

Propagation From seed.

Sciadopitys verticillata: A narrow tree with pyramidal habit. The needles are dark green and glossy, 8–12cm long and surround the branches like the spokes of a partially open umbrella. The tree flowers in May, the male inflorescences being grouped at the tips of the branches. The cones are green, but turn brown in the course of ripening, which takes as much as two years. The oval, mature cones are 8–12cm long.

Sequoiadendron

Mammoth Tree

In ideal conditions the mammoth tree may grow to a height of nearly 100m, when the base of the trunk will be no less than 10m in diameter. It grows at a rate of 0.5–1m a year. Needless to say this evergreen conifer is of majestic appearance.

Situation   Do not plant it unless you are able to provide a sheltered, very roomy position. In course of time the crown will grow to at least 20m across. Other requirements are full sun and damp, well-drained soil.

Soil   Nutritious soil, tolerates lime.

Propagation   From seed or cuttings.

Sequoiadendron giganteum (syn *Wellingtonia gigantea*), redwood: A narrow pyramidal tree, which in our part of the world may reach 70m. Its needles are 3–7mm long, awl shaped, blue green, turning brown after two or three seasons. The 4–7cm long cones take two years to ripen and are oval in shape. The soft, brown-red bark may be as much as 60cm thick in mature trees.

Sequoiadendron giganteum

Sinarundinaria nitida

Sinarundinaria

A magnificent fine-leaved bamboo species, evergreen in sheltered positions. Initially the stalks are erect growing, at a later stage they arch.

Situation   Provide a sunny or partially shaded position in adequately moisture-retaining soil. In summer wind is no problem, but in winter the plant will suffer; the foliage deteriorates and largely drops. *Sinarundinaria* may be used as an informal hedge; it looks very fine in a water garden or in a Japanese garden. Excellent in combination with large-leaved saxifrage, large-leaved foliage plants such as *Rodgersia*, irises, ferns and all types of grasses.

Soil   Standard garden soil.

Propagation   By division.

Sinarundinaria nitida (syn *Arundinaria nitida*): A vigorously spreading ornamental grass, to 2.5m in height, with green-yellow bamboo stalks, initially covered in waxy bloom. The leaves are 7–12cm long, up to 25mm wide.

Skimmia

Slow-growing, evergreen shrubs, grown for the sake of their striking flower buds and bright-red berries; not 100 per cent hardy. They are dioecious and in order to obtain berries it is therefore necessary to plant male and female specimens together.

Situation   Will do well in partially shaded positions, in moisture-retaining soil which must be on the acid side, especially in the case of *Skimmia reevesiana*. Provide a sheltered position, where they are protected from strong wind.

Soil   Acid soil, rich in humus.

Propagation   From seed and cuttings.

Skimmia × foremanii (syn *S. japonica × S. reevesiana*): Height to 1.25m and as much across. Leathery, broad-oval leaves and white flower plumes followed by red berries.

Skimmia japonica (syn *S. fragrans*, the male plant, *S. oblata*, the female): Height to 1.5m, 2m across. White flower plumes in May. Both flower buds and berries are retained for a long time.

Skimmia japonica

Sophora japonica

Sophora

Deciduous or evergreen trees or shrubs with pinnate foliage and butterfly-like flowers. The tree discussed below bears its flowers at a time when few other trees are in bloom, namely August. The seed has time to ripen only if the weather is warm in the autumn. An important characteristic is the sharp scent which one can smell if a twig is cut.

Situation   In a sunny spot *Sophora* is attractive planted singly, but it also looks well emerging from a group of shrubs. The flowers are visited by bees.

Soil   Nutritious soil, for example calciferous loam, is essential if the plant is to grow well.

Propagation   From seed.

Sophora japonica: A tree, 25m in height and 15m across, with dense, circular crown and bare green twigs. The alternate leaves are composed of 7–17 leaflets, 2–6cm long, oval, smooth edged and downy on the reverse. White flowers in up to 30cm long plumes; seeds in pods.

Sorbaria

False Spiraea

Strong, deciduous shrubs belonging to the rose family. They start into growth early in the year, have pinnate foliage, and in summer produce large terminal plumes of creamy-white flowers.

Situation *Sorbaria* plants grow in full sun as well as in shade, in poor as well as in rich soil. They develop numerous root-runners and may be used as soil-retainers. They look attractive in the shrub border, but are also very suitable for a free-standing position, for instance near a water garden. Before they start into growth in spring they should be severely cut back.

Soil Standard garden soil.

Propagation By removing root-suckers or from cuttings taken in summer.

Sorbaria aitchisonii: Height to 3m, 3.5m across, brown-red twigs. In July and August the shrub produces elongated white flower plumes. The berries are erect growing.

Sorbaria sorbifolia (syn *Spiraea sorbifolia*): A shrub to 2m in height and as much across, with erect-growing twigs. Erect-growing white flower plumes June–July.

Sorbaria aitchisonii

Sorbus americana 'Belmonte'

Sorbus

Mountain Ash, Rowan

Deciduous trees or shrubs with decorative foliage, sometimes with fine autumn colouring, and white flower umbels, followed by strikingly coloured berries. The leaves are alternate, simple, pinnate or of an intermediate shape. The flowers often have a disagreeable scent. The berries are white, yellow, orange to red, pink or brown.

Situation Rowans do not grow beyond 15m and the lower growing species, in particular, fit well into small gardens. They will thrive in sunny or partially shaded positions, in damp rather than moist soil. Birds adore the berries and it is therefore an excellent plant if you want to create your own bird sanctuary. Rowans are also popular for use as windbreaks, partly because of their rapid growth. The finest species look well planted singly; they do not create too much shade. *Sorbus aria* and *S. intermedia* are wind-resistant. Because they are sensitive to scab they are, for the time being, not planted on a very large scale.

Soil Undemanding; will grow in poor soil.

Propagation From seed, which has to be kept in damp

sand for a year before it will germinate. A number of species are bud-grafted on *S. intermedia* to create better anchorage and make them suitable for clay soil. Garden forms are grafted.

Sorbus alnifolia (syn *Micromeles alnifolia*): An erect-growing tree, to 12m in height, with glossy red-brown twigs and simple, oval leaves with a short point. Fine autumn colouring. White flowers May–June, followed by spherical red and yellow berries.

Sorbus americana, mountain ash: Height 8m, a tree with red-brown twigs and elongated, sticky buds. The foliage is composed of 13–17 spear-shaped leaflets. White flowers May–June and numerous fairly small red berries. The finest form is 'Belmonte', a compact tree with an oval crown, orange autumn colouring and a profusion of orange-red berries.

Sorbus aria, whitebeam: Height to 10m, a tree with grey, felty twigs and sticky green buds. Simple, oval, serrated leaves, felty and white underneath. White flowers in May and orange-red berries. 'Lutescens' has a broad-pyramidal crown and initially silvery foliage. 'Magnifica' is a large tree with a cone-shaped crown and large, dull-green leaves, white on the reverse, later turning felty green. Both strains are wind-resistant and prefer calcareous soil.

Sorbus aucuparia, native mountain ash: Height 10–15m; a tree with red-brown twigs and hairy, non-sticky buds; composite foliage, downy but later bare underneath; and orange autumn colouring. Grey-white flowers in May; red berries from late July to October. 'Beissneri' grows to 15m, develops a thin crown and has a red-brown trunk and twigs; yellow autumn colouring. 'Edulis' has larger berries than the species, edible, but acid. 'Fastigiata' is a slow-growing columnar form, to 7m in height.

Sorbus cashmiriana: A small tree with an open crown. The composite leaves consist of 17–18 serrated leaflets. Red-purple flowers and white berries in pendent clusters. They are retained for a long time.

Sorbus decora: A small tree with a compact crown. The composite foliage usually consists of 15 elliptical dark-green leaflets. White flowers in May, followed by large scarlet berries in large clusters.

Sorbus hupehensis: 'November Pink' is a fine cultivar, a 7m tall tree with an open crown and fairly long pinnate leaves. White flowers in May, followed by pinkish berries with a red point; they remain on the tree until December.

Sorbus vilmorinii. Height 6m with an open crown and arching branches. Fern-like pinnate leaves with fine autumn colouring. White flowers in June, carmine-red berries.

Sorbus aucuparia 'Beissneri'

Sorbus hupehensis 'November Pink'

Spartium

Spanish Gorse

Deciduous shrub, belonging to the pea family. Its yellow flowers brighten the garden in late summer. The reed-like green twigs give the plant an attractive appearance throughout the year, but unfortunately they are sensitive to frost.

Situation   This gorse enjoys a sunny or partially shaded position in fairly dry soil. It is attractive planted singly, but is also frequently planted in groups. It likes lime, something that should be borne in mind if you want to plant it in the heather garden, where the soil is usually on the acid side. If the shrub has been damaged by frost in winter, cut it back in March, being careful not to cut too deep into the old wood.

Soil   Standard, possibly calcareous soil.

Propagation   From seed.

Spartium junceum: A fast-growing shrub, to 3m in height and 2.5m across, with tough, reed-like twigs. The leaves soon drop. Bright yellow flowers in terminal clusters in September. The pods are brown.

Spartium junceum

Spiraea × arguta

Spiraea

Deciduous shrubs with alternate simple leaves and white or rose-red flowers in round or elongated umbels. Spring-flowering forms flower on the previous year's wood and are thinned out a little after flowering has ceased; summer-flowering types flower on new shoots and may be cut down to just above ground level in spring, though pruning is usually restricted to renovation.

Situation   Provide a sunny or partially shaded position. As a rule, the sunnier the position, the better *Spiraea* will grow. The finest species may be used as specimen plants. Low-growing species serve to form shrubberies or as edging plants. The very smallest might even be given a spot in the rock garden. Taller forms are planted in the shrub border.

Soil   Nutritious garden soil.

Propagation   From cuttings and by layering.

Spiraea × arguta: The result of crossing *S. multiflora* and *S. thunbergii*. A graceful shrub with thin, arching branches; height to 2.5m. Fresh green, spear-shaped foliage, and white flower umbels April–May.

Spiraea Billardii hybrids: The products of crossing *S. douglasii* and *S. salicifolia*. Height 2m and as much across. Round, felty, subsequently often bare twigs with oblong leaves, grey and felty underneath. Dense clusters of pink flowers June–August. There are several strains.

Spiraea bullata: Dense ramification; height to 40cm. Dark-green, oval, slightly curled leaves and dark-pink flower clusters June–July. Suitable for use as an edging plant.

Spiraea Bumalda hybrids: The results of crossing *S. albiflora* and *S. japonica*. To 1m tall shrubs with striped, often peeling twigs and oval to spear-shaped foliage. Dense umbels of rose-red flowers July–September. Profuse flowering will be encouraged if the plants are cut back to ground level in spring. The best known form is 'Anthony Waterer', with small leaves, often flecked with white, and red-purple flowers. Tolerates a fair amount of shade and is suitable for use in low hedges.

Spiraea chamaedryfolia (syn *S. flexuosa*): This species tolerates a great deal of shade. Up to 2m tall and as much across, it has arching branches and bare, grey-brown twigs, peeling at a later stage. Obovate leaves, bright green underneath. Dense umbels of white flowers May–June.

Spiraea × cinerea: A cross between *S. cana* and *S. hypericifolia*. Dense ramification; a shrub to 1m in height, with small, narrow, pale-green or grey-green leaves. Bright white flowers in small clusters April to early May. 'Grefsheim' is the best choice; it flowers profusely.

Spiraea japonica: Height just over 1m; purple-brown twigs and oval to oblong leaves, pale- or blue-green on the underside. Pink flowers in dense clusters in summer. 'Little Princess' does not grow beyond 50cm.

Spiraea nipponica: Height to 2.5m; a shrub with angular, arching branches. Oval to broad obovate, fairly small leaves, blue green underneath. White, semi-spherical flower clusters in June. 'Halward Silver', profuse flowering, and 'Snow-mound', very hardy with an exuberant inflorescence and also referred to as *S. nipponica tosaensis*, are beautiful cultivars.

Spiraea salicifolia: A 3m tall shrub with bare, somewhat angular twigs and oblong to spear-shaped leaves, pale green on the reverse. It tolerates a great deal of shade and prefers damp soil. Fast growing, therefore it may be used to create a tall hedge. Pale-pink flower plumes June–July, dense and elongated-cylindrical in shape.

Spiraea × vanhouttei: The result of crossing *S. cantoniensis* and *S. trilobata*. Height 2m, the same across; a shrub with bare, red-brown, more or less round twigs. The branches arch and bear oval to egg-shaped, often slightly lobed foliage. White flower umbels May–June.

Spiraea Bumalda hybrid 'Anthony Waterer'

Spiraea × vanhouttei

Staphylea

Bladder-nut

Large, deciduous shrubs with white flower plumes and strikingly shaped fruits.
Situation Attractive planted singly in a sunny or partially shaded spot. Also suitable as an edging plant or planted in groups in the shrub border.
Soil Standard garden soil, humus-rich in the case of *S. pinnata*. *S. colchica* requires damp, acid soil.
Propagation From seed and by layering. *S. pinnata* can also be increased from cuttings.

Staphylea colchica: Height over 3m, 2m across; a shrub with erect-growing, reddish twigs and 3- to 5-fold pointed oval, sharply serrated foliage, 5–12cm long. White flowers in large, erect-growing or slightly angled plumes in May, followed by oval fruits.
Staphylea pinnata: Height to 5m, 3m across; a shrub with erect-growing twigs bearing 5- to 7-fold leaves, 5–10cm long, oval and pointed, the underside blue green. White flowers in pendent plumes May–June. Spherical, inflated fruits with yellow-brown seeds.

Staphylea colchica

Stephanandra tanakae

Stephanandra

Small, deciduous shrubs with gracefully arching twigs and fine autumn colouring.
Situation A sunny or partially shaded position. The species illustrated is the tallest form and may be planted singly or in groups. *Stephanandra incisa* is also used in informal hedges and the strain 'Crispa' is a vigorous and very popular ground-covering plant.
Soil Rich in humus.
Propagation From cuttings and by division.

Stephanandra incisa: Just over 1m in height, 2m across. A shrub with dense ramification and red-brown twigs. The leaves are 2–5cm long, incised, lobed and serrated. Whitish flowers in up to 5cm long plumes in June. The strain 'Crispa' remains smaller, at most 60cm tall and 1.5m across. The twigs arch down to the ground and bear curled leaves, more deeply and irregularly incised than in the species.
Stephanandra tanakae: Height to almost 2m, the same across. The brown-red, angled twigs bear oval, pointed leaves, 3–8cm long, sharply lobed and serrated.

Stranvaesia

A partially evergreen shrub of broad-fan shape. The flowers are followed by attractive red berries. Unfortunately it is sensitive to scab.
Situation Beautiful planted singly; not suitable for small gardens. It will thrive in sun and in partial shade, in fairly dry as well as in dampish soil. *Stranvaesia* can also be planted in a large container, or in groups in the shrub border.
Soil Nutritious garden soil.
Propagation From cuttings or seed.

Stranvaesia davidiana: Height to 2.5m, as much across. A shrub with glossy green, leathery leaves which are retained for a long time. The leaves are 6–12cm long and 2–4cm wide, oblong to spear-shaped, bare. The leaf-stalk is hairy and reddish in colour. The white flowers appear in broad, downy clusters in June; the berries turn red late in summer. 'Lutea' has orange-yellow berries.

Stranvaesia davidiana

Styrax obassia

Styrax

Trees or shrubs with alternate foliage, the leaves often downy. Clusters of white flowers in spring, followed by one- or two-seeded berries. Although quite hardy, *Styrax* is not well known.
Situation Will thrive in sunny or partially shaded positions in light soil. Their size makes them unsuitable for small gardens. Attractive planted singly, but also in groups in the shrub border and as an edging plant.
Soil Sandy soil.
Propagation From seed, by layering or from cuttings.

Styrax japonica: Height to 5m and almost as much across; a shrub with thin, pliable twigs. The leaves are 4–8cm long, oval to oblong, dentated. Bell-shaped, delightfully fragrant white flowers in fairly short, pendent clusters May–June.
Styrax obassia: Height to 9m, 7m across; a shrub with erect-growing twigs. The round-oval leaves are 7–16cm long, delicately felted underneath. The fragrant white flowers appear in arching clusters May–June.

Symphoricarpos

Snowberry

Very well known deciduous shrubs, in autumn covered in an abundance of white or red berries.
Situation   The berries are produced in greatest profusion in full sun, nevertheless snowberries can be successfully grown under trees since they tolerate a great deal of shade. They will thrive in almost any type of soil. Many species make excellent hedges and *S. × chenaultii* 'Hancock' is a vigorous ground-covering plant. Twigs with berries will keep well in water.
Soil   Standard garden soil.
Propagation   The species from root-suckers; strains from cuttings.

Symphoricarpos albus: A 1–1.5m tall shrub with erect-growing shoots and elliptical leaves; round to oval white berries. The variety *laevigatus* grows a little taller and develops numerous runners. Bundles of pale-red flowers July–August. The berries will last until Christmas.
Symphoricarpos × doorenbosii: The strain 'Magic Berry' grows to a height of 80cm; it is one of the hybrids created by crossing *S. albus* var *laevigatus* and *S. × chenaultii*.

Symphoricarpos × doorenbosii 'Magic Berry'

Syringa komarowii

Syringa

Lilac

Widely grown shrubs with delightfully scented flower clusters May–June. *Syringa microphylla* flowers throughout the summer. Foliage is opposite, undivided; the flowers are always produced on the previous year's wood. Pruning is restricted to the flowering season, when the flowering branches are placed in water. In order to rejuvenate bare shrubs it is necessary to cut them back almost entirely.
Situation   Many of the modern hybrids are a little smaller than the species but can be used in fairly small gardens, especially if kept compact by pruning. They produce excellent cut flowers. *S. microphylla* 'Superba' is also suitable for a small garden. Other lilacs are planted at the back of a shrub border.
Soil   Nutritious, adequately moist garden soil.
Propagation   The species from seed, other forms by grafting or layering.

Syringa × chinensis, Rouen lilac: The product of crossing *S. × persica* and *S. vulgaris*. Height to 2m; a broad, erect-growing, bushy shrub with oval to spear-shaped foliage. Fragrant purple flowers in loose, pendulous plumes in May.

Syringa josikaea, Hungarian lilac: Height to 3m; a vigorous shrub with oval leaves, blue green on the reverse. Fragrant, short-stalked purple flowers in narrow plumes May–June.

Syringa komarowii: An erect-growing shrub with pale-brown, warty twigs, at least 4m in height and certainly no less across. Dense, oval plumes of pale-red flowers in June.

Syringa microphylla: Height to 1.5m; a shrub with round-oval, downy, grey-green leaves. 'Superba' is cultivated more widely than the species. This strain produces rose-red flowers May–October.

Syringa reflexa: To 3m tall shrub with oval-oblong leaves and large arching plumes of dark-pink flowers, a little paler inside, at the end of June.

Syringa vulgaris, common lilac: A vigorous, erect-growing shrub, 4–7m in height, with broad oval leaves, pale green on the reverse. White, pink or purple flowers in fairly narrow plumes. There are many magnificent hybrids, for example 'Charles X', single flowered, purple; 'Mont Blanc', with single white flowers late in the season. Double-flowered types are 'Charles Joly', purple red; 'Katherine Havemeyer', violet; 'Madame Lemoine', white.

Syringa vulgaris 'Charles X'

Tamarix chinensis

Tamarix

Tamarisk

Feathery, deciduous shrubs. Those flowering May–June are pruned after the flowering season; those that flower in mid summer are pruned early in spring.

Situation Tamarisks are resistant to wind, including sea wind; this is why they are grown on a large scale in coastal areas. *T. tetrandra* is not very winter-hardy and must be protected from frost in severe winters. All tamarisks enjoy a sunny or partially shaded position. They are beautiful free standing, but also in groups. Occasionally they are trained as espaliers.

Soil Nutritious, porous soil. *T. parviflora*, in particular, tolerates a high salt content.

Propagation From cuttings.

Tamarix chinensis (var *T. odessana*, *T. pentandra*, *T. ramosissima*): A shrub, 2–4m in height and 3m across, with arching twigs bearing bluish foliage. Pale-red flower clusters June–August.

Tamarix parviflora: Height to 3m and the same across; a shrub with dark twigs and dark-pink flower clusters in May.

Taxodium distichum

Taxodium

Swamp Cypress

Deciduous conifer which, at an advanced age and in adequately moist soil develops characteristic respiratory roots emerging from the soil or from the water like bent knees. They serve to supply the tree with oxygen. Young plants are not entirely hardy, but older trees will survive our winters without difficulty.

Situation Their size makes them suitable only for parks and large gardens. Provide a sunny position in damp or wet soil. Excellent for a free-standing position.
Soil Humus-rich soil.
Propagation From seed or cuttings.

Taxodium distichum: Height to 30m, 10m across; a tree with a symmetrical, cone-shaped habit. The bark is red brown. The pale-green leaves are 1–1.5cm long, awl-shaped and radially arranged on the long shoots, needle-shaped and arranged in rows on the short shoots. They turn brown in the autumn and drop together with the short shoots. Mature trees flower in spring and subsequently develop cones.

Taxus baccata used as a hedge

Taxus

Yew

Magnificent evergreen conifers, slow growing and long-lived. The flat needles are usually dark green, sometimes golden yellow. *Taxus* is very poisonous in all its parts though, contrary to what is generally believed, the red flesh of the berries is edible. However, beware of the seeds!

Situation Although the opposite is often maintained, *Taxus* will thrive only in full sun. Shade and dripping water are tolerated, but in such circumstances the yew will lose its beautiful habit and will turn into a withered monstrosity, reaching for the light. The golden-yellow forms in particular require plenty of light.

It is also a myth that *Taxus* is so strong and indestructible; in severe frost much of the foliage will turn brown. Fortunately the plant will start into growth again. This conifer also dislikes being touched. If rubbed against by passers-by, for example when it is used as a hedge, the foliage will die locally.

Nevertheless *Taxus* is an ideal hedging plant. It grows fairly slowly, 10cm per year, but grows to a ripe old age. The hedge in the photograph is several hundred years old. It is rather exaggeratedly tapered, but every hedge has to be tapered to some extent to avoid it growing bare at the base. The same applies if plants are grown close to a *Taxus* hedge; leave 0.5–1m space between. In addition to hedges, *Taxus* is also used for planting singly or for topiary. It is easily pruned into animal shapes.

Soil Will grow in any humus-rich garden soil, provided the water table is below 50cm. Annual feeding is essential in the case of hedges.

Propagation The species from seed; hedges are therefore somewhat variable in colour. Cultivars from cuttings taken in winter.

Taxus baccata, English yew: Height 10m; a tree or shrub with bare green twigs and 3cm long needles, glossy on the upper surface, pale green underneath. The seed is contained in red or yellow capsules. The following are well-known strains: 'Adpressa', a broad, fairly large shrub with dense ramification and fairly broad needles; 'Dovastoniana' has a broad-pyramidal habit, to 3m, the upper twigs arch; 'Dovastonii Aurea' has the same characteristics, but the twigs are yellow, the needles variegated yellow; 'Elegantissima' is one of the most popular variegated yellow strains, height to 10m; 'Fastigiata' initially has a narrow columnar shape, later a broad-elliptical shape with multiple tips; 'Fastigiata Aureomarginata' and 'Fastigiata Aurea' have variegated yellow needles; 'Lutea' is a small tree or shrub, to 10m in height, with yellow-orange berries and pointed green needles; 'Overeyenderi' develops a broader columnar shape with regular ramification and short, narrow needles; in 'Repandens' the horizontal branches adopt a broad, spreading habit, 50cm in height but sometimes as much as 3m across, its long, dark blue-green needles curving upwards; 'Semperaurea' is a fairly small, broad shrub with dense ramification and golden-yellow needles, beautiful all the year round; 'Washingtonii' has a broad, squat shape and yellow-green needles, bronze coloured in winter.

Taxus cuspidata: Resembles the previous species, but differs in that the bud-scales are sharply pointed and the needles are thicker, with an abrupt point. 'Aurescens' is a slow-growing dwarf form, to 1m in height, 3m across. The needles are yellow for most of the year. 'Nana' grows to approximately the same size and has short needles radiating in the shape of a star at the tips of the twigs.

Taxus × media: The result of crossing the two previous species. 'Hatfieldii' develops a broad, bushy shape and has dark-green needles, 'Hicksii' is broad-columnar, very suitable for hedges.

Taxus baccata 'Elegantissima'

Taxus × media 'Hatfieldii'

Thuja

Arbor Vitae

Thuja occidentalis

Thuja occidentalis 'Rheingold'

Evergreen conifers with fresh-green or yellow foliage and an unusual scent when rubbed. Flattened twigs, characteristically vertical in the case of the Chinese arbor vitae. The small cones are often hidden behind the foliage. Many *Thuja* become somewhat discoloured towards the approach of winter, or turn slightly brown after being transplanted. In spring, or once the plants have taken root, the colour will recover. Nevertheless the hardiness of *Thuja* is limited; in a severe winter many *Thuja* hedges may die, especially in positions unprotected from east winds and where the soil underneath has been carefully raked, allowing the frost to penetrate. According to an ancient European peasant custom, the placenta of a new-born baby is buried and an arbor vitae is planted on top.

Situation There are a number of *Thuja* species and strains which grow fairly rapidly and are suitable for creating a fine hedge, the more so as they are not very prone to becoming bare at the base. *Thuja* is moreover less expensive than, for example, yew. Plant in a sunny or partially shaded position in moisture-retaining soil. There are a large number of compact, small-growing ornamental forms suitable for small gardens or rock gardens, preferably planted singly in order that their fine shape shows to best advantage. Their natural shape is so attractive that pruning is rarely necessary, especially in hedges.

Soil Friable sandy or loamy soil.

Propagation The species from seed, cultivars usually from cuttings.

Thuja occidentalis, American arbor vitae: A pyramidal tree, to 20m in height and 6m across, with dense, fairly horizontal ramification. The twigs are covered in dull or slightly glossy, yellow-green scales, never white on the reverse. This species is particularly aromatic when the foliage is rubbed. Cones with 8–10 scales, to 1cm long.

Low-growing forms: 'Danica' is a spherical shrub, to 1m tall, with green foliage and practically vertical branches; in winter the foliage is somewhat brown green; 'Globosa' is similar, but has denser ramification and more grey-green foliage in winter; 'Golden Globe' is a low-growing, spherical conifer with sulphur-yellow foliage, particularly striking in winter; 'Holmstrup' has a squat habit in the shape of a broad cone, the dark-green foliage does not discolour in winter; 'Hoveyi' is egg-shaped, bright green; 'Little Gem' has a flattened spherical shape and dark-green foliage, larger across than in height it has very fine, sometimes slightly curled ramification; 'Pygmaea' has a dense habit, taller than it is broad, fairly flat twigs and somewhat glossy scales; 'Recurva Nana' is cone-shaped, the tips of the twigs twisted and turned upwards, fresh green; 'Rheingold' has a spherical to broad cone-shaped habit, with golden-yellow to bronze-coloured foliage, partly scale-shaped, partly needle-shaped; 'Smaragd' is not very vigorous, cone-shaped, the fine foliage fresh green even in winter; 'Tiny Tim' has a low, spherical shape, the foliage is grey green, bronze coloured in winter; 'Woodwardii' to 2m, fairly fast growing, is a spherical shrub with green foliage, turning brown in winter.

Taller forms: 'Aurea', height to 15m, is a broad cone-shaped tree with golden foliage turning more bronze coloured in winter; 'Elegantissima' develops a narrow cone shape, height to about 5m, the foliage dark green and glossy, but yellow-white at the tips, turning brown in winter; 'Europe Gold' has an erect-growing, pyramidal habit, but does not grow so tall, its golden-yellow foliage becomes more orange-yellow in winter; 'Hetz Wintergreen' is fast growing, cone-shaped, with dark-green foliage even in winter; 'Lutea' has bright yellow foliage and develops a dense, pyramidal shape; 'Pyramidalis Compacta' forms a fresh green column, as does 'Rosenthalii', which has dark foliage; 'Semperaurea' is broad, erect growing, to 10m, the glossy green foliage yellow at the tips, a strong strain; 'Spiralis' is unusual with erect-growing, slightly twisted twigs with fern-like ramification, pyramidal shape; 'Wareana' is fairly fast growing, with a broad pyramidal shape and blue-green foliage; 'Wareana Lutescens' is similar in shape, but has initially bright-green, later dark-yellow foliage.

For hedges: 'Malonyana', cone-shaped and of dense habit, has green foliage which does not discolour; 'Pyramidalis Compacta' is narrow, erect-growing in shape, with fresh-green foliage, even in winter; 'Rosenthalii' has a somewhat broader, erect-growing habit and green foliage; 'Skogholm' resembles the previous form, but retains its colour better; 'Techny' is a new cultivar for dark-green hedges.

Thuja orientalis, Chinese arbor vitae: A slow-growing, dense, egg-shaped shrub, to 8m in height. Planted less frequently than the previous species, since in severe winters it is damaged by frost. Because of the unusual ramification it is a striking conifer, well worth growing. 'Aurea Nana' is a popular dwarf form, egg-shaped, slightly flattened at the top, with bright-yellow foliage, bronze coloured in winter. 'Elegantissima' may grow to 5m; it is cone-shaped and has yellow foliage, turning golden bronze in winter.

Thuja plicata, Western red cedar, giant arbor vitae: Fast growing, it may reach as much as 60m in height. It is a pyramidal tree or shrub; at the base the trunk is very thick. Flat, usually erect-growing twigs, only slightly branched and strikingly parallel. The scales are green and glossy, whitish on the reverse. The cones have 10–12 scales.

In 'Atrovirens' the foliage is very dark green and glossy; 'Cuprea' is slow growing, with a broad, pyramidal shape to 1m in height, bronze-green foliage and twigs

Thuja orientalis 'Elegantissima'

Thuja plicata

which turn up at the tips; 'Gracilis Aurea' develops a loose cone shape and is fairly fast growing, to 6m, with conspicuous, graceful, fine golden-yellow foliage. 'Rogersii' is a true dwarf, to 1m in height, egg-shaped, pointed at the top. The foliage, dark green in the centre but with golden-yellow tips, is fine and dense and easily pruned. 'Stoneham Gold' is slow-growing, to 2–3m. The foliage is dark green in the centre, gold coloured at the tips.

Thuja standishii, Japanese arbor vitae: A pyramidal tree with yellow-green scales on round, slightly pendulous twigs. The foliage has white streaks or blotches on the reverse. The cones have 10–12 scales. Fairly loose habit.

Thuja plicata 'Rogersii'

Tilia platyphyllos

Tilia

Lime

Imposing deciduous trees which may reach a very great age. They are so large that they are found only in parks, very large gardens or lining avenues. The usually heart-shaped leaves are distributed and have long leaf-stalks. The flowers have a sweet scent and produce an abundance of nectar; they are followed by small, round or pear-shaped fruits. Limes have a deep root system; they are wind-resistant and fairly fast growing. They have the disadvantage that some species suffer from honey-dew and sooty mould, the former caused by aphids, the latter by the mould growing on the honey-dew. *Tilia cordata*, *T. euchlora*, *T. platyphyllos* and *T. tomentosa* are not very prone to these diseases.

Situation Limes will thrive in sunny or partially shaded situations, in well-drained soil. In view of their size they can be grown in gardens only if they are pleached. In that form they can protect a house from the sun.

Soil Standard garden soil.

Propagation The species from seed, cultivars by grafting or from cuttings.

182

Tilia × *euchlora*, Crimean lime: The result of crossing *T. cordata* and *T. dasystyla*. In winter it is clearly recognised by its green to yellow-green twigs. The lower branches in particular are pendulous. Silver-grey bark, with longitudinal streak. The glossy green leaves are serrated, with long, pointed teeth.

Tilia platyphyllos (syn *T. grandifolia*), large-leaved lime: Height to 30m; a tree with a dense, almost spherical crown and dull-green, regularly dentated leaves, downy on the reverse. The felty, thick-shelled nut-like fruits are sometimes retained in winter. 'Fastigiata' is columnar in shape; 'Aurea' is slow growing and has yellow foliage.

Tilia tomentosa, silver lime: A tree growing to 30m, with a pyramidal to egg-shaped crown and erect-growing branches. The leaves are dark green on the upper surface, initially downy, later practically bare; the reverse has a beautiful silvery colour.

Tilia × *vulgaris* (syn *T. europaea*, *T.* × *intermedia*), Dutch lime: A cross between *T. cordata* and *T. platyphyllos*. Height to 40m; a tree with bare, often pendent twigs and dull-green foliage. 'Pallida' has bright-green foliage; the twigs and buds redden in the autumn.

Tilia × *vulgaris*

Tsuga canadensis 'Pendula'

Tsuga

Hemlock Spruce

Evergreen conifers of graceful habit. The botanical species may grow to some tens of metres; but there are numerous smaller, slower growing cultivars. The species have a narrow-cone shape and horizontally spreading main branches, slightly curved at the tips. The lateral branches and twigs are pendent. The dark-green needles are soft and flat.

Situation Beautiful planted singly in a sunny or partially shaded position in not too dry soil. *Tsuga canadensis* and *T. heterophylla* can be clipped to form fine hedges; new shoots readily develop even from fairly old wood. The garden forms rarely need pruning, but badly placed branches should be removed.

Soil Humus-rich, slightly acid soil.

Propagation The species from seed, garden forms from summer cuttings.

Tsuga canadensis: Height to 30m; but in our part of the world the tree rarely grows beyond 15m, 10m across. Hairy, yellow-brown twigs and bright-brown pointed buds. Up to 2cm long needles narrowing towards the

Tsuga mertensiana

blunt tip and with whitish streaks and green margins underneath. 'Bennett', 1m in height and at least twice as much across, has a compact shape, flattened at the top. The twigs arch a little at the tips. 'Pendula' is a shrub-shaped weeping form, 2–3m in height and 3–5m across. A very graceful shape, with pendent branches. 'Albospica' has unusually coloured foliage and elongated, silver-white tips to the twigs. The needles are initially white, later turning grey.

Tsuga heterophylla: In its native country, the western part of North America, it may grow to as much as 60m, but here it remains smaller. A narrow tree with hairy brown twigs and blunt, grey-brown buds. Blunt, to 2cm long needles, the same width all over, with broad white streaks, but no green margins, on the reverse. The upper surface is green and glossy. Sessile cones, to 2.5cm long. 'Conica' is a beautifully shaped conical shrub with dense ramification; the tips of the branches arch a little; height to 4m, 3m across.

Tsuga mertensiana: Height to 30m, 12m across. A fairly slow-growing, pyramidal tree. The densely haired twigs are covered in blunt, blue-green needles to 2.5cm long, radially arranged. The cones are up to 8cm long. The rough bark is dark red-brown and scaly.

Ulmus glabra 'Camperdownii'

Ulmus

Elm

Decorative deciduous trees with alternate foliage, the leaves being oblique at the base and clearly arranged in rows. The tree flowers in the autumn, or in spring before the appearance of the foliage. The winged fruits soon drop. Dutch elm disease occurred for the first time at the end of the twenties; it is caused by a mould and is spread by the elmbark beetle. The disease abated after a decade and at that time more trees were planted. Unfortunately a much more aggressive form of the disease occurred in the late sixties, and many trees were killed. Affected trees are traced by means of infra-red photography. However, growers have succeeded in developing reasonably resistant elms, for example *Ulmus* × *hollandica* 'Groeneveld', 'Lobel', 'Plantijn' and 'Dodoens'.

Situation Most elms are fairly large and are used in parks or to line streets. The weeping forms are found on old country estates. The golden elm, though slow growing will in the course of time reach 9m and should therefore not be planted in very small gardens. Pruning may restrict its size, so that it will take up less space.

Soil Elms need a sunny or partially shaded position in adequately moist, but definitely not wet soil.

Propagation The species from seed, garden forms from cuttings, by layering or by grafting.

Ulmus × elegantissima: A slow-growing shrub, developing runners. In ten years it will reach a height of 2m. Dense ramification; the leaves, clearly arranged in rows, are elliptical, 2–3cm long, serrated and covered in rough hair. They grow close together. This clone is referred to as 'Jacqueline Hillier'. Suitable for small gardens.

Ulmus glabra (syn *U. campestris*, *U. montana*, *U. scabra*): A tree growing to 30m, with initially hairy, dark-brown twigs and buds covered in dark-brown down. Obovate leaves, to 16cm long, the upper surface rough to the touch. 'Exoniensis' has a cone- to pillar-shaped crown and somewhat curly foliage. A better known form is the Camperdown elm, 'Camperdownii', a tree to 5m in height and as much across, which forms a bower. The branches are pendulous, the tips often stretching along the ground. The foliage lies close to the branches and forms a thick thatch. Green flowers March–April as in the weeping elm 'Horizontalis', which resembles the previous type, but grows taller and broader, while the foliage does not cover the twigs. The yellow Scotch elm, 'Lutescens', has yellow foliage in spring.

Ulmus × hollandica: The result of crossing *U. glabra*, *U. minor* and *U. plotii*. Resembles the Scotch elm, but the leaf-stalks are longer and the twigs are practically bare. 'Plantijn' is fairly fast growing, to about 15m, with grey twigs. It grows very erect, but is less columnar in shape than 'Dodoens' or 'Lobel'. 'Groeneveld' remains a little lower and develops a dense, regularly branched crown. Grows more slowly.

Ulmus minor (syn *U. campestris*, *U. carpinifolia*, *U. foliacea*), smooth-leaved elm: A 10m tall tree with bare buds and twigs. The oval-oblong leaves are up to 10cm long, smooth on the upper surface. 'Dampieri' is columnar in shape when young, with somewhat rough leaves lying close to the twigs. 'Wredei', the golden elm, is similar, but has golden-yellow foliage.

These trees make fine specimen trees. 'Pendula', the weeping wych-elm, has an erect-growing trunk and smooth leaves. 'Sarniensis' grows to 9m in height and 6m across. It is a pyramidal tree with stiff, oblique branches and fine autumn colouring. Prone to Dutch elm disease.

Ulmus parvifolia: A tree with a broad, spherical crown; height to 12m. The oval green leaves are 2–5cm long. It does not flower until August or September; is resistant to elm disease. There are a number of miniature cultivars with tiny leaves.

Ulmus minor 'Sarniensis'

Ulmus minor 'Wredei'

Vaccinium

Blueberry

These deciduous or evergreen shrubs belong to the heather family. They have alternate, smooth-edged or serrated foliage, cup-shaped little flowers and red or blue berries, sometimes covered in bloom. The blue form is actually the only species found in gardens; the other species have become naturalised in marshes and woods. The cranberry is cultivated on a large scale in the United States; towards Christmas it is imported here.

Situation The blue form, bilberry, does best in sunny or partially shaded positions; the common blueberry and the cranberry dislike full sun and tolerate deeper shade. The bilberry is a beautiful shrub with striking autumn colouring. It can be grown as an ornamental shrub, but can also create a focal point in the vegetable garden. The other species are low growing and make excellent ground-cover, especially the evergreen forms. Moisture is essential if the plants are to develop well and produce a rich harvest of berries.

Soil All species are very demanding as regards soil; it has to be sandy and humus-rich or peaty, with no lime. The planting-holes should be filled with peat or conifer-needle compost.

Propagation From seed, by layering or division, and from cuttings.

Vaccinium corymbosum, American blueberry: A shrub to 2m in height and a little more across, with bare, yellow-green twigs and egg-shaped to oval, to 8cm long, bright-green leaves, turning orange and scarlet in autumn. White to slightly pink, urn-shaped little flowers in clusters, in May. The dark-blue berries are covered in bloom and are very tasty. There are a number of forms on the market; they vary in the size and colour of the berries and the time of ripening.

Vaccinium myrtillus, common blueberry: A small shrub, to 50cm in height; a native of Europe. Angular green twigs and oval leaves, to 3cm long. Bell-shaped, greenish-white flowers in May, followed by bloomed blue berries, very suitable for jam making.

Vaccinium vitis-idaea, cowberry: Evergreen, creeping ground-cover, to 30cm in height, with downy green twigs and up to 3cm long, dull-green leaves, paler underneath, and with dark spots. Bell-shaped white flowers in short clusters May–June. Acid red berries, which may be preserved, for example as a compote. 'Coral' is a beautiful strain with numerous large berries in pendulous clusters.

Vaccinium corymbosum

Vaccinium vitis-idaea 'Coral'

Viburnum

An extensive genus of evergreen and deciduous shrubs cultivated for their fine foliage, for their flowers or their fruits. The leaves are opposite; the flowers are often arranged in a spherical or umbrella-shaped inflorescence. As in the hortensia, the outer circle sometimes consists of larger, sterile florets. In autumn the shrubs bear juicy, colourful stone-fruits or have magnificent autumn colouring.

Situation Viburnums do well in sunny or partially shaded positions. Evergreen species are best kept out of bright sunlight in winter. Vigorously growing deciduous species are sometimes planted as undergrowth, in private bird sanctuaries or as windbreaks. They tolerate a great deal of shade, but in that situation will not produce such a profusion of flowers and fruits. The Japanese snowball is magnificent in a free-standing position but, like the other deciduous species, can also be used in groups in the shrub border. *Viburnum farreri* produces its flowers in autumn or late winter and for that reason deserves a special spot where it will show to advantage during that time. The evergreen species are beautiful planted singly in large containers, but also in groups. The low-growing *V. davidii* is used as an edging plant or to fill whole sections of the garden. Evergreen species need little pruning, but deciduous specimens are regularly given attention.

The hardiness of evergreen species, especially *V. davidii*, is limited. *V. rhytidophyllum* also suffers in severe winters. On the other hand the deciduous species, such as *V. carlcephalum*, are very hardy. Even the flower-buds will not be damaged in a temperature of −25°C.

Soil Well manured and well drained garden soil. Evergreen species enjoy humus-rich soil, on the acid side, especially *V. davidii*.

Propagation The species from seed; otherwise by layering or from cuttings.

Viburnum × *bodnantense*: The result of crossing *V. farreri* and *V. grandiflorum*. The form most frequently cultivated is 'Dawn', to 2.5m tall and often flowering in November, sometimes not until February or March, depending on the weather. White-pink flower clusters. Leaves to 10cm long, bare. 'Charles Lamont' is a little lower growing and has darker flowers, red when in bud. Flowering season November–January.

Viburnum × *burkwoodii*: The product of crossing *V. carlesii* and *V. utile*. A beautiful, partially evergreen shrub with arching twigs and to 10cm long, dark-green oval leaves, white and felty underneath. The pink flowers turn white as they fade in March or April. They are fragrant and are arranged in domed umbels. 'Chenault' is very similar, but the foliage is more sharply dentated and it flowers a week or two earlier.

Viburnum × *burkwoodii*

Viburnum × *carlcephalum*

Viburnum opulus

Viburnum plicatum 'Mariesii'

Viburnum × carlcephalum: A cross between *V. carlesii* and *V. macrocephalum*. A vigorous plant, to 2.5m in height and the same across. Broad-oval, to 8cm long, dark-green leaves, felty white on the reverse. Delightfully scented white flowers in spherical umbels, April–May.

Viburnum carlesii: Does not grow as fast as the previous species: height to 1.5m and the same across; the leaves are less sharply dentated. Often beautiful autumn colouring. Fragrant flowers, fading to white, April–May.

Viburnum davidii: Evergreen shrub, to 40cm in height and spreading to 80cm; somewhat sensitive to frost. White flowers in 7-part, broad umbels in June. If the plant is to produce its blue berries, male and female specimens must be planted together. The leaves are up to 12cm long, oval, 3-veined at the base, dark green, glossy and smooth-edged. Suitable for use as groundcover and in the rock garden.

Viburnum farreri (syn *V. fragrans*): A stiffly erect-growing shrub, to 2.5m tall, with red-brown twigs and up to 7cm long, oval leaves, initially brown, later turning green. Small plumes of strongly scented white flowers November–December.

Viburnum lantana: Height to 3m; a broad, erect-growing shrub with oval leaves, to 15cm long, densely haired, especially on the reverse. White flower umbels May–June, followed by red berries, subsequently turning black. Tolerates a great deal of shade.

Viburnum opulus, guelder rose: Fast-growing, bushy shrub, to 4.5m in height and as much across. The flower umbels which appear in May or June consist of fertile florets surrounded by large sterile ones. The berries are a magnificent red colour. Bright-green, to 11cm long, 3- to 5-lobed leaves, downy underneath. 'Nanum' is a bushy dwarf form, to 1m in height; it rarely flowers. 'Xanthocarpum' has permanent lemon-yellow fruits.

Viburnum plicatum, Japanese snowball: A spreading shrub, to 2.5m in height, with oval, to 12cm long, pointed leaves and a spherical inflorescence consisting of large, white, sterile flowers. Flowering season May–June. 'Mariesii' is lower growing; it bears fertile flowers as well and the inflorescence is flatter in shape. 'Rotundifolium' has broader leaves; all the flowers are sterile. It flowers two weeks earlier than the previous form.

Viburnum rhytidophyllum: An evergreen shrub, to 4m in height and 3m across. The twigs are densely covered in radial hairs. Oblong, practically smooth-edged leaves, to 18cm long, dark green and glossy on the upper surface, which is strikingly wrinkled. The reverse is white and felty. The white inflorescence survives the winter in bud and opens in May or June. Egg-shaped red berries, later turning black.

Vinca

Periwinkle

Very rewarding, vigorous, evergreen ground-covering plants with dense foliage and attractive flowers in spring. The simple, leathery leaves are arranged crosswise. The fairly large, axillary flowers have a flat corolla. *Vinca major* is less hardy than *V. minor* and in severe winters needs some protection from frost and drying winds. In very cold weather the part of *V. minor* above ground will freeze as well, but new shoots will grow from the roots in May and soon the plant will look as if nothing had happened.

Situation *V. minor* in particular, makes excellent ground-cover, forming a dense carpet which, in the course of time, is impenetrable to weeds. *V. major* has a somewhat looser habit; it develops much longer shoots and therefore is very suitable for planting in containers, on walls and in raised beds. Both species prefer a partially shaded position. The green-leaved species will thrive in deep shade, but will in that case produce fewer flowers.

Soil Standard, preferably with some humus content and not too dry.

Propagation By division and from cuttings.

Vinca major: Height to 40cm. The flowering shoots are 30–40cm long, the non-flowering shoots may grow as long as 1m. They are self-rooting. Satiny, dark-green, oval leaves, to 6cm long. Large, violet-blue flowers April–May. 'Alba' has white flowers. 'Variegata' is fast growing and has yellow-blotched and yellow-edged leaves. 'Reticulata' has yellow foliage with reticulate marking.

Vinca minor: A little lower-growing than the previous species. The stems are partially creeping, partially erect growing; the latter bear the violet-blue flowers, to 3cm across. The glossy dark-green, elliptical leaves, to 4cm long, are somewhat paler underneath. The main flowering season is April–May, but often odd flowers appear until autumn. 'Alba' is a little smaller and bears white flowers, as does 'Gertrude Jekyll', which has slightly narrower leaves. 'Plena Alba' has double white flowers. 'Atropurpurea Compacta' and 'Plena Purpurea' have purple flowers, in the latter they are double. 'Bowles' has a prolonged flowering season; the flowers are a deeper blue than in the species. 'Rubra' has red-purple flowers; there is a double form as well. There are also periwinkles with variegated foliage, for example 'Aureovariegata', with yellow-blotched leaves, 'Argenteovariegata', with white-blotched leaves – both with blue-violet flowers – and 'Alba Variegata', which has white flowers and white-spotted foliage.

Vinca major 'Variegata'

Vinca minor

Vitis

Vine

Vitis coignetiae

Vitis vinifera

Deciduous climbers, very popular because of their delicious fruit, but also because of the beautiful shape of the foliage which has magnificent autumn colouring. For a good grape harvest it is essential to take care in choosing the strain and the position where it is to grow. If the sole concern is to cover a wall or pergola in an attractive manner, the choice is large. Vines have lobed, dentate foliage and climb by means of the tendrils which grow opposite the leaves.

Situation Provide a position in full sun, sheltered against cold winds. A south-facing wall is excellent, but a sunny spot on a patio is even better. A good harvest can only be achieved by correct pruning. The vine may be trained in a U-shape, a new level being added year by year. The flowers appear on the side-branches of shoots developed the previous year. To obtain large grapes, surplus bunches must be removed as soon as possible and the remaining bunches thinned out. Unwanted shoots and axillary suckers must also be removed as soon as possible.

Soil Nutritious, calcareous soil. Dig a large planting-hole, especially if the vine is placed against a wall, and fill it with rotted cow manure, compost, leafmould, peat and other such material. Good drainage is also important.

Propagation By layering and from eye cuttings.

Vitis amurensis: A vigorous climber with fresh green, broad-oval to round leaves, turning yellow red in autumn. Insignificant greenish flowers, as in all vine species.

Vitis coignetiae (syn *V. labrusca*), crimson glory vine: A vigorous plant which may grow to as much as 15m, with brown, felty twigs. Round to egg-shaped leaves, 3- to 5-lobed, grey brown and downy on the reverse; beautiful autumn colouring. Flowers June-July; the fruit is black, non-edible.

Vitis vinifera, grape vine: A climber which grows to 15m, with initially downy, later bare, twigs and oval, fairly thin leaves, usually 3-lobed. The reverse of the leaves is green and smooth. The flowers which appear June–July are followed by grapes covered in blue, green or yellow bloom. 'Witte van Tol' is a good strain of white grape; 'Brant' is a reliable strain of blue. The latter grows to 7m and is one of the most winter-hardy strains, with edible fruit. The autumn colouring of the foliage is beautiful as well. 'Rembrandt', though hardy, produces acid fruit, usually on the small side. This is probably a *labrusca* cultivar.

Weigela

Deciduous shrubs, related to the honeysuckle. They are very attractive when in flower, but less so when only in their green foliage. This problem can be solved by planting a variegated type. Opposite, short-stalked, serrated leaves. The flowers develop on the previous year's wood and are bell- to funnel-shaped, white, pink or red. After the normal flowering season in late spring or early summer there is often a second flowering in September.
Situation Weigela will thrive in a sunny or partially shaded position. Forms with unusual foliage colouring are attractive planted singly; others look well in the shrub border. There are low-growing forms for small gardens.
Soil Nutritious garden soil.
Propagation From cuttings.

Weigela floribunda: Height to 3m; a shrub with hairy twigs and egg-shaped to oval, pointed leaves, densely haired on the upper surface, less so underneath. Sessile, often isolated flowers. In 'Grandiflora' the flowers are particularly large; white or pale red. Flowering season May–June.
Weigela florida (syn *W. rosea*): A 2m tall shrub with yellow-brown twigs and pointed oval leaves. The underside is hairy only along the central vein. Pink flowers, slightly paler inside, isolated or in twos or threes, May–June. 'Nana Variegata' grows to just over 1m and has yellow-blotched foliage and a rich inflorescence. 'Purpurea' is fairly slow growing, compact with arching twigs and brown-red foliage, and a profusion of deep-pink flowers.
Weigela hybrids: This group includes shrubs growing to 1.5–2m, flowering May–July. 'Bristol Ruby', 'Eva Supreme' and 'Newport Red' have red flowers. 'Abel Carrière', 'Ballet', 'Boskoop Glory', 'Conquête', 'Féerie' and 'Rosabella' have a pink inflorescence; the latter's is particularly profuse. 'Bristol Snowflake' and Candida have white flowers. 'Ideal' flowers early, bright red-purple.
Weigela middendorffiana: Height 1.5m and approximately the same across. Oval-oblong, pointed leaves and grey-brown twigs with two rows of hairs. Yellowish flowers with orange blotches inside May–June.
Weigela praecox: The bare twigs of this 2m tall shrub bear green leaves, densely haired underneath. The flowers are deep pink, yellow inside. As the name implies, this species flowers very early, in early May. 'Bailey' produces a profusion of flowers in short clusters.
Weigela venusta: A little known species with red-brown branches and elongated, tubular flowers from late April onwards. 'Dropmore Pink' is the finest choice.

Weigela florida 'Purpurea'

Weigela hybrid 'Ideal'

Wisteria

Wisteria sinensis

A deciduous climbing shrub with clusters of white or blue flowers. It requires support and is not entirely winter-hardy; it must therefore be protected in severe winters.

Situation Provide a sunny or partially shaded position against a wall, pergola or, as is done in Japan, along a bridge. Sometimes *Wisteria* produces scant or no flowers, often because the wrong strain has been selected. Shortening the lateral branches in June or July, and omitting the nitrogen fertiliser for a year, may help.

Soil Nutritious soil. Make a large planting-hole and fill it with good soil.

Propagation From cuttings, by grafting or layering.

Wisteria floribunda: The twigs twist to the right and May–June bear violet-coloured, lightly scented flowers in pointed clusters. 'Alba', 'Issai' and 'Issai Perfect' are beautiful strains.

Wisteria sinensis: The shoots wind in a left-hand direction and bear strongly scented, violet-blue flowers in blunt clusters. The flowers appear before the foliage. 'Alba' and 'Prolific' are beautiful strains.

Zelkova abelicea

Zelkova

Deciduous trees or shrubs belonging to the elm family. Smooth trunk and alternate, coarsely dentated foliage. Striking greenish inflorescence and round fruits.

Situation Beautiful planted singly in a roomy, sunny position. Most species tolerate some shade.

Soil Nutritious soil.

Propagation From seed and by layering.

Zelkova abelicea (syn *Z. cretica*): Height to 10m, 6m across; a tree branching at a fairly high level. Smooth trunk and an oval crown. Fine autumn colouring.

Zelkova carpinifolia: Height to 24m, fairly low branching. Dark-green oval leaves, 2–7cm long, pointed, with blunt teeth. The underside is hairy along the veins.

Zelkova serrata: The best known species. Short trunk and erect-growing branches. The dark-green, egg-shaped leaves, 3–9cm long, pointed and sharply serrated, have bronze-coloured to red autumn tints. Both upper side and reverse are bare.

TABLES

Shrubs suitable for a situation in full sun

Abelia × grandiflora
  triflora
Abies
Acer (most species)
Amorpha
Araucaria araucana
Berberis 'Bunch o'Grapes'
  thunbergii
  wilsoniae
Betula
Buddleia
Campsis radicans
Carpinus betulus
Caryopteris
Catalpa
Ceanothus
Cedrus
Cercis siliquastrum
Chamaecyparis
Cladrastis kentukea
Clerodendrum trichotomum
Cotinus
Crataegus
Cytisus
Datura suaveolens
Davidia involucrata
Deutzia
Empetrum nigrum
Erica cinerea
Escallonia hybrids
Eucalyptus niphophila
Exochorda giraldii
  racemosa
Fagus sylvatica
Ficus carica
Forsythia
Fraxinus
Genista
Ginkgo biloba
Gleditsia
Gymnocladus dioicus
Hebe
Hibiscus syriacus
Indigofera
Koelreuteria paniculata
Kolkwitzia amabilis
Larix
Lavandula angustifolia
Lavatera olbia
Liriodendron tulipifera
Lithodora diffusa
Magnolia
Metasequoia glyptostroboides
Nothofagus antarctica
Nyssa sylvatica
Ostrya
Paeonia
Pernettya mucronata
Perovskia atriplicifolia
Phellodendron amurense
Photinia villosa
Picea
Pinus
Platanus × hispanica
Populus
Prunus
Pseudotsuga menziesii
Pyrus
Quercus
Rhus
Robinia
Rosa
Salix
Sciadopitys verticillata
Sequoiadendron giganteum
Sinarundinaria nitida
Sophora japonica
Syringa
Tamarix
Taxodium distichum
Taxus
Thuja
Tilia
Tsuga
Ulmus
Vitis
Weigela
Wisteria
Zelkova

Shrubs for partial shade (where necessary)

Acer
Actinidia
Aesculus
Ailanthus altissima
Akebia
Alnus
Amelanchier
Aralia elata
Aristolochia macrophylla
Aronia
Arundinaria
Aucuba japonica
Berberis (most species)
Broussonetia papyrifera
Buxus
Callicarpa bodinieri var giral-
  dii
Calluna vulgaris
Calycanthus
Camellia japonica
Carpinus betulus
Castanea sativa
Celastrus
Cephalotaxus harringtonia
Ceratostigma
Cercidiphyllum japonicum
Cestrum
Chamaedaphne calyculata
Choenomeles
Choisya ternata
Clematis
Clethra
Colutea
Cornus
Corylopsis
Corylus
Cotoneaster
Cryptomeria japonica
× Cupressocyparis leylandii
Cydonia oblonga
Daboecia cantabrica
Daphne
Decaisnea fargesii
Dipelta
Elaeagnus
Enkianthus campanulatus
Erica (most species)
Euonymus
Fagus sylvatica
Fallopia aubertii
Fothergilla
Fuchsia magellanica
Gaultheria
Halesia carolina
Hamamelis
Hedera
Hippophaë rhamnoides
Holodiscus
Hydrangea
Hypericum
Ilex
Jasminum nudiflorum
Juglans
Juniperus
Kalmia
Kerria japonica
Laburnum
Lespedeza
Leycesteria formosa
Ligustrum
Liquidambar styraciflua
Lonicera
Mahonia
Morus alba
Osmanthus
Pachysandra
Parthenocissus
Paulownia tomentosa
Philadelphus
Picea
Pieris
Poncirus trifoliata
Potentilla fruticosa
Pseudosasa japonica
Pterocarya
Pyracantha coccinea
Quercus
Rhododendron
Ribes
Rubus
Sambucus
Skimmia
Sorbaria
Sorbus
Spartium junceum
Spiraea
Staphylea
Stephanandra
Stranvaesia davidiana
Symphoricarpos
Vaccinium
Viburnum
Vinca

Shrubs tolerating shade

Acer campestre
Berberis verruculosa
Hedera
Hydrangea anomala
Ilex
Ligustrum
Lonicera
Mahonia
Pachysandra
Prunus laurocerasus
  lusitanica

Sarcococca humilis
Vaccinium
Vinca

Shrubs tolerating or requiring dry soil

Ailanthus altissima
Berberis koreana
Betula (most species)
Clematis montana
  vitalba
  viticella
Cytisus ardoini
  decumbens
Daphne cneorum
Gleditsia
Lavandula angustifolia
Lespedeza
Perovskia atriplicifolia
Pinus
Robinia
Spartium junceum

Shrubs tolerating or requiring damp soil

Acer palmatum
  pensylvanicum
Amorpha
Arundinaria
Betula ermanii
  jacquemontii
  nana
  nigra
  pubescens
Cercidiphyllum japonicum
Chamaedaphne calyculata
Choenomeles japonica
  speciosa
Cornus amonum
  sericea
Dipelta floribunda
Dipelta ventricosa
Erica cinerea
  × darleyensis
Fothergilla gardenii
  major
Gaultheria
Hydrangea aspera ssp sargentiana
  macrophylla
Kalmia
Liquidambar styraciflua
Mahonia aquifolium

Rhododendron
Rubus
Salix
Taxodium distichum
Vaccinium

Shrubs needing protection from strong wind

Abelia
Acer japonicum
  palmatum
  saccharinum
Alnus incana
Araucaria araucana
Camellia japonica
Campsis radicans
Ceanothus
Celastrus orbiculatus
  scandens
Enkianthus campanulatus
Eucalyptus niphophila
Exochorda giraldii
  racemosa
Ficus carica
Fothergilla gardenii
  major
Ginkgo biloba
Gleditsia
Hamamelis
Hebe
Hibiscus syriacus
Ilex
Jasminum nudiflorum
Kolkwitzia amabilis
Liquidambar styraciflua
Magnolia
Mahonia
Morus alba
Paulownia tomentosa
Poncirus trifoliata
Pseudosasa japonica
Rhododendron (most species)
Robinia

Shrubs needing frost protection in severe winters

Abelia
Acer palmatum
Araucaria araucana
Arundinaria pumila
  simonii
Aucuba japonica
Berberis 'Bunch o'Grapes'
  darwinii

  linearifolia
  wilsoniae
Broussonetia papyrifera
Buddleia davidii
  Nanhoensis hybrids
Callicarpa bodinieri var giraldii
Camellia japonica
Campsis radicans
Caryopteris
Catalpa
Ceanothus
Ceratostigma
Cercis siliquastrum
Cestrum
Chamaecyparis obtusa
Cytisus ardoini
  decumbens
  purpureus
Daboecia cantabrica
Daphne cneorum
  laureola
  pontica
Datura suaveolens
Erica ciliaris
  cinerea
Escallonia hybrids
Eucalyptus niphophila
Exochorda giraldii
  racemosa
Ficus carica
Fuchsia magellanica
Genista lydia
Hebe
Hydrangea macrophylla
Hypericum calycinum
Indigofera
Jasminum nudiflorum
Lavandula angustifolia
Lavatera olbia
Lespedeza
Ligustrum quihoui
Liquidambar styraciflua
Lithodora diffusa
Lonicera nitida
  × tellmanniana
Paeonia suffruticosa
Paulownia tomentosa
Pernettya mucronata
Prunus laurocerasus
  lusitanica
  subhirtella
  × yedoensis
Pseudosasa japonica
Rhododendron (most species)
Sarcococca humilis
Sequoiadendron giganteum

Skimmia
Spartium junceum
Viburnum davidii
Wisteria

Evergreen shrubs

Arundinaria
Aucuba japonica
Berberis buxifolia
  candicula
  darwinii
  gagnepainii var lanceifolia
  × hybridogagnepainii
  julianae
  linearifolia
  × stenophylla
  verruculosa
Buxus
Calluna vulgaris
Camellia japonica
Cestrum (several species)
Chamaedaphne calyculata
Choisya ternata
Cotoneaster dammeri
  salicifolius
Cotoneaster simonsii
Daboecia cantabrica
Daphne acutiloba
  cneorum
  laureola
  pontica
Elaeagnus × ebbingei
  pungens
Empetrum nigrum
Erica
Euonymus fortunei
  japonica
Gaultheria
Hebe
Hedera
Ilex
Kalmia
Ligustrum amurense
Lithodora diffusa
Lonicera nitida
  pileata
Magnolia grandiflora
Mahonia
Osmanthus
Pachysandra
Pernettya mucronata
Pieris
Prunus laurocerasus
  lusitanica
Pseudosasa japonica

Pyracantha coccinea
Rhododendron
Sarcococca humilis
Sinarundinaria nitida
Skimmia
Viburnum davidii
Vinca

All the genera of conifers dealt with in this book

Abies
Araucaria
Cedrus
Cephalotaxus
Chamaecyparis
Cryptomeria
× Cupressocyparis
Juniperus
Larix (not evergreen)
Metasequoia
Picea
Pinus
Pseudotsuga
Sciadopitys
Sequoiadendron
Taxodium
Taxus
Thuja
Tsuga

Ground-covering shrubs

Arundinaria pumila
Berberis × media 'Jewel of the
   Park'
Calluna vulgaris
Ceratostigma plumbaginoides
Choenomeles speciosa
Cotoneaster adpressus
   dammeri
Cytisus ardoinii
   decumbens
Empetrum nigrum
Erica
Euonymus fortunei
   japonicus
Gaultheria
Hedera helix
Hypericum calycinum
Juniperus chinensis
   conferta
   horizontalis
   sabina
   squamata
   virginiana

Lithodora diffusa
Pachysandra
Stephanandra
Vaccinium vitis-idaea
Viburnum davidii
Vinca

Shrubs suitable for hedges

Acer campestre
Berberis buxifolia
   × media
   × ottawensis
   × stenophylla
   thunbergii
   vulgaris
Buxus
Carpinus betula
Chamaecyparis (most species)
Cornus mas
Cotoneaster simonsii
Crataegus
× Cupressocyparis leylandii
Cytisus × praecox
Elaeagnus multiflora
   pungens
   umbellata
Escallonia hybrids
Euonymus fortunei
Fagus sylvatica
Ilex × altaclarensis
   aquifolium
   crenata
Juniperus communis
Larix kaempferi
Ligustrum obtusifolium
   ovalifolium
   vulgare
Lonicera nitida
   pileata
Mahonia
Potentilla fruticosa
Prunus laurocerasus
Pyracantha coccinea
Ribes alpinum
Sinarundinaria nitida
Spiraea × vanhouttei
Symphoricarpos
Taxus (most species)
Thuja

Climbing shrubs and those that can be trained

Actinidia

Akebia
Aristolochia macrophylla
Campsis radicans
Celastrus
Cestrum (several species)
Clematis (several species)
Euonymus japonicus
Fallopia aubertii
Forsythia suspens
Hedera
Hydrangea anomala
Jasminum nudiflorum
Lonicera (several species)
Parthenocissus
Pyracantha coccinea
Vitis
Wisteria

Shrubs suitable for a free-standing position

Abies koreana
   lasiocarpa var arizonica
Acer cappadocicum
   griseum
   japonicum
   palmatum
   pensylvanicum
   platanoides
   pseudoplatanus
Aesculus
Ailanthus altissima
Aralia elata
Araucaria araucana
Betula
Buddleia
Calycanthus floridus
   occidentalis
Camellia japonica
Castanea sativa
Catalpa
Cedrus
Cercidiphyllum japonicum
Cercis siliquastrum
Chamaecyparis
Cladrastis kentukea
Clerodendrum trichotomum
Clethra alnifolia
   barbinervis
Cornus (most species)
Corylus avellana
   maxima
Cotinus coggygria
   obovatus
Cotoneaster salicifolius
   Watereri hybrids

Crataegus
Cryptomeria japonica
Davidia involucrata
Decaisnea fargesii
Eucalyptus niphophila
Exochorda giraldii
   racemosa
Fagus sylvatica

Shrubs suitable for a free-standing position (cont'd)

Fothergilla gardenii
   major
Fraxinus
Fuchsia magellanica
Gaultheria shallon
Ginkgo biloba
Gleditsia
Gymnocladus dioicus
Halesia carolina
Hamamelis
Hibiscus syriacus
Holodiscus
Hydrangea macrophylla
   paniculata
Ilex
Indigofera
Juglans
Juniperus chinensis
   communis
   recurva
Juniperus sabina
   squamata
   virginiana
Koelreuteria paniculata
Kolkwitzia amabilis
Larix
Lavatera olbia
Ligustrum obtusifolium
Liquidambar styraciflua
Liriodendron tulipifera
Magnolia
Mahonia
Malus (most species)
Metasequoia glyptostroboides
Nothofagus antarctia
Nyssa sylvatica
Ostrya
Paeonia
Paulownia tomentosa
Phellodendron amurense
Philadelphus
Photinia villosa
.Picea

Pieris japonica
Pinus
Platanus × hispanica
Poncirus trifoliata
Potentilla fruticosa
Prunus
Pseudosasa japonica
Pyrus
Quercus
Rhododendron
Rhus
Robinia

Salix
Sciadopitys verticillata
Sequoiadendron giganteum
Sinarundinaria nitida
Sophora japonica
Sorbaria
Staphylea
Stranvaesia davidiana
Taxodium distichum
Taxus (most species)
Thuja (most species)
Tilia

Tsuga
Ulmus
Weigela
Zelkova

Trees (up to 5m) suitable for small gardens

Acer ginnale
  japonicum
  palmatum

Aralia elata
Betula pendula 'Youngii'
Broussonetia papyrifera
Chamaecyparis lawsoniana
  (several species)
Cydonia oblonga
Koelreuteria paniculata
Malus (several species)
Photinia villosa
Poncirus trifoliata
Prunus (several species)
Rhus

Shrubs requiring special attention as regards pruning

a Small shrubs which quickly grow bare at the base and therefore need to be cut back drastically at regular intervals, ie at least every second year. They include heathers, such as *Calluna* and *Erica* species, and also *Daboecia* and *Lavandula*.

b Taller shrubs of which only older branches have to be cut back drastically every second or third year. This treatment is called rejuvenation. It is essential in deciduous *Berberis*, *Cornus alba* and *C. stolonifera*, all species of *Cotinus*, *Exochorda*, *Forsythia*, *Hydrangea macrophylla* and all climbing roses.

c Shrubs in which the branches that have ceased flowering have to be removed just above young side-shoots: *Buddleia alternifolia*, *Ceratostigma*, *Clematis alpina* and *C. montana*, all species of *Cytisus*, *Deutzia*, *Dipelta*, *Philadelphus*, *Ribes*, all species of *Spiraea* with the exception of summer-flowering forms (see next group), *Weigela*.

d Shrubs which must be cut back to 10cm above ground every spring before they start into growth: *Buddleia davidii* and *B. Nanhoensis* hybrids, *Campsis radicans*, *Caryopteris*, *Ceanothus*, *Clematis flammula*, *C. jackmanii*, *C. tangutica*, *C. vitalba* and *C. viticella*, *Escallonia* hybrids, *Fuchsia magellanica*, *Hydrangea arborescens*, *H. aspera* ssp *sargentiana* and *H. paniculata*, all species of *Hypericum*, *Indigofera*, *Lavatera olbia*, *Lespedeza*, *Leycesteria formosa*, *Perovskia atriplicifolia*, all shrub roses, *Sorbaria*, *Spartium junceum*, *Spiraea bumalda*, *S. japonica*.

INDEX